Angela Gheorghiu

Angela Gheorghiu

A Life for Art

ANGELA GHEORGHIU

WITH

JON TOLANSKY

• • •

ForeEdge

ForeEdge

An imprint of University Press of New England

www.upne.com

© 2018 Angela Gheorghiu

All rights reserved

Manufactured in the United States of America

Designed by Eric M. Brooks

Typeset in Whitman by Passumpsic Publishing

For permission to reproduce any of the material in this book,
contact Permissions, University Press of New England, One Court
Street, Suite 250, Lebanon NH 03766; or visit www.upne.com

Library of Congress Cataloging-in-Publication Data

NAMES: Gheorghiu, Angela, author. | Tolansky, Jon.

TITLE: Angela Gheorghiu : a life for art / Angela Gheorghiu
with Jon Tolansky.

DESCRIPTION: Lebanon, NH : ForeEdge, [2018] |
Includes bibliographical references and index.

IDENTIFIERS: LCCN 2018023843 (print) |
LCCN 2018025317 (ebook) | ISBN 9781512603071
(epub, pdf, & mobi) | ISBN 9781611689129 (cloth)

SUBJECTS: LCSH: Gheorghiu, Angela. | Sopranos (Singers)—
Romania—Biography. | LCGFT: Autobiographies.

CLASSIFICATION: LCC ML420.G379 (ebook) |
LCC ML420.G379 A3 2018 (print) | DDC 782.1092 [B]—dc23

LC record available at https://lccn.loc.gov/2018023843

5 4 3 2 1

CONTENTS

Acknowledgments vii

Preface ix

1 • Poems of Childhood 1

2 • Study, Study, Study 24

3 • Communist Romania and the Path of Music 49

4 • Romance and Revolution 76

5 • Falling in Love with Covent Garden 89

6 • A Star Is Born 107

7 • New Beginnings 126

8 • Dramas and Traumas 141

9 • Royal Encounters 161

10 • Becoming Tosca 174

11 • Choices and Launches 187

12 • Restoring My Faith in Love 198

Timeline of Career Highlights 213

Discography 217

Index 221

Illustrations follow page 102

ACKNOWLEDGMENTS

This book could not have been produced without the devoted assistance of Mihai Ciortea, whose fastidious care and scrupulous application in detailed fact checking, textual refinement, and meticulous proofreading have been indispensable.

I must express my gratitude to Sorana Savu for conducting in-depth conversations from which substantial portions of this book have been furnished. Also, my gratitude to Alexander Gerdanovits for his crucial help during the formative stages of this book.

I must also thank Maite Pernas and Federica Rayman for translating contributions that were written in Spanish and Italian.

I would like to express my appreciation to all the contributors who have given their commentaries providing invaluable insights and recollections.

In the case of eight of the photographs reproduced in this book, though every possible effort has been made to trace the photographers, their identities remain unknown. In the case of one other photograph, though every possible effort has been made to trace the estate of the deceased photographer, this remains unknown.

Finally, a debt of profound gratitude is due to the artist, Angela Gheorghiu, for her candid thoughts and recollections that have enabled the writing of this authentic chronicle of her life.

Jon Tolansky

PREFACE

I have long postponed starting to work on this book. Those who know me closely remember how I used to tease them, jokingly, about the time when I would write my memoirs—how I used to tell them that they still have to wait, as that time had not yet arrived.

The perfect moment may not have arrived even now. The book you are about to read, if you have the desire and patience, is not *the story* of my life, but rather *a story* of my life. It does not end with "Sfârşit" or "The End" or "Fine," but with "To be continued."

As in the world of opera, everything is carefully planned and contracted years and years ahead. I know already, for example, what "to be continued" has in store for me in the next three years, at least professionally speaking. But my intention with this story is to tell you in my own words, in my view, *a modo mio*, about the facts, people, emotions, worries, places, successes, struggles, which over a quarter of a century have been captured in thousands of short stories that others have written or told about me. And of course, to all these, I want to add the missing pieces of the puzzle: experiences or events that, until now, have never been shared publicly.

I tell it all through dialogue, a format that I'm already familiar with, after the hundreds of interviews I have given in the past decades. Specifically, what you are about to read is a series of dialogues, all honest and detailed, following on the one hand the most important moments of my life and, on the other hand, those roles that defined my career or have been closest to my heart.

In reality, my life and art have always been intertwined and have always strongly influenced each other. For me, every stage appearance, every interpretation of a character, and every score I bring to life feed on my feelings and emotions.

Angela, of whom you may have heard a thing or two, is a continuation of Gina, of whom you are about to read—Gina is the name my family has called me since I was a child—and, reciprocally, Gina is a continuation of Angela.

Even now, when I prepare to answer questions, I have one week before recording a new disc, I answer emails regarding a new opera, I plan how many performances I am to sing, when and where.

I am still very much active in my profession, I am still living my biography, and in my spare time I am trying to commit some of it to paper. That's all.

The curtain rises and, for the first time, the libretto is all mine.

Angela Gheorghiu

CHAPTER 1

Poems of Childhood

• • •

*Y*ou were born in 1965, a year in which Romania was going through a time
of great change.

I came into the world in a time of hope, at the beginning of September 1965. Romania had been out of the domination of Soviet troops for
several years now, the wartime wounds were beginning to heal, and, in
Bucharest, the Communists had elected a new leader in whom, at least
for starters, everyone placed high hopes.

At the time of my birth, my parents were already living in Adjud in a
big and beautiful house with six rooms in the new area of town, which
we all used to call "the neighborhood." But Ion and Ioana Burlacu were
both originally from Adjudu Vechi, a nearby village, and before moving to "the neighborhood" it was in Adjudu Vechi that their romance
had begun.

In the countryside, the people's greatest joy was to attend the *hora*,
the local folk dance event. There, each time, my mother went chaperoned by her own mother, as girls were not allowed to go unaccompanied. The youngest of five siblings, Ioana Sandu was very loved,
protected, and pampered.

As she was very beautiful, my mother was intensely courted by the
village lads. With dark brown hair and green eyes, she was getting a lot
of attention. She was also very elegant and always dressed in clothes
she had cut and sewed for herself, because she had solid tailoring training with the merchants in Adjud.

She used to make clothes not only for herself, but also for the village
girls, for whoever asked her. There were nice clothes, cut from good
fabrics, chosen with impeccable taste. Whenever she helped out her
friends with her skills, she never asked for any money. Seeing her seriously inclined toward tailoring, her eldest brother gave her a Singer

sewing machine—specifically for her to use later on, if she ever decided to become a professional seamstress.

Do you still have this sewing machine?

Yes, I still have it, now it's just a nice piece of antique furniture, but I have kept it carefully.

How was Ion Burlacu back then?

My father was six years older than my mother. He was a charming man, intelligent and ambitious, with a penchant toward poetry and a passion for flying.

Were there siblings in his family?

He was the second of six. He attended the Vocational School CFR,* and initially wanted to become a pilot. But a career in aviation would have meant too many years of school and a service that would have led him away from home and his family. Also, in those times, the elder brothers had a great unwritten duty to begin work early so that they could help their parents and younger siblings.

So his decision to abandon aviation was not really what he wanted?

Grandma Victoria, my father's mother, used to tell us how she had begged my father, tears in her eyes, to stay home after the war and get a job at the newly established railway company CFR Adjud, as the town had recently become an important railway junction. Serving an apprenticeship as a fireman on a steam engine for a year and four months was very tough.

According to Grandma, Dad would come home from work all black and greasy. He later managed to apply to the train drivers' school in Iași,† and once his studies were completed, he returned to work in Adjud with a new status. As a driver in uniform he belonged to one of the few categories of "working people" who were rewarded with good wages for hard work.

They had the same special treatment as the miners. . . .

Yes, railway workers and miners were part of a special wage category, receiving much more than teachers, for example, but it is true that their work was very demanding.

---

*CFR stands for Căile Ferate Române, the Romanian Railways.
†Iași is the largest city in eastern Romania, the seat of Iași County, located in the historical region of Moldavia.

Coming back to the dance events in the village, my mother must have been very impressed with my father, who is to this day a very garrulous person. In Adjudu Vechi, compared to all the other lads of the village, he stood out. The time he had spent in various towns provided him with an unparalleled life experience. He was educated, handsome, with curly hair and merry eyes, and moreover—as per the secret dream of all girls at that time—he had a hat, a uniform, and a bicycle: three criteria that would have endeared him in the eyes of any adolescent.

Have you kept photos from that time?

It so happens that I have, indeed, some photos of my mother from that time. They were made by a team of journalists and photographers from a Russian magazine. The Russians were keen to present the beautiful villages and towns in the Communist countries in their publications, and those journalists wrote a feature about Adjud and the Siret River Valley.

My mom and Tănţica, a friend of hers, were chosen as models for the photo shoot to accompany the story. As Mother used to make the clothes for both herself and her friend, they may have seemed the most stylish girls in the village. This is how, right after the war, my young mother had a genuine, *avant la lettre* photo session.

So both your mother and father were, each in their own way, quite some characters in Adjudu Vechi. How did the grandparents view their relationship?

My maternal grandfather, Ilie Sandu, did not attend the meeting with my father and his parents.

A fairly radical gesture. . . . But why?

When Dad came with them to ask for my mother's hand in marriage, to state his serious intentions about her, Grandpa did not accept him— there was something about him that he did not like. Maybe he thought he had a malicious or arrogant air. . . . Maybe it was just instinct. . . . Maybe he knew his family, we would never know. It was hard to not like my father, but my grandfather had his vast experience with people and he judged my father through this. Quite harshly, I'd say.

Grandma Sanda Sandu, on the other hand, would have agreed with everything my mother wanted—"As you wish, dear," were her words. As for my mother, she was adamant: she told her parents that she only wanted Ion, otherwise she would go to the monastery. And so it was. Ioana and Ion were married in 1962.

Did your maternal grandfather accept Ion Burlacu eventually?

Yes, sure. Even though he had objected before the wedding, my grandfather did not hesitate to help my parents after they had become a family and moved to Adjud. A mason by profession, he built the house, while my father's parents, Constantin and Victoria Burlacu, bought the land. Each side of the family had its own contribution. All were extremely hard workers and loved us enormously.

Therefore, courtesy of our grandparents, our home in Adjud was very large and very well made.

This was something quite unusual at the time, when people were building small houses both for lack of money and also for fear that they would not be able to keep them warm, or maintain them in general.

Our house was really big. We had no fewer than six rooms, plus a separate kitchen, a storeroom, and a cellar. We had a lot of space, every room was big, everything was built with love. In summer, we would spread out and take over the entire house while in winter we would gather in only two or three rooms, so we could warm them up.

Having spent my childhood in such pampering conditions also created some problems for me later on. When I went to boarding school in Bucharest, as I was not used to living in small spaces, I thought I would suffocate.

Not only our home, but the entire neighborhood where I grew up was new. It was known as the railwaymen neighborhood and had developed in just a few years because, with the establishment of the railway junction in Adjud, a lot of new jobs were created and many people from the neighboring villages had come to settle in town.

For all of them, moving to the town was a logical move, as commuting was more a question of luck. At that time there were no buses, no public transportation, so the people had to march to the town or hitchhike with a horse-drawn cart—that is, if they were lucky to find one. The time and effort spent, at each beginning and end of day, were huge. And also huge was the difference between the villages and the town. For all railwaymen, as for my parents, this move was a sign of progress, a step forward.

Times were not easy, certainly, but in those early years we had everything we needed, because we were living in a house on a plot of land and we could be self-sufficient. Around the house, my mother worked

ANGELA GHEORGHIU

in no fewer than four gardens—one with vegetables, one with living birds, a little vineyard, and the front yard, which was full of flowers. All were my mom's work.

How did she have time to do everything? Did she also have a job?

No. Despite all her rigorous tailoring training made with the Jews of Adjud, my father did not allow her to take a job. Such were the times, such was my father's judgment. . . . In the railwaymen neighborhood, in most families, things were pretty much the same, and if Mother had wanted to do something differently, like earning money by sewing clothes for others, people would have noticed and frowned upon it.

From the time of the marriage to the birth of the first child, three years went by.

In the early years of her marriage, besides the household chores, Mother struggled to give birth to a child, but without any luck. After several unsuccessful attempts, when my time came, Mom had to stay in bed and take injections in order to make sure she could carry me to the term.

I was the first born after three hard years of failed attempts. A much awaited, much loved child. Mother did everything she could so that the pregnancy was successful. A year and four months later, when my sister was born, Elena, she had no more problems, both pregnancy and birth went normally.

How was your mother coping with two babies and a husband who had such a demanding job?

With great difficulty. I remember my father's job type was called *turnus*.* We would see him leave at any time of day or night, whenever he was called for, working as a train driver both on passenger and freight transports. Moreover, each year the railway timetable used to change, so everything was fluid in my father's life, everything was moving. Pretty much the way it would be for me, much later.

At home, on the other hand, things had to be very well organized for him. My father had his briefcase and his tiny food containers, which Mom used to fill up. There was no other way, nobody would stop the

*A *turnus* job involves a work program organized in units or workplaces where it is necessary to ensure, during certain periods, a different number of employees (increased or diminished compared to the usual number) for the provision of services to the population, due to requests coming unequally at different times.

train for him to eat. He had to carry his food with him, so that he could be always on the move.

While we were still in our infancy, my mother had to stay with us. Later, she tried once more to convince my father to let her take a job, but Dad still did not agree. He was educated in this silly belief that women should be kept at home . . . and Mom had to give in . . . at first because she had to, then to keep things nice and quiet at home. . . .

Wouldn't it have been better for both of them to work? They could have brought more money to the family and she could have had an occupation, especially since she was so gifted at tailoring. . . .

My mom had us two in her care and money issues weren't too many in my family because the four gardens provided for us, and my father had a large-enough salary. His job was very hard indeed, but also very well paid. I do not know how much money he made exactly, but I know they used to talk about it.

As we grew older, however, things began to get worse in the country, and shortages of all kinds appeared—especially of the simple things: food, clothing and footwear, everyday things.

Through the efforts of my parents, but also thanks to the generosity of those around us who had discovered us and helped us ever since we were very small, we did not feel the hardships for a very long time. We lived in a bubble, protected, isolated from what was happening in the country.

Perhaps this protective circle appeared around our family because of us. The fact that I was a child with a special talent determined all our relatives and teachers, and everyone I met really, to want to support me somehow. They would create a shield around us—me and Elena—even if disaster was lurking about.

The age difference was not great—how well did you get along?

From the moment Elena—Nina as we used to call her—was able to set her eyes on me and know who I was, we were always together.

We used to have a hard time convincing people that we were sisters, because we looked nothing like each other, but we were always treated and dressed like twins. Angela and Elena Burlacu. Gina and Nina. Whoever knew our family was able to understand where each of us had borrowed her features. Elena was blonde with green eyes, and had curly hair. Our father's sister was blonde and curly like her,

ANGELA GHEORGHIU

but Nina's eyes and mouth were from our mother. Everyone was saying that she was more beautiful, that she was more . . . and that's exactly how she was.

I was brunette with very straight hair. I took more from my father's side and from Grandma Victoria, his mother. I remember that I always had my hair short and my fringe was caught in a hairpin, to prevent it from covering my eyes. Nina, with her curly hair, looked great irrespective of her haircut. I did not. I was not too good-looking when I was little, or at least this is how I saw myself. . . . Only later on I improved.

In terms of personalities, we could not have been more different. My sister was voluble, outspoken, whatever space you would give her she would take it all. She always wanted to be different from me and was much fiercer. At school she was very intelligent, a quick learner, she had good grades and was always best in her class. My grades, by comparison, were not quite at the same level. Still, that did not bother me—on the contrary, it suited me to let her take the limelight. For fear I would embarrass myself, I preferred to sit in my corner and say nothing, to go unnoticed as much as possible.

A very big difference compared to today's Angela Gheorghiu . . .

Believe it or not, at the time, wherever you'd put me, there I stayed, and things remained this way until much later. I had no courage to speak up. If we knew each other and we would get close to each other, I would open up, I would speak, but otherwise not. Elena, on the other hand, was a whirlwind of joy. Whenever guests came to our house, usually colleagues of my father, I used to shut down or lock myself up physically, in another room. I dared not utter one word the whole time; I was afraid that I could embarrass myself, that I did not know enough things so that I could properly hold a conversation. I was extremely shy.

Rather than have the world misjudge me, I preferred to remain silent. I was very much aware of what I was doing and I was even wondering if I would ever get to talk the way I would have liked. I was suffering from huge stress as I was afraid I did not know enough, could not do enough, was not beautiful enough, was not learned enough. In short, I thought I was not enough. . . .

Also, in our household, obedience and respect for the school, for learning, was an obsession, almost like a disease. Any child had to achieve more than his or her parents. More than just . . . enough. In my turn, I had to be the cleanest, best groomed, best clothed, and, of course, I had to take the highest grades.

None of this was easy. We used to heat our home with wood stoves. Up until I was eighteen, we had no running water and no sewage system inside the house, but only a water pump in the yard. We used to bathe in *bălii*, some large water tanks. The water used to be warmed in some huge pots and poured in the tanks. Bath time was an entire ritual, for sure, just not in the sense we understand it today. It was much more work and much less relaxation. Mom always had to wash and starch everything, we had to be eternally spotless clean and have everything ironed to perfection. That, at some point, ceased to be fun for us—it demanded a lot of effort and patience on the part of children.

It was a great pressure to place on children. . . .

This obsession with being impeccable was not only my parents'. All people who sent their sons and daughters to school were in some sort of competition. And among themselves, the children were competing as well.

It was a climate of rivalry, then?

We had no rivalry within our family, quite the contrary. From early childhood, my sister was my first and best friend. I have never had any elder sister complex, although sometimes I did feel that my parents' attention focused rather more on her than on me. I loved Nina and we both wanted to be together wherever we went—at play, in kindergarten, at school, and later on at the High School of Art and the conservatory. We completed each other perfectly and were completely honest with each other, just like in a mirror.

We even looked like in a mirror when we were together, because our mother used to make us identical clothes. We used to have the same coats, the same shoes, the same dresses. . . . A little later, when the hardships became more serious, it happened that some of my clothes were handed down to her, but this was only for a short time, because we were about the same age and we grew at about the same pace.

We were normal children, growing up in a neighborhood of normal people. Our life was quite ordinary.

The fact that my mother was a seamstress was enormously helpful to us. Especially for two girls, that meant something extraordinary—it meant we could always be dressed in nice and clean clothes, even after clothes had started to be very hard to find in stores.

Where did she find her tailoring patterns? In the '70s and '80s, fashion magazines no longer existed in Romania and there was no chance to bring in or order anything from abroad.

Mom knew her patterns by heart, because her schooling had been truly serious, sewing with the Jewish craftsmen and merchants in Adjud, but also with Madame Vergina Mărcuța, in Adjudu Vechi. She was quite skilled and reached a point where she would cut based on principles and rules, not by following patterns. Tailoring patterns were very hard to find anyway.

She knew exactly what she wanted in a dress, how it should be—fitted to the body, cloche, conical, with raglan or puffed sleeves. . . . These things, these tailoring rules are, in fact, valid to this day. The combinations are different, of course—as are the fabrics, the bodies, the rigors of fashion—but the way a dress, a blouse, a coat, or a skirt is cut has basically remained the same.

Where did she get her fabrics from? Good fabrics were never easy to find, not to mention ready-made clothes.

We were lucky with the fabrics as well. Mother had brothers who were living in Bacău and Bucharest, Romania's capital, so she could go to them to buy whatever she needed. She would not let anyone choose the cloth for her; she was the only one to know exactly what she was looking for. In time, I discovered I had inherited this gift from her—an eye for beauty, the attention to detail. She always had this, and to this day she has incredibly good taste.

Meanwhile, was your father only busy with his job, or was he also able to help around the house?

With his demanding job and full travel schedule, across the country, Dad used to give a hand, whenever he could, to the so-called manly chores of the house. Whenever he was home, he did part of the more difficult gardening chores. Most times my parents worked together, because when cultivating plants or vines, nature is not waiting for you. Ploughing, weeding, harvesting, all these agricultural works must happen in their due time, you have to keep up. Seasons do not give you any respite—nature grows.

During the rest of the time, Mother would take care of our little farm—of the yard, as we would call it. And she made clothes for us, or for others, if relatives or friends would ask her to. She would not even think of making any profit out of it. It was not until many years later when we were both in the boarding school in Bucharest that she was forced to sell some of her work, but at home in Adjud, when we were kids, we were her favorite "customers."

Were you naughty or nice when you were kids?

When we were little, I remember that my parents left us together alone in the house, in our crib which was placed near a glass-paneled cabinet where our mother kept all of her wedding gifts. There was tableware, china plates, all the good glassware that she used only on Sundays or when she had guests over. Her little treasure . . .

And once, when both my parents returned home, they found all these in pieces. We had taken a methodical approach, throwing down and breaking everything from the shelves below, which were easier to reach, all the way to the top shelves, for which we had to climb onto the cabinet.

But that was usually what happened when we goaded each other: nothing stood in our way, good or bad. We must have liked the sound of glass and china on the floor, I do not know, but we never stopped until we managed to throw the last piece of china we could get our hands on, so when Mother returned, there were only two or three pieces left, the ones that had been placed very high, completely out of our reach.

What did you like to do?

We liked to sing, indoors or in the garden. When I went out into the yard, I used to climb into an older sour cherry tree, first by myself, then with Nina. That sour cherry tree felt like a place where nobody could judge me, where I was free, in my own world. There I could be myself, carefree, without anyone knowing. There I worked on my breathing and honed my natural technique as I used to try singing the longest phrases and hitting the highest notes, making my voice sound as loud as possible. While no one could see me, everyone could hear my voice. . . .

There in that sour cherry tree I used to sing my heart out all the time—from when I was little to the time I went to school. I would try out all the songs I heard, imitating everything that was playing on the radio, and the songs I loved best were those which allowed me to hit the highest notes. That sour cherry tree cast a special spell on me, I still don't know why. Maybe I liked the way the sound trickled through its branches, maybe it was the fact that I could hide from everyone but still be heard. . . . I do not know, but that tree was my dearest place, our dearest place.

Our childhood imagination provided us with broad stages and audiences. The road in front of our house was not paved. Every year, trailers full of gravel were unloaded and had to be spread evenly onto the ground, so that cars could drive by and not sink into the mud. When the gravel was unloaded, before being spread out, it was left in large heaps on the roadside. Those mounds of pebble were our stages.

We would gather all the neighborhood kids, we would climb onto the gravel stage and sing with all our hearts, all the songs we knew; and the children would applaud, not by clapping their hands, but by hitting their bare legs with their palms, to make it sound louder and as if it were coming from a larger audience. They were trying to imitate the real applause that we were all hearing on the radio. When they liked a lot whatever we were singing, they knew how to say "Bravo!" Even though there were only three or four children, their clapping hands could be heard loud enough, and we loved it, and that would fire us up to sing even more, even louder. We would sing for hours and hours. Nobody could stop us. We had a show to perform.

We would descend from our mound only if our parents called us with a job to do. House chores, and later on homework, took precedence. Otherwise we had the right to go to play—and singing was part of playing. While playing we learned, for instance, I do not know how and from whom, to sing in two voices. Everybody was fascinated by our duets, yet to us it seemed only natural.

If we had no gravel mounds for the roads, then we had the woodpiles for the stoves—one way or another, we still found something to build our stages from. As the whole town, including our house, was heated with tiled stoves, which burned wood, every autumn wood was brought down from the mountains. Whole stacks of logs were unloaded in front of the houses. When the pebbles were not available, we would climb on the woodpiles, and somehow we managed to find a way to sing for our friends.

During the winter holidays, did you go out caroling like all the children?
In those years when we were both very young, my dad taught us our

first carol, because we wanted to tour all our neighbors for Christmas. It is a carol that I still sing and love—"O, ce veste minunată!" (Oh, what wonderful news!). It is a rather unusual song for the children's repertoire, probably because it is the most vocal of all. We did learn it, however, because we wanted to impress, because we were happy to see that people liked what we sang and how we sang. We did not care to receive any money, anyway. Whatever we received we would give to our parents when we came home. We cared more about Santa Claus, who would bring us lots of presents at the foot of the Christmas tree every year—those were far more appealing to us than cash. But the money was relevant for us from another perspective—we saw it as a kind of measure of success, and the fact that we received more, a lot more than other children, amused us greatly.

In winter, numerous groups of carolers were going door to door to sing, for many evenings. The custom was to welcome them, to let them sing in the porch or outside the door, and repay their effort with some coins. But because we both sang beautifully, people would not keep us at the door, but rather invited us in and asked us to sing several Christmas songs, not just one. At the end of the recital, instead of coins, we received banknotes.

What did your parents think of this? Were they happy?

Yes and no. They saw things a little differently. At one point, Dad was a little upset—in his opinion, we made too much money for a kids' job. He was slightly embarrassed by this. He feared that somehow the neighbors might get a wrong impression about us, and therefore, from a certain point on, he no longer allowed us to go out and sing. We suffered greatly, we cried, as caroling was our kind of tour. . . . But from that time on, up until I was fourteen and left home for the High School of Art in Bucharest, he no longer allowed us to go out singing alone for Christmas. He only made an exception for the New Year, when we would go singing "Plugușorul," a sort of rejuvenation folk song.*

We enjoyed sweets greatly as children, and the visits of peddlers with their loaded carts were such important events for us that I can still remember them. A sweets van used to pass by on our street and

---

*"Plugușorul" is a Romanian New Year's tradition and carol. *Plugușor* literally means "little plough" in Romanian.

we adored it, because during summer it was selling ice cream while in winter it was bringing us homemade halva. On summer days, the van would usually be parked somewhere near the high street, on the merchants' street, but when he got bored, the driver also used to drive through our neighborhood.

Coming back from his frequent trips, Dad never forgot to bring us something in his bag. Most often, the surprise was a little chocolate bar with rum filling, which I still like.

Our neighbors were about 90 percent railwaymen, at least in the beginning. They had all moved to Adjud to work at the railway junction. The vast majority kept their wives at home with their children. To me, this was and remains a great injustice. Those customs simply bound all women to their homes. At the same time, by leaving men as the sole providers for the families, the same customs would give them a position of power within the family, while also putting enormous pressure on them.

Was musical talent a family trait? Did your parents sing?

With all the worries my parents had to face, there was not too much singing in our home. Mother can't sing too well; she does not have a musical ear. Father could hear well enough, but did not have too much of a timbre. In the village of my grandparents in Adjudu Vechi, there was just one woman with an extraordinary voice—a cousin of my mother, Axenia Radu—and all the time I was told that I should learn to sing like her if I were to make my living by singing in the church. She was the only singer the village could hear and whose songs everyone appreciated.

Since you were so close to Elena, I imagine it was hard for you to be separated when you had to go to kindergarten.

In Adjud, the kindergarten and the Elementary School No. 3 were in adjoining buildings. Being born in September, just as the school year began, I was sent to the kindergarten at five, not four years old as is usual, because I was too small compared to the other children. At age five, I was already very close to my sister, so when my mother left me alone with the teacher in my group, I began to shout my lungs out, because staying somewhere away from her was something I could not conceive.

Anticipating what reaction I might have after her departure, Mother left me in the kindergarten activity room and went quietly through the gate, hoping I would not notice her. As it happened, however, I was just looking out the window when I saw her sneaking out of the kindergarten building, walking slightly bent, desperately trying to keep away from my sight. When I understood that she must go and I must stay there all by myself, I started to cry like crazy. The teacher did not know what to do with me. Perhaps a few days went by and I was not appeased, so my parents thought about it and concluded that they had to bring Nina with me to keep me appeased. As soon as we were back together, my protests ceased. I kept quiet and they could leave us there at the kindergarten without any further incident.

For the same reason—being born in September—I stayed in kindergarten until I was seven years old, not six. And toward the end of the course's time, I remember that we had several graduation celebrations. I was still very small, but in preparation of the festivities, our teacher made us sing—first in a choir, to test our voices. I cannot recall what exactly we sang then, but the fact is that the teacher (my neighbor's sister), Ms. Roșca, heard me and invited me in front of all the children to sing a solo.

Did you know at that time that you had a different type of voice?

I was not aware I was singing loudly or softly, I had no idea my voice sounded different. I sang the way I was usually singing, with all my confidence, just like any other child. But perhaps, for my age, I did sound very loud—and it may have sounded surprising to my teacher's ears. All I knew was that if I wanted to be really loud so that everyone could hear me, I had to sing in a different way than the way I was talking, and this "different" way of singing was the vocalization. As much as I try, I cannot remember ever to have uttered a musical sound like the other children. I have never sung the way I talked.

But obviously no one had ever told me that, so I just thought that was the proper, the only, way to sing. Ever since I was born, this had been my reality. And then, upon hearing me, my teacher took me out of the chorus and appointed me as a soloist; furthermore, she asked the music teacher in the school next door to come over and listen to me as well.

Luckily, Mr. Mihail Armencea was a real music teacher, a graduate of the conservatory in Iași. He used to teach the pupils of the Adjud School No. 3—the school that many years later was to bear my name.

Generally, small-town teachers were not necessarily people with academic musical studies, but with just some high school degree in music or a certain inclination toward music. But Mr. Armencea was a special character; he was a graduate of the Department of Education at the conservatory. Furthermore, although not all music teachers loved or love classical music, this man was particularly fond of opera, so my voice caught his attention.

For later as well as now?

I reunited with him in primary school, as my teacher there, Mrs. Nistor, felt I had a unique musical aptitude and believed I could sing songs that were technically way above my age. One day, Mrs. Nistor asked me if I wanted to sing in a show organized at the House of Culture by the school's music teacher and choir director—the same Mihail Armencea. Of course I wanted—unlike my piles of wood and gravel, the House of Culture was a proper concert hall with stage lights and a real audience.

From the stories of Mr. Armencea, I know that after he saw me once again, he went back home, looked through his vinyls and tapes, and kept pondering what to give me to sing, to suit both my voice and my age. Thus he ended up choosing "Wiegenlied—'Guten Abend, gut' Nacht,'" a lullaby written by Brahms, which he had in both the Romanian and the original German version. I studied with him—he let me listen to the tapes several times—and I quickly learned the song, in about twenty minutes. I learned both its versions by ear. I could not speak German, but I managed to memorize the words to the music, phonetically.

Dressed beautifully by my mother, singing a lied that fitted my voice and which had never before been performed in a children's show, I enjoyed great acclaim. I believe that was the first time that I got onto a stage in an official capacity, but it was so early in my life that I did not fully realize what was happening to me.

At home and on the street anyway we were pleased to give "performances"; at school we had countless celebrations and festivities where we could sing and we were always part of the casting. For a while I sang my Brahms lied and the Romanian folk song "La oglindă"* with

---

*"In front of the mirror," by George Coşbuc.

backing vocals from the children's choir. Later, when my repertoire expanded and when the teacher thought I could handle more, I started to sing on my own. Childhood performances and celebrations were great sources of joy for me and at one point they became a habit. I liked them a lot because they gave me a reason to dress up every way—I would wear a swallow costume or a peasant costume, and so on—and provided me with an audience, which supported me and cheered for me.

However, with or without a proper stage, with or without a fancy costume, we kept on singing. As our house was on a small street on the outskirts of the town, near a cereal warehouse, we were close to a romantic, green, and sheltered area. The place in question was, in fact, nothing more than a ditch, but as it was covered in grass, it looked nice and was a magnet for couples in love. There we sang for countless lovers . . . we sang our hearts out.

At home, did you have any radio, any records you could listen to?

We had no device that could play music recordings, at least not until we were seventeen or eighteen. Apart from the TV set and the radio speaker, we had nothing. On the radio there were just a few programs, while the television shows were increasingly just about the Ceaușescu family and Communism. At first, in the early '70s, one could still find something to watch . . . so I was always glued to the screen; I've suffered from "televisionitis" ever since then. Every Sunday at eleven, Leonard Bernstein's music show was aired. Our family adored him and we never missed any episode.

Where were you spending your holidays?

Just like any other child, I spent many of my holidays in my grandparents' village, Adjudu Vechi. There we would meet with our cousins. I had and still have many, about twenty-five, but out of them, we were the closest to Zoica and Florentina. They were the children of my mother's sister, Safta. From my father's side, we were closest to Mariana and Adriana, daughters of my father's sister, Joița. Later on, Gina, Nina, and Florentina developed an extraordinary relationship of friendship and innocent complicity in games and book reading.

Our folks were happy to send us to our grandparents because there we were no longer fussy about the food and we could play in the wild, freely and safely. We were happy that we could trek the forests all day long and sit on the riverbank, in a place of our own, marked by three poplars. Apart from the backyard sour cherry tree, those three poplar trees on the river have heard a lot in their lives, the Burlacu chirping sisters. We would sing anything we could think of—as the forests and the Siret River Valley were ringing with our songs. We were living radio stations, singing everything from simple songs, children's songs, to ballads and pop and folk music. We would stage fantastic performances, pretend we were real singers or put together theater plays using our mother's large shawls for period costumes.

At the same time, every summer our parents would take us to the seaside, to the Black Sea. This happened until we were about seventeen. Afterwards, they allowed us to go on our own. The Romanian seaside was *the* holiday place at that time. To us, it was the epitome of joy every year. We would visit all the resorts, attend all the shows performed in the so-called summer theaters, go to the restaurants, and walk on the promenade. I was in heaven and to this day I love the seaside wherever I can find it.

And during the school year, how was it at home for you?

My father was a very educated man, who had love and respect for learning. Until I was fourteen, I used to study a lot with him after school. We would discuss mathematics, Romanian language, geography, history, even drawing. He helped me with my homework, filled me in with details about the topics I had learned in school, and he tested me. I do not recall having too many books at home, but when I wanted to read, I would go to the library and borrow from there. We loved reading.

Everything that I had learned in school, I would go over again, with my dad, at home. He was patient with me and supported me, so I did not need any tutors; I knew I could always count on him. Artistically speaking, besides music I had no other talents. I'm not good at all at drawing, for example. My sister, on the other hand, yes—she was indeed talented, excelled at school, she got all sorts of awards. . . . Compared to her, I was less expansive both in relation to the school and everything else. The only subject that really fascinated me was music.

You were frequently cast in the school performances. I guess you were very popular for this reason and maybe a little different? What did the teachers and your classmates think of you?

At school I never noticed any jealousy from my classmates. I've never been very combative, never raised my voice, never fought. At home, there was a different story: I would have childish quarrels with my sister, because if one of us wanted something, immediately the other wanted the exact same thing, at the exact same time. This was how we were, we could not help it. . . .

Mother dear continued to dress us in clothes sewn by her during all our school years. Even if we had to wear mandatory uniforms, ours were always a bit special. School uniforms sold in stores were made of cheap materials or synthetic fabrics, so that they could be affordable to everyone. Matters pertaining to how they looked or how the child felt dressed in such poor materials were considered unimportant. For our uniforms, Mother found better fabrics; she would cut them carefully and tailor them to our measurements, up until we were eighteen, so we were able to ignore the clothes that were provided by the gray and dull shops of that time, all state-owned and all imposing the Communist austerity.

Not only our uniforms were different, but also the way we were regarded by our teachers—all this thanks to our voices. From my teachers in the secondary school—irrespective of their teaching field—I was left with memories and lessons related to music that I have never forgotten. Miss Maxim, for instance, was our math teacher. She was about forty years old back then and was crazy about classical music. Knowing that she had a talented student in her class, during breaks she would gather us and talk about Wagner, Verdi, and Beethoven, her favorite composers. She was very strict, excellent as a teacher, so she would never speak about anything else but math while she was holding class, but during the breaks she would love to talk about music. The winters were very cold at school, so during these breaks we would gather around a huge terra-cotta wood stove and listen to her and talk to her.

The school building was made in such a way that the stoves warmed only the classrooms, while the hallways remained icy cold. There was no running water or sewage installed in the school, as it was very old. We would only get one bucket of water and a cup in each classroom, so that at least when we were thirsty we would not have to go out in the cold.

Weren't these dangerous conditions for children—weren't you cold all the time?

We were not thinking about that back then. These are details that I remember only now, as I am looking back, and they make me understand how hard it really was, and how hard it must have been for my parents. But at the time, they were my normality—they were all I saw and all I knew, and even if they were, indeed, serious, I would not notice them.

During one of these breaks near the stove, at school, Miss Maxim explained to us why she liked Verdi more than any other opera composer —because, she said in simple words, "he does not have sudden changes of tempo, everything happens gradually, both during the lyrical and the dramatic moments." Any fracture of rhythm was bothersome to her, as she loved order and method.

My teacher of Romanian language and literature, Mrs. Nica, would sometimes come to help me with my lessons in secondary school, and she was keeping an eye on me all the time. Whenever I had a moment of respite, she would send me to the piano, to study and learn the notes. This is how, when I arrived at the High School of Art, I could already tell the notes and had a basic knowledge of music. I would read scores with difficulty, but I would indeed read them. I had learned the G key, the F key, I had even tried my hand at playing the piano.

How was the cultural life of Adjud back then?

Whenever I had completed my homework, I went to all the performances that were organized in town. In those years, given the Communist government's policy of promoting culture all over the country, the House of Culture in Adjud was visited by many actors and singers. Among them, I remember that there was a famous singer of Indian music whose stage name was Naarghita. In fact, she was born in a village near Adjud, so each time she came to town, Naarghita used to give a concert. I was impressed to see a Romanian woman without any particular musical studies who had managed to acquire so much of the Indian culture and sing so well.

Whatever show was organized at the House of Culture, I would not miss it. As for my own debut there, that obviously happened soon enough with Mr. Armencea's show and the Brahms lied. I understood that, just like the grown-up artists on stage, I was also able to do something different, something special. Even though, in the classroom, children made fun of me sometimes—they called me the Little Froggy, because whenever I sang, it seemed to them that my voice sounded like the croaking of frogs.

In parallel with my lessons at school, I went to the House of Pioneers —a kind of place where you could further your studies with specialized teachers if you were considered to be a child with special artistic inclinations. Whenever the regular school teachers discovered a talent, they would send him or her there by default, so they could progress faster and further in the topic of their interest. This may seem strange today, but looking back I think it was and would continue to be extremely useful for the gifted children.

This was also a life-defining experience for me. At the House of Pioneers, I noticed a very good and kindhearted teacher, Mr. Nica. He was the principal there and, in his turn, he noticed me as well. His wife was the professor of Romanian language and the principal of the secondary school in Adjud at that time. They both believed in me from the first moment. They had no doubt that I would have an important career. They were my mentors and my benefactors during all the four years of secondary school.

Watching me evolve, all of these teachers—Mr. Armencea, the music teacher, the Nica family, and even the physical education teacher, Mr. Catrinescu—helped me to develop my repertoire, came up with new scores for me to read, encouraged me and admired me, gave me great advice, and, in the last years of school, came repeatedly to our home to tell my parents that they must surely send me to the High School of Art in Bucharest. They were thinking big for me.

At fourteen years old you won the national finals of Song to Romania (Cântarea României), the only big festival that was organized in the country.

Yes, it was the most important artistic competition at the time, but I did not know what it meant; to me it was just a contest in which I had the opportunity to sing. To be sure that I really had a special gift and I could sing better than normal, the Nica family begged my parents to let me take a test with another teacher before the competition. My parents agreed, so Mr. and Mrs. Nica took me by train to Focşani, where they knew a teacher who had graduated at the conservatory in Bucharest and could tell them whether I could face the competition or not. The professor listened to my singing and encouraged me to go further.

So I did. At fourteen, I won the national competition of Song to Romania. The national competition was practically the final stage, which determined the big winners from the hundreds of participants, and that year was held in Piatra Neamț. The cheers and applause of the audience in Piatra Neamț were stuck in my memory for a long time.

Although it had just a little over 250 seats, The Youth Theater Hall seemed huge to me. As per the rules of the Song to Romania contest, I was no longer allowed to wear dresses cut by my mother, but a plain Pioneer uniform: white shirt, black pleated skirt, and the customary red tie with tri-color trimming. All I had was my voice and . . . "Voices of Spring," the aria from *Wiener Blut*, the operetta by Johann Strauss, the son. Even so, in the dull uniform and with huge nerves, I still won, letting my folks know clearly that music for me was not a mere adolescent fantasy.

Was this still an issue up for debate? After all, there were already many teachers around you who had noticed your exceptional vocal skills and with whom you were talking about music.

I was talking about music even with those who were not strictly related to music, sometimes even with people who were not part of the school. Still, their words have remained good lessons for me. Mr. Feraru, my neighbor, for example, was a forestry engineer who played the violin as a hobby. He explained to me that I would have to sing opera, not operetta. He had heard me, of course, singing this and that, but he would tell me that I should not sing operettas, because the operetta as a genre was neither as difficult nor as valued as the opera. To him, the opera was the *summum*. And this opinion, as simple as it was, remained stuck in my mind.

When I grew up a little, I began to look differently at the world around me; I began to see through the things that I was afraid I'd never understand. I was just thirteen or fourteen, but my thinking was already very mature. Listening and weighing it all by myself, I began to understand at that age, even before I left Adjud, a lot of things about life. Many of the lessons I learned then, many of the conclusions I drew then, right at the beginning, about the world and the people in it, have not changed at all later.

I was not talking too much with other people. There were, therefore, many things that I had not discussed with anyone, things that no one had explained to me. I just made sense of them on my own. Maybe because I was so much inclined to listen and weigh things in my mind . . . maybe because I had an unusually keen instinct. . . . The only person I would talk to about the deep and intimate facts of life was my sister, Nina. I used to share all my thoughts and all my revelations with her; she knew everything I knew. And vice versa.

As already in sixth grade my teachers had let my parents know that I was to go to the High School of Art in Bucharest after graduation, it was obvious to everyone that music would be my destiny.

What did an artistic career entail back then?

Mr. Armencea, who had so much faith in me, was telling me all about my professional music career and explained to me, from this perspective, everything I needed to do. Obviously, in his scenario, the most important thing was to get a soloist contract for a full-time job as a singer somewhere. "In order to be hired anywhere, you need to have the proper education. Without the conservatory diploma, no one would sign you up," he used to tell me, as some sort of encouragement. "If you do not have a solid foundation of theory and solfeggios and do not know how to sing properly, so you can build your repertoire, you will fail. To get hired by the National Opera or any other music institution as a lyrical artist, you must graduate from the conservatory." He repeated this so many times to me that he managed to instill in me a kind of obsessive striving for performance, for success, both in high school as well as, later on, at the conservatory. To achieve all I had to achieve was the only thing I knew and the only thing I wanted.

In fact, as I was a kid, everyone around me had treated my talent with great care and attention and with—or as a—great responsibility. Everyone told me, "Your voice is not for now, you have to study, you must learn first, you need to succeed in your exams." My family and my circle never thought about fame or fortune; they rather thought of my talent as my key toward a steady job, a lifetime career. Yet no one knew for sure how I was supposed to achieve that.

My dad seemed to be able to understand more of what was to come, but my mother was just worried about everything and would not have wanted to send me away from home. When eventually we all decided that I had to go to Bucharest, my mother was thinking, skeptically, that it would have been good for me to end up at least as a chorister, to be one of the ladies who appeared on television accompanying opera performances or vocal-symphonic concerts. At that time, anyone who was featured on television, in whatever context, was, in our eyes, a star, a very important person. My mother did not dare to hope for more for me.

But that did not prevent *me* from dreaming. I used to tell Mother even then, "Mom, I'll be the best, the most famous, the most admired, I'll come to you with the most wonderful car filled with gifts." Cars, let's not forget, were a major occasion for excitement and celebration in the streets of Adjud at that time. During Communism, as if the enormous price of a Romanian automobile was not enough, any customer who wanted to purchase one had to order it and wait for it for years. Promising my mother that I would return by car in Adjud—of course, having conquered the world first—was, in other words, showing how much of a dreamer and an optimist I was. But I also had, truth be told, more and more confidence in the gift God had bestowed upon me—my voice.

Encouraged by teachers and public reaction wherever I went to sing, I was also starting to plead with my parents to let me go to the High School in Bucharest. I reminded them of the words and the frequent visits of my teachers from school and from the House of Pioneers, of the contests in Focșani and Piatra Neamț. I would tease them, challenge them, even accusing them of speaking only in pretense when they seemed to agree with everyone else. I would directly reproach them that, in fact, they did not want to send me to school in another city.

And then, one day, to make me stop, my parents took a train and went to Bucharest to see what documents they needed to provide and which exams I had to pass in order to get me to the High School of Art.

CHAPTER 2

Study, Study, Study

◆ ◆ ◆

*S*o your mother and father had to go to Bucharest in person just
to make enquiries about the high school? Was there no one to help them
with information at the school in Adjud?

At that time, everything was very complicated. There were no
phones where you could call for information, no one knew how to help.
For any little thing you had to make a trip to the capital, to go to the
information desk of the high school and make your enquiries in person.
Thus, my parents went together to Bucharest, to the High School of
Art which was headquartered in Lemnea Street, near Victory Square.
The secretary there received them. They told her that they had a gifted
child back home and that they had been advised by all her teachers in
secondary school and in the House of Pioneers to send her specifically
to that high school. At just fourteen years old, I was quite small; I could
normally join the High School of Art only in the second stage, for the
junior and senior years, but the problem was that in my school I had
never studied music in a structured way and there were already things
I needed to catch up with, academically speaking.

Admission to the high school singing section was based, of course,
primarily on talent. So, the first advice of the secretary to my parents
was to bring me to Bucharest, so that one of the high school professors could assess the level of my aptitude. Seeing them come from a
small town with a child who was so young, the secretary never thought
for one moment of classical canto, but rather of folk singing. Moreover, there were no seats available in the classical canto specialization
for children of fourteen, as it was considered to be too early for them
to study such a discipline. Therefore, the teacher my parents were directed to was the folk singing professor.

She was Mia Barbu....

Mia Barbu had, in her turn, a history of classical canto. She was a graduate of the conservatory and had been a colleague of the great baritone Nicolae Herlea, but since she did not have a voice that was big enough for opera, she ended up singing and recording lieder and romances. Her heart, of course, was still in opera. In the '50s, her specialization, folk singing, was created specifically for the great, famous Romanian singer Maria Tănase as part of the Division of Folk Music —singing and playing. The first classes were taught by Maria, but later on, when she gave up on teaching, she personally recommended Mia Barbu to take her place.

In 1979, the Music School No. 1 had just gone through a process of merger with the Music School No. 2 (the current George Enescu College of Arts) and the School of Choreography (the current Floria Capsali Choreography High School). All three institutions had merged under one name—the George Enescu High School of Art. Over several years, this measure would have many implications for the buildings where I had to take my classes and live. But the first of them was that even though the school information desk was in Lemnea Street, the music classes were held at 63 Principatele Unite Street, an old and stylish building that had previously housed a girls' boarding school, a military base, and an Orthodox school. There my parents found Mia Barbu and, using all the power of persuasion they were able to conjure, they organized a subsequent meeting which I too was to attend.

My mother was already sick with nerves, she would think of nothing else but my exam, so she was the one to bring me to the aptitude test with Mia Barbu. Toward me, however, she had a special talent of soothing me and keeping me in a good mood. I was very emotional— only much later would I learn to control myself—but back then when I was nervous, nothing pleased me, nothing suited me. My mother was very accommodating; she used to make me feel good and help me get into shape.

How was the first meeting with Mia Barbu? Were you aware of what was at stake?

I went straight to her classroom in the building at 63 Principatele Unite Street. She held her classes in a nice room, which had high ceilings and stucco, and a very nice, baroque mirror hanging on one of the walls. Mia herself was, for me, the embodiment of elegance. She was dressed superbly in light blue, with a perfect posture and an aristocratic attitude. In my turn, I was also prepared and dressed up by my mom, to the best of her abilities, as she understood quite well the importance of this meeting.

Mia Barbu's first question was, of course, related to my age—fourteen. I began by singing her a folk romance, "Ciobănaş cu trei sute de oi"—Little shepherd with three hundred sheep—as I had been advised that she liked romances.

Then she went to the piano, to do some scales and some arpeggios with me, asking me to follow the piano and go as high as I could. As I kept going higher and higher without stopping, she stopped at one point and exclaimed, "But you're not here for singing folk music!"

I confirmed, slightly confused. "No, I am not here to sing folk music, I am here for classical canto."

"But of course, classical canto it is!" she replied. Only then did Mia Barbu reconsider the information about my age. "Well, my dear, but you're too young for classical canto."

In one voice, my mom and I explained to her what we had been told for years by my professors in Adjud—that I had to go directly to a specialized high school, that I could not afford to lose two more years instead of making music, because otherwise the junior high school would have been too difficult for me and I could never catch up with musical theory and solfeggio.

Mia Barbu agreed with us, but anyway we all had a problem: for the first two years of high school, that is, for the students aged fourteen to sixteen, there were no classical singing classes in the curriculum. We were not allowed to practice for this kind of singing while we were so young—it was against the school curriculum, and the current belief was that it was somehow unnatural.

Why? They did not know that you had already won a national competition with an aria from an operetta?

The system was based on rules, not on exceptions. A child was allowed to start singing classical music only at sixteen. By tradition, it was considered that before that age children were insufficiently developed from a physiological point of view. I, however, was sufficiently developed, and my voice was already formed. That was the truth, and even Mia Barbu confirmed this to me at that meeting, when, after our scales and interpretation, she tested my breathing technique and told me in very simple words, "You are ready. From now on do not change a thing."

As exceptional situations call for exceptional solutions, after some thought about my schooling, Mia Barbu told us flatly that she would try to create a seat just for me. Although I was to be enrolled in a class of folk singing, I was to take only classical singing lessons from her. "For a child like you," she said, "we must all do something."

What did she mean, exactly?

She had to find a way for me to join the high school at fourteen, that is to say a bit early, and to make sure that throughout all my studies I would follow classical singing and nothing else. In the past, there had been only one similar situation with a student of classical singing, Bianca Ionescu, and Bianca managed thereafter to be admitted to the conservatory. So the path was well known; Mia Barbu's only concern was to ensure that she could keep on teaching me classical canto throughout the entire duration of high school, from freshman to senior year.

After that first meeting, Mia Barbu drafted the entire academic plan for me, everything I needed to do prior to my admission into the high school. I was to have private lessons of theory and solfeggio, I had to take a few singing lessons, and last but not least—in order to pass the examination and not present myself differently from other children before the admission committee—I also had to learn some folk songs. "Honey," Mia told me, "you learn the songs and I will send you to a teacher who has very good taste and who can really show you how to sing authentic folk music."

How come you followed her recommendation? She was, still, a mere stranger, a person you had just met. . . .

That first meeting had been sufficient for me to have as much faith in Mia Barbu as I had in God. And as it happened, the same thing happened with my parents. Mia was able to recommend a professor in Vaslui*—Mr. Didulescu—because she was acquainted with many musicians and professors all over the country. Following her instructions, I left home for the first time in my life. I was hosted in the house of

---

*Vaslui is a city in eastern Romania, the seat of Vaslui County, in the historical region of Western Moldavia.

an army captain in Vaslui for two to three weeks and studied the folk songs that were to ensure my access to the George Enescu High School of Art.

I learned those songs, I took the exam. Among all the Romanian songs, I managed to sneak in "The Trout" by Schubert ("Die Forelle"), but of course only in its Romanian version—"În apa cea curată" ("Păstrăvul").

How tough was the competition for admission?

I remember that there were many candidates for each seat. The seats in the art institutions were fewer and fewer, but Mia Barbu had assured my parents that I would have no problem passing. Even the secretary in Lemnea Street predicted that I would pass the admission examination. Besides, were I not fully confident myself, I'd probably not have ventured to Vaslui to study for the admission.

For folk music singing I certainly had enough voice and in fact admission could not have been a problem for me, because there was no need for musical knowledge. We only had our vocal abilities and sense of rhythm tested—there was no test for theory or solfeggio.

But for all my confidence in my own natural gifts, the stakes were enormously high and my efforts before admission were just as intense. The year before, there had been two places in classical singing, but in my year there was only one place, and I had to take it. In all those months before the exam, I studied like crazy. There was nothing else but music, as far as I was concerned. My success was my main obsession—as well as the obsession of my family, my teachers, of pretty much all the people who met me or spoke to me. That was that. Nothing else. So, after all the excitement and preparations, in 1979 I went to the George Enescu High School of Art.

And for the first time, you left home to go to boarding school in Bucharest.

The shock was not so great at school and in the classroom as it was in the boarding house. There, for the first time, I felt really lonely after the separation from my family. In the early weeks, I would cry my eyes out. And unlike in the previous situations, when the presence of my sister was always my consolation, I could not bring Nina with me to high school, at least not in the early years.

Moreover, up until this time I had not really understood the hardships of life, as I had not been touched by them. Staying in a nice big house, looked after by my mother, having a father who earned a good salary in a small town, having been provided with good food and elegant clothing—the very things that were most acutely missing on the market—I had lived a sheltered life. During the '80s, Ceaușescu tried to repay the country's foreign debt at any cost, including that of starving and humiliating an entire population. That was the darkest period of Romania's Communist era and those were the years that affected our daily lives in the most severe way. It was exactly at that time that I left home to go to Bucharest alone for high school and boarding school. It was a very drastic change—I was torn from a community where everyone knew me and sent to a completely new place, which had fixed rules and where no one cared about me.

What were the rules?

Back home, I had never been a morning person, but here at seven o'clock the reveille was sounded and you had just about fifteen minutes to dress up and reach the cafeteria. If you did not eat during the open hours of the cafeteria, you would go hungry. If you sold your food tickets to get some money for a book, a movie ticket, or a perfume, you would go hungry. If you received a parcel with food from home and finished it immediately, with the enthusiastic participation of your roommates, you would go hungry.

In the boarding house, when we were not in classrooms, we were constantly under the watchful eye of the "supervising professors," as they were called. My life was "shared," completely deprived of quietness or privacy, as I was in a room with four or six beds, and the days when I was on duty, patrolling the corridors, were endless and exhausting.

It was only then, in the first year of high school, that I began to understand what hardships really meant.

And how did you react? How did you cope with all this?

I did not see these hardships like everybody else did. Perhaps because I was a bit of a dreamer, perhaps because I had been indoctrinated for so many years by the people around me that my purpose in life was to sing and that I had to do everything I had to in order to fulfill my purpose. . . . Whatever the reason, it seemed to me that if the school and the life in the boarding house was tough, the only way to reach a better situation was to work even harder, to outdo myself in order to show to all the people the value of my voice, to let them all hear how beautifully I could sing. This belief was the only thing that helped me and motivated me enormously, making me overcome the sordid details of life in high school, including hunger, food pinching, and begging.

The boarding house was built right inside the old yard of the high school. At the time, it was the newest and best building of its kind in Bucharest. It had just been completed in 1977 and had 170 seats in rooms of four to six people. At first, all the seats were reserved for music students, but then in the tenth grade, following the merger of the three high schools, the ballet students from the Choreography High School joined us. Each had half a building—music students and those from ballet. I remember there were long corridors, interrupted in the middle, so that boys and girls could remain separated. That boarding house also hosted secondary school children, aged six to twelve, all with extraordinary talent and sensitivity.

The mentality of the time was not very different from that currently promoting the British boarding schools—parents left their children to live on campus, greatly believing in their talent and putting all their hopes in the school to provide the necessary training for them. In these institutions, with specialized teachers and a very strict discipline, almost military, a gifted child was not put in the firing line: the more talent one had, the more she or he had to study. Everyone studied—the studying was of paramount importance. It was such a struggle to get admitted and stay in the School of Art, as we can hardly imagine now.

Do you remember any of your classmates? Have you kept in touch with any of them?

In 1980, when I went to the High School of Art, in that folk singing class, on that seat that was especially created for me following Mia Barbu's idea, I had only one colleague. During my year we were the only two students in this specialization and only one of us had serious thoughts about a career in folk music. Eugenia Moise was a gorgeous blonde, and she remains fair to this day. I got very close to her in those high school years—we were like sisters, inseparable. I was trying to show her the world of classical music and she was introducing me to the charms of folklore. At one point, even, she began to flirt with the idea of taking classical singing classes—she was an alto, she had a very beautiful voice with a beautiful timbre.

We even spent our holidays together. Eugenia's parents had a farm, they were hardworking people and were doing very well. Wherever we went, during our individual study time or during our walks around the city, we would sing or talk about opera and folklore. This is why today I am fond of both genres, as I know full well that good and authentic folk music requires a lot of study and exquisite technique. There are so many valuable folk areas in Romania, with so many distinctive features and influences so diverse that you would need several lifetimes to study them all. I still find the Romanian folklore very interesting, not only with its songs and musical modes, but also with its costumes, its arts and crafts.

Among my older colleagues, all in the department of folklore, I remember Dana Dragomir, who studied pan flute with Cornel Pană and later on left Romania to become the first professional pan flute player. My world had two sides, one consisting of classical music and the other one of folk music.

After so many years went by, I wore Eugenia Moise's folk costume during one of my piano recitals at La Scala, in 2014. . . . That's quite something if you think about it.

So the coursework and the classmates were as expected, unlike the boarding house. . . . .

The dormitory had its unwritten rules I had to learn—some the easy way, others the hard way. At the beginning, my mother, whose greatest concern was whether or not I had enough to eat, instructed me to keep all the food parcels she sent me just for myself, given how much effort they were costing her. Big mistake. The unwritten rules of the boarding house stated that food was supposed to be shared immediately with everyone else.

On one of the first days of school, I did not even get to *see* what she had brought me. After she left the food in my room, we had to go downtown together, and until our return I had locked the food in my closet. Another boarding house "rule" was that you were not supposed to lock up anything. The mere fact that my closet was locked indicated I had something to hide from the others, and therefore my roommates punished me promptly: while we were out, they found and ate the whole package. When I returned to the room with my mother, there was nothing left. Not even the bag where the food was packed. As I was saying, just like anywhere else in the world, life in the boarding house was tough. . . .

EUGENIA MOISE

Romanian folk singer Eugenia Moise Niculae was Angela Gheorghiu's dormitory roommate during high school, and they developed a strong friendship that lasts until today. Together they have also recorded the Romanian song "Ciobănaș cu 300 de oi" (Little shepherd with three hundred sheep).

◆ ◆ ◆

My precious Gina,

I thank the good Lord for making our lives intersect, for us to meet and to remain friends and sisters for life. I thank you for being in my life! I've learned that every single person in this life has their own journey: one should only follow it!

In June 1980, when I took the admission exam for the George Enescu High School of Art in Bucharest, in the school's yard (on the Strada Frumoasa entrance) I met a girl with black hair, a luminous face, and eyes that shined like diamonds. It was the admission exam for popular canto (traditional Romanian singing)! Unlike all of us who were there for popular canto, this girl was singing not the *doina*, nor the *hora* and also not the *sârba* . . . she was singing "The Trout" ("Die Forelle") by Schubert and her voice was flowing as if it were a mountain stream. Her intonation and style were so natural and innate! It was for the first time in my life that I heard a girl of her age singing cultured music. From the very first moment I knew she was something else, that she was an exception to the rule! It was a voice you couldn't often come across. We both passed the exam and we met up in September as colleagues in the same class, sitting next to each other, both students of Madame Professor Mia Barbu, inseparable as Siamese sisters.

From the first moment, I felt Angela was made for singing: the vibrations of her voice and the way she sang were different from the other girls I had listened to up until then but also up until now, as I write these words. I will never forget her eyes which, when singing more profoundly, were shooting diamond flashes. I loved it when she was studying with Mia Barbu and I was able to watch her and listen to her. Her talent was already immense back then when she was singing a tougher excerpt, her voice flowing beautifully and, as it would seem, even more amply. The girl Angela was very conscientious, she was not giving up on work. . . .

We were laughing and laughing, but when it came to singing everything became serious. Nothing was hard for Gina, she was a girl with an adult's voice—she was perfect. But she didn't stop working until everything was perfect for her. When the songs were laid out, she would go to the rehearsal with Mrs. Nistor, the piano teacher, and we were listening to one another, giving each other advice.

On one wonderful night at the Romanian Opera Angela and I went to see *La traviata*, with the great soprano Eugenia Moldoveanu as Violetta. After the performance we went to get autographs as we often did. On that particular evening, Eugenia Moldoveanu didn't care for the crowd of fans who were there to congratulate her; her gaze was fixated just on Angela. . . . She hugged her and told her that she was extraordinary and wonderful!

Angela was spectacular, I don't think she needed any teachers, everything was right from the first try and she gave so much emotion, up to the point of tears. She was who she was supposed to be. She was born to be a star!

I thank the good Lord and I thank you, Angela, for our "Ciobănaș"—your gift to our everlasting friendship! I love you, I adore you! I wish you strength and courage to keep going forward!

The first winter—at the end of the school quarter and beginning of December—at home we were celebrating St. Nicholas. Father Christmas (Santa Claus) was officially not to be mentioned, because the celebration of Christmas was obviously a religious one. In his stead, the Communists had invented Grandpa Frost, perhaps taking him on some sort of cultural loan from the Russians. But on December 6, we were still allowed to celebrate St. Nicholas, as he had the same name as that of the Communist president. Quite complicated . . .

In Moldova we did not have celebrations for St. Nicholas, or at least not in Vrancea County, where I come from. When I was growing up at home, I had never heard of him. With so many naughty girls around me at school, someone caught wind that I was not aware of this winter holiday and thought of a practical joke to make sure I would never forget him. For St. Nicholas, the custom required us to clean our footwear and leave it by the door, so that overnight they could be filled with little surprises (fruit, candy, small toys). In the morning, I also received a surprise—my boots were completely ruined, as they had been filled with fruit preserves and toothpaste, in the spirit of the dorm.

It was quite a nightmare to be left without boots in the beginning of winter, particularly during that time when you could not find anything even remotely decent in any clothing store. If I remember well, all the stores had to offer were plastic overshoes. . . . I tried to clean my boots as best I could, but there was nothing I could do to save them, so that winter I had to borrow a pair from someone else. It turned out to be a rather common practice, as people tended to understand such issues, and I had no way of buying a new pair right away.

In the first two years of high school, we were not allowed to leave the school during class hours. In the afternoon, if I was not on duty, I had a bit of time to go for a walk in town, but I was obliged to be back in the room at nightfall. Only on Sundays did we have time and money to go to the sweet shop on the nearby Boulevard June 11, where we would eat savarin cakes or chocolate-coated peanuts. Otherwise, we were not allowed to get out of the dorm; we were not allowed to miss the roll call, much less go home to our parents. For any misbehavior, we risked having our folks called by the headmaster for a discussion in Bucharest, and this was extremely serious. For other, lesser offenses, the punishments were clear and cruel: we were grounded in our rooms and forced to clean the toilets.

In the senior years, with all the risks, I would venture taking a train and going home, taking my parents by surprise. Once, during a very heavy winter, I was so homesick that I could no longer resist and took the train to Adjud without telling anyone. I arrived late at night, struggling through huge piles of snow and slipping on the ice. When I was just about home, I found the front gate locked and frozen. There was no way to call someone inside the house, so I figured I would jump over the fence. When I reached the other side, my coat got stuck in it. Finally I slipped, I fell, I hurt myself quite badly, so, instead of being happy that I took my parents by surprise and that I could finally enjoy winter from the comfort of my home, I found myself screaming in pain, yelling at my door for my mom to open it. It was tragicomic. . . .

One other winter, in my first years of high school, with only a few

ANGELA GHEORGHIU

days before the holidays, I played truant with two classmates. One of them was, of course, my dear Eugenia Moise, from folk singing, and the other was a harpist. We three went downtown to watch some movies on Kogălniceanu Boulevard in Bucharest, where all the cinemas were lined up. That very day, Mom had decided to surprise me and come to the dormitory with some of the great food she had already prepared for the holidays. She would come pretty much every week, with bags of food, taking advantage of the fact that my father could provide her with free train tickets from his workplace. All that food would now be finished that very day, or in two days maximum, as per the unwritten laws of the boarding house. By now, I knew and observed them.

Meanwhile, to make ends meet, my mother had collected all her courage and, with the help of her brother in Bucharest, she learned to make shearling coats. She would cut and sell the coats, bypassing the decision of my father, just so she could keep me in high school and make sure that I had something to eat.

As if it were not enough that I had played hooky from school that day, upon our return I did not go directly to my dorm room, but stayed some more with the girls in the harp room. This was one of the most beautiful rooms in high school, with beautiful moldings, so after the movie, to keep the magic alive for a little longer, we asked our colleague to play something for us. The harp recital took a good while, and we had lost track of time anyway, so when we returned, we were greeted by our panicked colleagues, who were shouting, "Angela's mom is here! Angela's mom is here!"

Ouch!

I immediately realized that the end of the evening would not be nearly as pleasant as its beginning, but I was not at all prepared for my mother's reaction.

She was awfully mad at me, scolded me, wept and cried. She told me that if this was how I intended to repay her efforts to keep me in high school in the capital and help me follow my dream, I could always go back home, to the Adjud Agricultural High School. I was so terrified, I suffered so much, and I felt so guilty that I did not know what to answer. "You're here for an extraordinarily important purpose—have you got any idea how much is at stake?" she kept telling me with tears in her eyes.

IOANA SANDU

Ioana Sandu, Angela Gheorghiu's mother, was always meticulously concerned with Angela's and her sister's education and care in every respect. She still lives in Adjud and is always next to Angela, with all her heart, for many events, performances, and holidays.

◆ ◆ ◆

As a mother, you are always incredibly nervous, the mix of emotions is immense, one cannot describe the feeling in words, constantly breathless. Two hearts wouldn't suffice to hold these feelings!

From a very young age, in kindergarten, Gina stood out with her voice —even in the children's choir she was put right in the middle, the first voice, the one who guided all the rest and, on occasion, even conducted the choir. Various festivities and celebrations and contests followed and my Gina, and later Nina, were the only ones who were admired for their incredible voices. My legs were shaking from nervousness when I saw and listened to them sing.

It was only after Angela was successfully admitted into the music school in Bucharest that I realized that she was going to leave home forever at the age of fourteen. I started crying and was understandably upset and at first I could not bear the thought of my Gina going away. . . . I finally embraced the idea that music was her life and with a very heavy heart I accepted it, and so began my daughter's destiny.

I was always present, from kindergarten festivities through to the end of her studies at the music conservatory, I was there for all the exams and all the performances—my daughter's concerts—I was never absent and I could never imagine it otherwise! I was the proudest mother for my daughters, I wanted them to be the best at everything: the best in class, the most elegant, the most beautiful, impeccable from head to toe. And so they were! Gina had dark hair and brown eyes and Nina had blonde hair and green eyes. They would see the latest fashion on television in the films and I would tailor those clothes especially for them, be they dresses, skirts, blouses, coats, etc. I would do anything to make my girls happy and I would watch them as they left the house until they were no longer in sight, that's how much I adored them!

The first time I ever heard Angela sing live on national television was on Iosif Sava's show in 1985, and the first time I saw her sing on a big stage was on *Vă place opera?* (Do you like opera?), the series of televised concerts at the Radio Hall in Bucharest, where I remember that I created a light blue dress for her, and because I was so nervous for her, I barely managed to finish it on time. These first important public appearances were greeted with the greatest emotions on my part.

I would happily go back to those times, although I know it is impossible, and of course all chapters in life have their beauty and charm—they are all unique moments that I would gladly relive! I continue to have the same flow of overwhelming emotions when I see Angela onstage and I am incredibly happy and grateful to still share so many beautiful moments with my daughter, my life!

This episode left a really strong mark on you.

I was totally shaken by this meeting with my mother. I was deeply moved and, in retrospect, I think I had a moment of sudden insight and maturity. A time when, finally, I asked myself honestly, "Lord, why am I here?"

From that moment on, it no longer mattered what state I was in—the only things I could think of were, "You must study," "You can do it." I started a real fight with myself, an honest and continuous fight, the kind of struggle that only a girl who wants to show the world what she is capable of can start. I suffered a lot after this conversation with my mother and then I got down to do some very serious work.

Apart from Mia Barbu, who became your main mentor, how were the other professors at George Enescu?

For musical and other disciplines, we had very good teachers in high school. There were people with such tact and dedication that during their classes even the brainless students behaved like lambs. Our Romanian language teacher—Ligia Constantinescu—had a perfect elegance, both physical and mental. I admired everything about her, including the way she spoke, the way she was able to make our lessons attractive, the way she instilled the passion for learning in each and every one of us.

During one such class, we were studying with her a poem by our national poet, Mihai Eminescu—"In the Evening on the Hill" (Sara pe deal)—when she asked the class, "Did you know that there is a romance written based on Eminescu's lyrics? Anybody studying canto?" All fingers pointed at me. I was seventeen. . . . "Do you know it?"

"Yes I do."

"Can you sing it to us?"

"Gladly."

I sang the whole romance in front of my colleagues. It was kind of a long poem, but I was so pleased with how everyone responded to my voice that I sang all the verses both for their pleasure and my own. I had time to look at everyone and record all of their reactions, as later on I did during the rehearsals for La traviata at the Royal Opera House, Covent Garden. From a certain point on, everyone was moved, my colleagues were crying, the professor was also weeping, although the lyrics were not so sad. It was clear to me that this was the effect of interpretation, and it inspired me to stir them even further and to convince them even more. In the end, everyone was standing up, cheering and applauding me. It was a magical moment during a normal literature lesson, and the teacher gave me a special "10" for my performance.

The mark was captured in the grade book; the moment was captured forever in my soul.

Mia Barbu was known to shape not only the singing, but also the singer.

All the things she told me—not only about musical theory and vocal technique—I can still remember and I have used them many times in my life. I studied singing with her following the methods of Vaccai, Concone, and Lutgen, but besides that, during all our sessions, she would correct my posture, my attitude, and most of all, the artistic expression.

Vocalizations, for her, were an exercise in concentration and expressiveness. I can still hear her telling me, "When you do your scales, you are not allowed to look relaxed, neither in the way you sound nor in the way you look. Do not sit on the chair! When you're in front of someone, you have to be always alive, vibrating, not only with your voice, but with your whole being. If you're tired or you do not feel up to it, you'd better stay home!"

This was surprising advice for a girl of fourteen to fifteen years.

Yes, but when I fully understood them they became very helpful. She also was the one to draw my attention to the importance of mimic and gestures, of the acting craft, which needs to support the vocal interpretation so that the opera could become the complete show that it was intended to be—"The eyes are the ones that must express what you sing, not the hands," she used to tell me.

We often went to her home, in the block of flats behind the Intercontinental Hotel, across the Batiștei Street, to continue our lessons quietly. She had a beautiful apartment, elegantly furnished with impeccable taste. In the midst of it there was a grand piano. Those rooms were in themselves a lesson in style for me, but also an extraordinary setting for study. Every time I got there and I approached the front door I could hear the sound of classical music.

During your school years, you had many appearances in shows, at Adjud. Were there opportunities at the high school for singing in public?

In the two years of high school when I worked with her, Mia Barbu first brought me to sing in Bucharest, before an audience at the military academy. I was sixteen, there were just students in uniform in front of me, and I was so excited and nervous that I could not distinguish anything: I was only able to see various shades of blue. It is then that I sang the first opera aria in my life, as I had repeated it and practiced it professionally, with a piano accompanist. It was the aria of Susanna from Mozart's *The Marriage of Figaro*, "Deh vieni, non tardar." My first little aria . . .

At the end of the second year, there was another exam for the second stage of high school, the final two years. After this exam, I could officially transfer from folk singing to classical singing. Again, there was only one seat and several candidates for it, seven or eight, I do not know. They were all girls. Among us there was a candidate from Oradea, who fared better than me at theory and solfeggios. Those were my biggest problem, and that was the test that worried me the most. But I got a 10 for canto, this being the highest grade, and around 8 for theory and solfeggio. The other candidate scored considerably less than me in singing. In short, I passed the examination and succeeded in reaching the second stage of high school, and I think that was my most important victory. This result, obtained in a very competitive situation, mattered more to me than many of those that followed.

After that, were the last two years of high school somewhat easier?

During my junior year, the discipline in the boarding house relaxed a bit and I really felt I could enjoy more freedom, even though in the meantime our classes had moved to the headquarters in Lemnea Street and that meant I had to walk across downtown Bucharest every single day. We were now allowed to be outside the boarding house a little longer, and so I eagerly began to go to the theater, opera, and concerts. I was taking full advantage of the power of our High School of Art badge, which offered us free access to all the theaters in Bucharest.

After the exam, Mia Barbu retired, but I continued to study with her for my admission to the conservatory. I was assigned to the class of Ion Fălculete, a powerful tenor with a good career, who used to sing with Marcela Slătinaru and had made several records. He, however, was also approaching retirement and so he had become a teacher.

Unquestionably, Mia Barbu's influence on me had been tremendous, and the education I received from her in all aspects—artistic, technical, stylistic, and personal—was by far the most important and most valuable for me.

What about Ion Fălculete?

Ion Fălculete, together with his pianist, Manuela Terescu, had a huge passion for opera and saw in me a future artist. They put together a plan to promote and support me in every way possible. And from this perspective, their efforts to help me be seen and heard ever since high school were great, and I will always be grateful to them for this.

In the junior year, Ion Fălculete organized an important moment for me at the Athenaeum during the annual high school concert.* The high school orchestra was there, with Diana Popescu as a piano soloist. Diana was the daughter of Paul Popescu, who conducted the Radio Orchestra, so it was entirely a students' concert, but it was held at the Romanian Athenaeum, and the place, for us, was magic. That year I sang "Se tu m'ami" by Pergolesi and "Solveig's Song" from *Peer Gynt*, by Grieg. Mr. Fălculete was very excited, and as he was a tall man, he walked like a caged lion throughout the Athenaeum, introducing me to everybody—"My student." He was so proud of me, and I was so excited.

---

*The Romanian Athenaeum (Romanian: Ateneul Român) is the capital city's main concert hall and the home of the George Enescu Philharmonic Orchestra.

We had rehearsals in the morning but during the evenings, of course, concerts were held there, as per the regular program of the Athenaeum. As on the night of one of our rehearsals there was a concert with a famous foreign pianist, playing something very romantic, together with a colleague I decided to stay in hiding in the Athenaeum until then. Our magic high school badge could not help us with every single concert, so the only solution for us was to hide somewhere during lunchtime, after our rehearsals were over, in order to remain in the building.

Where?

We kept looking for a hiding place in the Athenaeum, a little corner where no one could see us during that afternoon until the evening concert. And obviously, we found one. The royal box has, on one of its sides, a hidden little door. Luckily that door was open and had a tiny key left in the lock, probably because nobody was using it. The little space under the royal chairs looked like a mouse hole, but it managed to accommodate us both.

In the evening, when the pianist was invited to the stage in the midst of the applause, we also came out without anyone noticing. And this is how we enjoyed an evening's piano concerto at the Athenaeum that I would remember for the rest of my life.

What about other international artists—were you discovering celebrated singers?

In those two years of high school and a little earlier, I had already started to complete my education by listening to as many valuable records in the history of opera as possible. From the outset, Mia Barbu sent me to the Central State Library, which is located somewhere near Amzei Food Market. It was a beautiful building, with a huge reading hall like any good old-fashioned university library, and it was full of treasures. Everywhere around me in that hall there were shelves filled with art albums covering all fields—paintings, sculpture, architecture, along with an extensive discography including opera records of all kinds, from Virginia Zeani, Maria Cebotari, Nicolae Herlea, to Montserrat Caballé and Plácido Domingo. All these in a Communist Romania where not only food and clothing were scarce, but also good books and discs were rare, expensive, and hard to find and where any printing or recording could be suddenly censured or removed from the market without further comment.

At the Central State Library I discovered Virginia Zeani with the two vinyls she had done with Electrecord, the only recording label at the time in Romania. As I was a soprano myself, the first record that I wanted to listen to was, of course, *Traviata*. And this was what I asked the librarian to give me. She recommended to me the disc with Zeani, Ion Buzea, and Nicolae Herlea, the only recording of this opera made by Virginia in Romania. Nicolae Herlea was the greatest star in Romania, the most beautiful baritone voice, a *monstre sacré*.

When I got the disc in my hands, I was *bouche bée*. I initially thought that the photo on the cover was of some actress, some beauty, placed there for commercial reasons. But reading what was written on the back of the disc, I saw that the photo was from the Metropolitan Opera and it was featuring the lead soprano, and gradually I began to learn about Virginia Zeani.

I would stare at that picture for hours and hours, listening to that disc so many times. That photo revealed to me an entire world—the attitude, the dress, the makeup. . . . Not only did Virginia Zeani have a crystal-clear voice and impeccable phrasing—her eyes had the magic of a Hollywood star. Her image inspired me and motivated me extraordinarily. Her discs where she was singing Tosca and Violetta were endlessly on my playing list. She was a diamond, shining bright from every angle. . . . Those discs influenced generations of opera lovers in Romania and left their mark on me too.

Throughout the school years, up until the conservatory, I would listen to everything I had to sing either at the Central State Library or in the live performances of the National Opera or the local concert halls. I had no other option. We are talking about a girl between fourteen and eighteen years old who was living in a boarding house without any cassette player, tape recorder, or any other recording or playback device available—neither at home, nor at school. I had no opera records of my own and it would be quite some time before I started to buy some.

The first tape recorder we bought in Adjud was a Sanyo. Once we learned how to use it, we started recording whatever we needed. There were no prerecorded tapes with good sound quality. We just had empty cassettes that we would record crudely, sometimes just by placing the tape recorder near the TV set or the radio. So in all my high school years, I went to the library and then, as soon as I was allowed, I began to go as often as I could to the Opera, the Athenaeum, and the Radio Hall. Those were years when I would be avidly attending every classical music performance I could.

After high school graduation, the great aspiration was admission to the music conservatory. I know there were very few seats and that the exams were very difficult. Each year the competition was colossal both for the conservatory and for the acting college—I do not think there were other colleges where admission was so tough and the stakes so high.

The admission to the music conservatory was indeed very serious. We had to go through three tests, of which the third was pretty much a full-fledged recital and was eliminatory. The recital meant that you needed to study and sing before the committee no less than eight songs, lieder or arias. For that, I prepared with two teachers. And of course, I worked on two different repertoires! At the High School of Art I was preparing with my teacher, Ion Fălculete, and in private Mia Barbu was also working with me.

For the other two tests, in addition to the courses held in high school, I would take private lessons of theory and solfeggio with Mr. Țuțuianu. Married to an interesting contemporary music composer—Irina Odăgescu-Țuțuianu—he was a professor of music history, theory, and solfeggios right in the conservatory. Mia Barbu had advised me to work with him. Even before admission, in order to face the competition of the exam, I had to be there already, at college level, and have a real college professor train me.

The Țuțuianus made me feel like I was in heaven in their home. It was an old-style house, where everything was a dream—the atmosphere, the way the lessons were held, the way they welcomed me and treated me. I was always in a dream. I only woke up when I was hungry, back to the dorm and my poor bagels.

The feeling I had back in the dorm could not be more different from the way I felt in my professors' homes. I had two colleagues who were studying wind instruments and because they both had portable instruments, they could bring them back to the room and continue to practice. One was playing the oboe, the other one the horn. That horn was particularly driving me mad. But of course, I had to let them study; everyone was under huge pressure and worked incessantly.

So for admission, I trained for two recitals in parallel: one proposed by Mia Barbu, the other one by Ion Fălculete.

How did you make that work?

I continued to follow the guidance and teachings of Mia Barbu—and it was clear to me that I would register for the exam at the conservatory with her repertoire. But because I also respected Mr. Fălculete very much and did not have the heart to disappoint him, I did not say anything to him and I let him choose another program for me and prepare me. He was so pleased with my voice and so confident in my career. . . .

I remember that, in time, Mr. Fălculete wrote countless letters to my father to explain how talented I was and how much it mattered that he should do whatever he could to help me fulfill my musical destiny. One day, as he maybe saw me a bit uncertain in his class, I do not know, the fact is that he said, "Tell your father to come and see me." . . . And I did indeed call my dad, I had no choice. But in preparation for this meeting, I talked to him and I asked him that, no matter what any teacher told him, he should answer with, "Whatever she wants."

I was already studying very intensely and working very hard in high school and during the private lessons. Any extra pressure would have been too much for me. Fălculete kept on giving me new scores to learn and identified new opportunities for me to sing, created small shows for me at the Museum of History, at the Dalles Hall, at the Small Hall of the Palace. . . . All this was very nice, but also very tiring, and I had a feeling that the discussion with my father would only have brought more work on my plate.

I was in the eleventh grade, that is to say junior year, one year to go before graduation and the big exam. Dad came to school and was called to the faculty room, in front of all the teachers, the headmaster, everyone. Then, according to the stories my father told me, Mr. Fălculete said, "Mr. Burlacu, you have in your house the best voice that was ever born in this country—how could you believe you could stand by or how would you not want to do anything in your power for her to go to the conservatory?"

"Whatever she wants . . . ," my father replied, as per my instructions.

"How is that, sir, whatever she wants? See this coat on your back? Sell it if you have to, dear sir! Sell it if you have to, but keep your daughter in school," Fălculete insisted, all exasperated.

Tensions rose to the highest level, but my father repeated until the end, unfazed, "Whatever she wants." After his departure, God knows what the professors must have thought about him. . . . "Poor girl, what a father she has. . . . He is irresponsible . . . does not know who he has brought up in his own house." Anyway, they all mobilized. And, just as I had feared, every week, on top of my already full program of study, at the initiative of Fălculete, the theory and solfeggio professors in high school gave me extra lessons for free.

The private lessons were the main source of income for teachers back then. Their wages were not very high even at the university level and they had to make a living with such lessons. So wasn't it a bit unusual for them to offer to help you for free?

Of course it was. But Mr. Fălculete's power of persuasion and their sincere desire to support me were sufficient arguments.

Together with Mr. Fălculete, I also met the pianist he worked with, Mrs. Terescu, who during the last years of high school was like a mother to me. She brought me sandwiches to school, loved me very much, rehearsed with me during every break, and also found for me opportunities to sing. They would both say, "We have a miracle girl in our class, you should hear her sing." And Fălculete knew I needed more exercise, so he would always tell me, "You should sing, no matter where or to whom, you must always sing." At eighteen, after so many performances and appearances, I already had a repertoire. He would always tell me to sing with care—not too much, not too hard. "The only thing I want is for you not to hurt your voice," he kept saying. I was left with this "obsession" from him. It proved to be a very useful obsession.

Near the time of the entrance examination to the conservatory, Fălculete started to prepare me even more intensely, and I had to take it. The repertoires chosen by him and Mia Barbu were both very good, but they were very demanding, and until the twelfth grade (the senior year), when I had to send the track list chosen for my recital to the conservatory, I prepared for both.

What was the outcome? Did you finally tell Mr. Fălculete that you were registering for the exam with Mia Barbu's repertoire?

When the deadline for the registration approached, Mr. Fălculete said to me, "I am going to the secretariat to hand them your repertoire in person." He had prepared a really, really nice repertoire that I had rehearsed for months and months. I probably said nothing, not even in the last moment, though I felt awful. I could not tell him anything to his face, I could not hurt him. I let him go. . . .

He went to the conservatory and met with the pianist, Marietta Leonte, who, in the meantime, had already been allocated to me, to accompany me with Mia Barbu's recital. When she saw him, she told him, "My dear professor, Angela Burlacu already has a recital program." And that was it. From that moment, I think I've seen him only once, by chance, and that was it. . . . He never scolded me, never reproached me for anything, but simply faded away, disappeared. . . .

What did you finally sing in the recital exam?

For the exam, I sang the short aria in *La traviata*, "Addio del passato," the main aria of *Eugene Onegin* (Tatyana's letter scene), some Schumann lieder, the jewels aria from *Faust*, the Countess's aria in *Le nozze di Figaro*, and also a Romanian song, "Doina stăncuței," by Tiberiu Brediceanu.

I wasn't too great with languages back then—there were few books, and there was no way to practice speaking in a foreign language in a country whose borders were quasi-closed. I had to learn everything phonetically. I would first sing the score note for note, just like any other solfeggio. Then I would translate the text or have it translated for me, and little by little, I would start associating words with notes. I studied very much; I was able to sing an aria for two hours on end, without feeling the slightest effort. It was hard to get me out of the rehearsal room. I could sing forever and my voice never tired.

I knew that I could sing an aria well rather quickly, because I was a quick study. But to tell you the truth, I was so thrilled with the way my voice sounded that I would sing just for fun, a thousand times. And I would try all sorts of technical fireworks—trying to hear how a phrase might sound if I sang it like I was breathless, applying a particular vibrato, trying to sing faster, or with a legato—all these just because I could do pretty much anything.

When Mia Barbu told me, at fourteen, word for word, "Breathe! From now on, never change anything," she was neither exaggerating nor joking. There were many technical topics that we never even discussed, like they never existed. I had a very good instinct, which I've cultivated since and on which I knew I could count. I would study the scores directly, by myself, and sing them back to my teachers, and the only discussions we had were like, "Beware of that note or articulate that sound like this, take it there, make it so." Nothing more than this.

It was just me with my scores, with what I felt. I was obsessively recording the reactions of those listening to me. I remember their reactions—"Look at her, look how she does it, listen to how she sounds." For me, it was more of a reflex, but the way the people around me responded to my interpretations helped me improve.

Was Nina wanting to follow in your footsteps?

Yes, my sister came after me to the same high school. According to our tradition, she wanted to do exactly what I did. Moreover, she was not the only one to want to follow in my footsteps. At one point, everyone who was close to me would have wanted to pursue classical singing, I do not know why. I had friends who secretly tried to switch to my section where I was studying, but they were not necessarily successful. They were better suited to the career they had initially chosen and eventually they went back to it, but they had a temptation. . . .

Mia Barbu agreed to work with Nina too, just as she had done with me, although she noticed that we had a similar timbre and this, in her opinion, was not necessarily good for our future careers. For a good while, I perfectly understood Nina's decision, because she also had a beautiful voice; she could take the high notes even easier than I could. But her explosive personality was not helping. She did not have enough patience, vocal or emotional strength. Her nervousness was affecting her greatly. She could become completely another person, could freeze completely.

Other than that, she also passed all exams with flying colors: it was not a problem for her to follow me, on the exact same way. But all those around her who knew her and were worrying about her future realized that the nervousness and the lack of patience might turn into real issues later on.

How was Nina as a teenager?

Beautiful, spiritual, joyful . . . I was the opposite. She was charming, witty—all these were her innate gifts. All the boys were courting her and I liked it, I would feel very proud of her success. I was thinking about her just like a mother would—that's why I would also warn her occasionally. Just like a mother, I wanted just the most wonderful suitors for her. I had an old-fashioned mentality and never considered anyone good enough for her. I dreamed of Prince Charming on a white horse for her: for me anything less than that for her would not do. She used to laugh at me.

During all this time that we spent together in high school she had, as I recall, one boyfriend who was a student of theology and with whom she wanted to come home for the holidays. I completely forbade her, I told her she should be ashamed. I regret doing so to this day. But this was the way I was educated in my family and this was how I thought, even after I had left home—I was very strict, very *coincée*. During all my adolescent years, I was the most scared person in the world. For me there were no boys. At eighteen, I was trying to get to college, I had something better to do, I ignored anything that could have deterred me from achieving my goal.

Were there no exceptions?

Just one, so very romantic and childlike. . . . At one point, I decided that I liked a long-haired blonde from theology school, who was walking his dog on the Metropolitan Hill (Dealul Mitropoliei) in Bucharest every evening at a certain hour. I would go to see him on the hill, which was deserted at that hour. There would be just the two of us and the dog. I never said a word to him, but I would watch him from a distance and that was about all the boldness I could muster. We never met properly, we never exchanged two words. We merely breathed the same air and for me that was enough.

Throughout this period of high school all my emotional feelings were mostly related to music and live performances. I was a saint, and this was not a façade. My mind was pure and innocent. Music was really everything to me.

CHAPTER 3

Communist Romania and the Path of Music

◆ ◆ ◆

*S*eptember 1984—*after winning the highest grade on your admission examination, you entered the Ciprian Porumbescu Conservatory in Bucharest (now the National University of Music Bucharest). How were the professors there?*

Even before entering the conservatory, everyone who knew I was going to be in the classical singing department advised me to stay away from a particular professor—her name was Arta Florescu.

Comrade Arta Florescu was a plant of the Communist regime in the world of opera and, as I was to learn very soon, a plant of the Securitate, the secret police agency of the Communist regime, which was monitoring any opinion, attitude, or movement that was at odds with the policies and measures taken by the "unique party" or the "most beloved leader," as Ceaușescu was called, by some in earnest, by most in mockery. Extremely well connected politically, she was holding the lectures on classical singing in her capacity as the head of this department within the conservatory. Basically, all those who wanted to pursue a serious career in opera had to go through her.

How did you end up in her class—wasn't there any way to avoid this, to choose another professor?

Among the privileges Arta Florescu enjoyed was the right to select each year the best students, those who had the best results at the admissions exam. This allowed her right from the start to have an impressive "portfolio" of disciples, one that was more or less deserved. All the others, who were considered less interesting, were taken care of in the other classes of singing. The right to choose belonged entirely to her, and no one could get past her. Ironically, although recognized as a representative of the party and of the Securitate within the conservatory,

Arta insisted on being called "Mrs." and not "Comrade." For everyone else, such a requirement would have been heresy, but the party trusted her loyalty completely and tolerated all her eccentricities.

As for me, ever since I entered the conservatory, I knew that I was what I was. Mia Barbu had confirmed to me once again that it no longer made sense to continue her lessons with me, so after the admission we continued to be on very good terms, but more of friendship, not professional. We would meet regularly for coffee, I would sometimes consult her, but the real training had stopped, as Mia considered that my education was now complete.

At the admissions examination I was very self-composed and precise and I succeeded to be first on the list. I had prepared as much as for two exams, not just one, so everything I had to perform in front of the admission committee sounded wonderfully, I was in very good shape. There were five seats altogether that year and fifty candidates, ten for each seat, a real madness. I was not only competing with people from my generation, but also from previous generations, because for the Theatre Institute and the conservatory there were often situations where you would have to try several years on end in order to enter.

In the summer before the freshman student classes were created, Mia Barbu advised me to go see a professor who could be a model to me, from whom I could further learn. All said and done. In order to avoid any problems and to keep secret the fact that I "dared" want a certain professor, I had to meet with Mrs. Georgeta Stoleriu in the city, the park more precisely, as if we were clandestine. In those years, even walls had ears; people could have genuinely or maliciously misinterpreted my initiative and Mrs. Stoleriu could have been in trouble as well. We did not want to risk anything, so we met in Cişmigiu—the park behind the building of the conservatory—as if we had both acted in a spy movie.

Maybe this sounds ridiculous, but at that time the idea of trying to avoid a professor who was confirmed and supported politically was a great gesture of rebelliousness. From the several discussions and recommendations I had received from Mia Barbu, Georgeta Stoleriu seemed the mentor I needed—competent and relaxed. I went to the secretariat, I wrote a formal request letter asking to be assigned to her class, and waited quietly for the semester to begin in the fall.

Had they taken into account your letter of request?

On the first day of class, I came dressed very elegantly, in an outfit that was specially created by my mother. . . . I remember she even knitted me a handbag, in keeping with the fashion of the time. I was delighted with the new beginning, very optimistic. I left my mother waiting for me at the dorm, opposite the Canadian embassy, and I went to the conservatory to meet my new professors and fellow students. In passing, I stopped by the secretariat to ask if everything was okay with my application letter. It was not.

With my top grade at the admission exam, I had been allocated to Arta Florescu by default. Ironically, that year she was not even on the admissions committee, but her implicit right to take the best students was still observed. The news took all my air. I started to cry, I cried all day, I could not stop. I was so down and disoriented after this that I forgot about the bag my mom had made for me and I lost it somewhere. The fact is that I went back to the dorm with red eyes and empty hands. To this day, I am not sure Mrs. Stoleriu knows how much I suffered that I could not get into her class and how helpless I felt with the prospect of my spending—all against my will—six years with a professor with such a dark reputation.

Meanwhile, did you get to know Arta Florescu?

No, I had never met her, but there was no person in the classical singing business who would not know something awful about her. "Keep away from her . . ." was the only advice they had given me, without exception. Later on I learned that I had no way to escape her, because, even before the admission, everybody in the conservatory knew that a completely unusual voice was about to appear. My arrival had been intensely commented on, and this drew Arta's attention.

In my year, my colleagues were Mihnea Lamatic, a bass; Alexandru Badea, tenor; Roxana Gaiane Tapacian, a soprano; Adriana Urechescu, also a soprano; and, later on, Atsushi Onoghi, a Japanese tenor who converted to Christian Orthodoxy and was to become the husband of Iulia Isaev, our colleague from the classical singing class, a soprano with a beautiful career and a great friend. We were part of a small but good group of students who have remained friends over the years, tight as brothers. In the first five years of study there were only five of us.

Roxana's father took the first professional photos of me and Nina. He was a photographer, and we were good friends with Roxana; we would often invite her over, in Adjud, for holidays. Mihnea Lamatic, the bass, married operetta soprano Gladiola Nițulescu, with whom I was also a colleague in the classical singing class, and both of them are still my friends after more than a quarter of a century.

How was Arta Florescu in the classroom?

Just as I was told—very cold, harsh and vulgar, with a contemptuous attitude supported by her political power, of which she was very sure. At our first meeting, maybe because she wanted to shock me, maybe because she wanted to show us who she was, I recall so clearly how she told us, "It is not enough to be able to sing—you have a lot to learn if you want to become an opera singer. Whoever does not like this is free to leave, go back home to your pots and pans! This job is a whoring job." I was dumbstruck and my amazement must have showed on my face. I was a child, completely unable to hide my feelings.

Certainly, I had not worked like crazy for four years in school to take something like that. Also I did not need this kind of motivational speech. Seeing that I was white as a sheet, as the blood had drained from my face, she singled me out—"Take a look at this one, she looks as if she has fallen from the moon"—making me feel even more horrible.

How often would you have class with her? I presume canto was the most important course. . . .

She held open lessons, every day, from 10 a.m., with all the students from canto (classical singing), claiming that they could learn more from each other, but, in fact, preferring to have a wider audience for whenever she decided to humiliate someone. Without spectators, she would behave more reasonably, and would not make any scenes. She had, however, a very good and gentle accompanist, Doina Micu—the most talented pianist in the entire conservatory. With her we had a completely different relationship, much closer, and the way she talked to us and taught us was far more balanced and beneficial.

The main courses, the singing ones, were a disappointment, and so was the dormitory of the conservatory. We pretty much had the same routine as in the high school dorm, with several roommates in every room and spartan living conditions. The major difference now was that my roommates were not specializing in disciplines that required breathing, so they were smoking from dawn to dusk, which for me was both disturbing and harmful.

In those early days, while I was trying to adjust to my new circumstances, which were no better than the previous ones, I would cry, once again, incessantly. In the meantime, I had discovered the powder and the mascara and did not let it show to those around me, but the truth is that every single night I would fall asleep on a pillow which was wet with tears.

How did you manage, though? Such stress is unbearable, especially when it goes on and on for six years.

It so happened that from the very beginning I also made the decisions that would help me go through the conservatory courses without suffering from a professional and artistic point of view. I concocted an entire strategy to protect myself from Arta Florescu's lessons while not arousing her suspicions. The didactic activity in the conservatory was not very well organized at the time, so with a little diplomacy, I managed to find ways to build my own repertoire, in addition to what she imposed on us—which was mostly ballads or romance, patriotic songs, and contemporary music.

In class, I would always tell Arta that I had already done my scales and I did not need to practice any more, although I can now say that was not true. By the grace of God, my voice has never had the need for vocalizations. Up until now in my fifties I have not done any scales, but of course at that time I could not tell this to anyone because no one would have believed me. In fact, to me the vocalizations were tiresome and boring. My voice was exactly where it was supposed to be, regardless of the repertoire and irrespective of vocalizations.

This rarely happens with an opera singer—to have a perfectly formed voice, without needing special exercises. . . .

Surely this is not an example to follow: everybody works and trains his or her vocal instrument the way that's needed and as it feels good, but for me this was the nature of my voice and this was my instinct. And when it came down to my instinct, I would obey whatever it was dictating me, religiously, to this day.

At Arta's classes, apart from my year group of colleagues, I would usually work within another group. This was a kind of elite group of very good students she had selected from several years. There I met

Leontina Văduva, Iulia Astanei, Iulia Isaev, Mioara Manea, Ruxandra Donose, Gladiola Nițulescu, Cristina Iordăchescu, Florența Marinescu, and Cristina Măgureanu, whose father was very good friends with Arta Florescu. All these colleagues—some from the year group, such as Alexandru Badea and Mihnea Lamatic, some others from the canto classes—have remained my greatest friends until today. Wherever we are, we are like a family, we adore and respect each other wholeheartedly, and over time we have given each other so much. We were those that Arta used in order to organize patriotic poetry and music shows, following her main mission as a Communist propaganda agent.

There was no way you could say no, no way to stay away from this. . . .

The same way you could not avoid being in her class if you had good results, the same way you were forced to participate in any program of concerts she would organize. All this for the entire six years of studies at the conservatory.

Ever since the early semesters, under her control, I ended up singing in patriotic concerts in all the factories and all the universities in the country. During the wintertime in particular, these "shows," with all the necessary quotation marks, were a traumatic experience for everyone—artists and spectators alike.

The large conference halls of the factories, where workers would hold their general meetings, were not kept warm during winter. For the show, of course, we were obliged to dress nicely and remain exposed to the severe cold, while everyone in the room was wrapped up with gloves, hats, and coats. Because of the gloves, even the most enthusiastic applause would still be stifled. It was tragicomic.

In all these tours, we had some minimalist stage directions, which required very little movement from our side. I usually stood in one corner of the stage and took a step forward only when I was singing. . . . In freezing cold temperatures, in full concert dress and immobilized for hours onstage, we were frozen to the bone at the end of every evening. One colleague ended one such tour with frostbite on her toes. Another one had a nervous breakdown, wept spasmodically, and refused to appear onstage until she was allowed to put a fur on her shoulders, to alleviate the cold.

Wasn't this dangerous for your voices? Somebody must have thought of that, particularly since we are talking about the best young voices in the country.

We exposed our voices to unspeakable conditions, we would risk getting sick and hurting our voices for the rest of our lives, but nobody cared about that, of course. The only thing that was important for the organizers was that in the songs we had to sing we were to mention and extol Nicolae Ceaușescu and his wife Elena as often as possible.

Instead of bringing joy, as we could have with our performances, we were just enacting a tragedy. . . . Sure, people liked at least some part of what they saw onstage, sure we were all young, beautiful, sang beautifully, and we would mix valuable scores with the Communist rubbish, but instead of rejoicing with a shared passion for music, we were all part of a collective obligation. They were forced to sit in an ice-cold hall, we were forced to shiver onstage, singing things which nobody believed, and even worse, that we were sick of. It's really hard to describe that atmosphere. I hated it with all my heart and it embittered my college years in a way that few can comprehend now.

That was Arta's doing—this was her mission as a Securitate agent. A mission of which, until today, people in Romania are reluctant to speak, although it is well known in musical circles.

At that time, however, you also started to appear on television—how did this happen?

Fortunately, not all things were black even at that time in the country, and during the first semester of the conservatory I also found the way out, the solution to most problems that had arisen.

Already in the first month of study, Arta took us to the state television, the only one in existence, to have a live broadcast on TVR2.* I had to sing a baroque piece called "Music for a While," by Henry Purcell. I studied it with a piano, but in the television studio they brought a spinet, to make it sound like it used to when it was originally written. We were all invited onto the show of Iosif Sava, a famous and highly respected music critic and producer of cultural programs in Romania, with an unmistakable baritone timbre and a unique presence on the sad, small, black-and-white TV screens of the time. His shows were watched and commented on constantly by the Romanian intelligentsia, with a unanimous admiration that has not manifested henceforth in relation to any other television personality in Romania.

*TVR is Televiziunea Română, Romania's national television network.

In the TVR2 studio, with the song written by Purcell, Mr. Iosif Sava heard me singing for the first time. And I think I was a genuine revelation for him—as soon as I finished singing, he literally jumped from his chair and began to bestow upon me a torrent of praise and compliments as I had never heard before. That this scene was not a mere circumstantial outburst, I became convinced of very quickly. From that moment on, whatever awesome show Iosif Sava put together, I was invited directly, without involving or even telling Arta Florescu.

As Sava organized not only TV shows but also high-class live performances, through him I had the opportunity to become acquainted with the best actors of my country, usually those trying hard to bypass the Communist regime—Victor Rebengiuc, Leopoldina Bălănuță, Carmen Galin, Ovidiu Iuliu Moldovan, Ion Caramitru, and many others. . . . Iosif Sava was, himself, a man with backbone, integrity, and respect for art, and sought to surround himself with people like him. Only he knew what he had to endure in order to be able to do what he wanted to. He was a great personality.

Among the great musicians of the country, during Sava's shows I met the pianist Dan Grigore, the soprano Eugenia Moldoveanu, and jazzman Johnny Răducanu. As his programs were cultural, so somewhat targeted to a limited audience and broadcast on the secondary television channel, he was careful not to show on the radar of the party apparatus. Because he admired my voice and style of interpretation, he gave me ample opportunity to sing in theaters, concerts, and TV studios. He would invent special themes for the shows, so that he could invite me as often as possible. He was a man with a rare force of persuasion, undeniable purity of character, and an unerring flair for discovering talent. If Iosif Sava said about something or someone that he or she was "extraordinary," that was the truth.

Therefore, I was absolutely impressed when, shortly after we met, he encouraged me and told me, "After you finish the conservatory, I am sure you will sing at the Metropolitan Opera." For a moment I thought that he was kidding me, just to motivate me. At that time, I dared not even dream to go to London or Milan, in free Europe, because any break from the Communist camp was strictly forbidden. Dreaming of the most important opera stage in the United States was also forbidden, especially to us, the younger generations. Very few Romanian artists had managed to travel and sing abroad while still living in Romania. Those who had would then give more than half of their fees to the state and were also required to report back to the Securitate. But Iosif Sava believed in me so much that he gave me the courage to dream.

Along with his shows and concerts, another breath of fresh air during my student years was the *Vă place opera?* (Do you like opera?) series of concerts. In 1984, the first edition took place. I watched it on TV, but as I was not yet a student, I had not been invited. For the second edition, in 1985, to my great joy, I was invited, because in the meantime I was in the conservatory, and more than that, I had been discovered by Iosif Sava.

These twice-yearly concerts were produced by Luminiţa Constantinescu for the Romanian state television. Under this name, *Do You Like Opera?*, Luminiţa Constantinescu organized great concert performances, gathering the best Romanian artists of all generations, and the working atmosphere during rehearsals was very pleasant and professional. To me, they were not only a great joy, but also meant incredible pressure when next to me onstage were artists like Eugenia Moldoveanu, Maria Slătinaru-Nistor, Nicolae Herlea, Mioara Cortez, Octavian Naghiu, Ionel Voineag, Alexandru Agache, Leontina Văduva, Felicia Filip, Ruxandra Donose, and Liliana Nichiteanu. When rehearsals would begin at the Radio Hall in Bucharest, a wonderful collegial feeling was created, just as happens within the great artistic ensembles. I would never feel any generation gap. And I would watch all the others with great admiration and joy.

The first *Do You Like Opera?* gala in which I participated was live, and for the preparations I could not ask for anyone's help. All preparations fell to my responsibility alone. My mom had made me a gorgeous, vintage-inspired dress. It was a wonderful blue taffeta, and for such an important occasion I think my mother was just as nervous as I was, because although she was a very experienced seamstress, she had worked particularly hard on this dress. Everything she did one day, she would undo overnight, just like a modern Penelope. Her hands were shaking, and she barely managed to finish it on time. But on the evening of the performance, with the dress from my mother and some sumptuous jewelry borrowed from Mia Barbu, I looked like a princess.

What did you sing that evening?

For the gala concert, we chose the small aria from *La traviata* —"Addio del passato"—from the moment when Violetta is reading her letter out aloud ("Teneste la promessa"). Angela Burlacu was making her debut on national television at nineteen.* Everything was produced with five cameras, and the broadcast was live. I was in front of a national audience, in exceptionally good company; I was not allowed to do anything wrong. I sang it all and . . . *bis!*† Three times the audience called me after my aria ended. I was extremely confused, because I had not prepared anything else. . . . Nor could I have thought about an encore, being a debutante in a concert of well-established artists. . . . However, the fourth time I had no choice, and with the support of the conductor, I resumed the aria. . . .

Immediately after the performance, phone invitations for all sorts of concerts and broadcasts began to pour my way. Obviously, there was cause for celebration: I had given a great performance in such an important context that now people were responding to it. But there was also cause for concern. I had to decline, with all the tact that I was able to muster, the requests of patriotic music composers, and, in doing so, avoid attracting even stronger dislike from Arta Florescu's side. I had already heard stories of the past about how far Arta could go when someone became too popular or tried in any way to break away from her influence.

Then how could Arta Florescu retain this great image that she has as a professor in the history of Romanian opera?

People are still reluctant to talk about these dark things. I also avoided talking about Arta Florescu for years, preferring instead to talk about Mia Barbu, who was indeed my mentor and my tutor. But, as you say, this reluctance perpetuates a false image of a woman who not only did not help, but rather tried to destroy some of the greatest voices of Romanian opera. It is true that she did not manage to hurt everybody, and because there are two or three great sopranos who were not subjected to such treatment from her and who sing her praises today, it is

---

*Do You Like Opera? was aired on the main national channel, unlike Iosif Sava's programs, which were shown on the TVR2 channel for a limited, select audience.
†"Again, once more!" Used by audiences in France and Italy instead of "Encore!"

generally believed that she was a good person. I will let people judge according to their own conscience.

Maybe some of us were not directly affected by her harassment—but I was an important target for her from the very beginning.

In addition, in my later years of study, I witnessed private conversations in which she literally raged with anger, especially against those who had chosen to leave Romania. It was just then that I was able to observe her true personality, some facets of her character that my colleagues did not know. I was lucky, however, to work with her pianist, Mrs. Doina Micu, whom I had met on the first day of class. It was with Doina that we rehearsed and prepared for exams. We used to go to her house quite often for our classes, as there we felt more at ease, it was nice and pleasant. Otherwise, in the classroom, all we received from our professor were caustic comments and negative remarks that did nothing to help us.

So then, how did you study?

I would do the study of the actual text and score as I always did it, by myself. Discovering each aria, exploring the vocal possibilities it provided, I was my own singing teacher, coach, pianist, everything. To this day I do all the preparatory work alone—no one hears me until the first official rehearsal or directly in the recording studio, when the red light is on.

Wasn't it difficult to study without getting any reaction from any audience or any teacher?

I had no other way. I now count twenty-eight years of career, plus the six spent in the conservatory . . . all in all thirty-four years of solitary study, with a blind trust in my musical and artistic instinct.

It's not just a matter of instinct, but also of tenacity and sharp self-criticism. . . .

To get to succeed and to convince when you are onstage, during auditions and especially in front of the audience, you need many kinds of talent and quite a few qualities. Your voice is not enough, no matter how good it is. The timbre and the vocal capacity should be supported by musical and artistic intelligence, by flair and a real desire to get where you think your strength and talent can take you.

But surely other colleagues did require help from these professors. . . .

Of course—I had colleagues who were unable to project some acute notes, and then the professor, instead of adjusting their repertoire and solving their problem, would ask them to keep on singing the same aria, obsessively, although it was clear that the voice could not hold it up. The idea was not necessarily to help them progress, but rather to demonstrate and cultivate their inferiority. There were girls around me who had obvious flaws, who sang with a crooked mouth, who would force their jaw, who really needed someone to watch over them and correct them.

How did Arta Florescu get to be a professor at the conservatory?

She used to be, in her time, quite a valued artist. I listened to records and she was obviously good for the Bucharest Opera. She had never reached the level required for an important international career, but she managed to be quite convincing in those years, because she had just a bit more class and always tried her best to improve herself. She had, in fact, briefly studied with the same teacher who had also prepared Virginia Zeani—Lydia Lipkowska.

At the moment I met her, she could still give you some sound stylistic advice, tell you how to dress, how to present yourself onstage, although her tastes were a little outdated. Yet she was neither able nor willing to really help someone in terms of vocal technique. However, as most girls who arrived in the conservatory were really working hard and were talented, many of them could do well even without her assistance.

What other courses did you have in the conservatory?

In addition to our singing lessons, we were studying harmony, counterpoint, history of music, opera, lieder, foreign languages, and acting —actually, both acting and dance, or rather stage movement. For acting and stage movement, our teacher was an actress who had studied ballet in her youth, so that she could teach both classes. Her name was Mihaela Gagiu. She was blonde and beautiful; I loved her very much. We were working quite seriously with her, and additionally we also had elocution lessons with teachers from the Theater Institute, the IATC.* Moreover, we would have yoga classes for mobility and meditation and concentration techniques. For exams, we would act in all kinds of plays,

*The IATC is the Institutul de Artă Teatrală și Cinematografică—the Institute of Theater and Film.

ANGELA GHEORGHIU

we would interpret all sorts of characters. The role that I loved most in my acting class was Nora, from Ibsen's play *A Doll's House*.

As an actress at the Bulandra Theater, Mihaela Gagiu was able to have the gates of her theater wide open for us. Seats were reserved for us in the balcony on the right of the stage. People knew that the conservatory students of Mrs. Gagiu would be there for every performance. I would never miss any major play—between 1986 and 1990 I saw everything that could be seen at the Bulandra Theater. Of course, we would also go to other theaters—whenever we could find tickets, because finding theater tickets was also a problem. But it was to the Bulandra that we went most often.

What were you doing in acting classes?

All sorts of things. At the class of acting techniques for instance, we had fun with our colleague Roxana Gaiane Tapacian when we had a yoga lesson for concentration and mobility. Our group consisted of five men plus a girl from Timișoara,* and another one from Bulgaria, Carmen, married to a colleague, Ștefan Popov. We all had to lie down, face up, and the teacher asked us to close our eyes and imagine that we had an invisible material. We were to create something out of this material with our hands and she had to guess what it was that we were making. It was a creative exercise, both fun and relaxing.

Roxana was special, she had a keen sense of humor, and as she was making something we could not see, as our eyes were closed, Mrs. Gagiu asked her what it was she was making. "Bread," she said. We left her to make her bread, and minutes later Roxana asked, "May I put the bread into the oven?" As we heard her we started to laugh like crazy and could no longer continue our class.

Besides the classes, you were building a serious television career. . . .

Trying to reconcile the rigors of school with what I loved to do most —get ready for the shows and performances organized by Iosif Sava or Luminița Constantinescu—I started to develop my own repertoire. Every time I had to choose something to sing in such a program, with such a high artistic standard, I was trying really hard to pick particular arias that were not only suited to my voice but also able to create

*The capital city of Timiș County, the main social, economic, and cultural center in western Romania.

a special moment, to help me go a little further and, why not, let me stand out a little bit in the eyes and ears of the audience. That meant not only that I had to study a lot outside the classroom, at home, late in the evenings, but I also had to get the scores that I wanted, from wherever I could find them. In Socialist Romania, the printing and distribution of opera music, especially for those works that were seldom produced, was not a priority. If I wanted to sing *Louise*, *Anna Bolena*, *Madama Butterfly*, or *La rondine*, for example, I needed someone to transcribe the orchestrations by ear, because otherwise I could not have been accompanied.

Who could do this?

Fortunately, in Bucharest, there was such a person with a unique talent. He was a tenor, his name was Ion Stoian, and it was he who could write down, by hand, entire orchestral scores, just by listening to old recordings from the archive of the National Radio. A tenor who is able to pull off such a feat is highly unusual. . . . But he had absolute pitch, did not miss any instrument, and when orchestras played from his scores everything was in place, exactly as it should have been. I remember I did not even pay for his efforts—I think this was fun for him, rather like unraveling an enigma. Then he would give me his handwritten scores and I would go to the concerts or the television studios with them. He was an extraordinary man; we remained friends for years.

Obviously, these scores did not enter into my singing class—I was carefully avoiding doing anything to arouse suspicion, malicious comments, or observations. But still, Arta Florescu would watch me on TV, and she had taken the habit, after each TV appearance, to stop me in the hallway, take me in a classroom or anywhere she could find a piano, and ask me to sing the arias again to her. Only to her. "Come, darling, let's hear you," she would say. So I sang to her *Louise*, *Butterfly*, *Anna Bolena*, *La traviata*, all very difficult arias, everything I was preparing for the shows. She wanted to hear me live, right in front of her, as though she doubted that I was able to repeat the performance.

From the moment I discovered that apart from these private performances there were no other consequences against me, I was actually looking forward to meeting her and singing to her. "But where did you learn that, honey?" she would ask me dryly.

"I have learned it by myself . . . ," I would tell her, truthfully. If I happened to sing in the presence of another person, she would constantly interrupt me with strange comments: "Oh, would you listen to that . . . ," as if I were an exotic creature. She had childish reactions. . . . She would just listen to me and then go. . . . And that was that. . . . But she somehow wanted to be convinced that my interpretation was real; she wanted to hear "how I did it."

How were the exams with her?

All examinations were taking place in front of all professors, month after month, and this helped us get used to a live audience. For each exam we had to present one aria and one lied. Everything was recorded and, fortunately, now I have all these records. I would start by introducing myself in a small voice, my last name before my first name, in the Communist fashion—"My name is Burlacu Angela and I will sing . . ." In all the years of conservatory, after so many exams, I gathered quite a rich repertoire. Then I would make recordings at the Romanian Radio Hall, in the T8 studio. I would frequently appear on television to make some real video clips of opera and operetta arias for them, also other arias. I did *Madama Butterfly*, *La traviata*, *Louise*, *Porgy and Bess*, Rossini's *Stabat Mater*, and so on. The national television archive has preserved all these records and some of them have been posted on You-Tube in the meantime.

I was singing in the shows of Iosif Sava and Liviu Tudor Samuilă,* traveling the country with the patriotic or romantic concerts of Arta, and every year I was invited to appear in the two extraordinary gala concerts of *Do You Like Opera?*

Wasn't it a bit too much?

I did not feel any particular effort when I sang what I liked. Quite the contrary—and as well as all these, since my first year, together with my colleague Mioara Manea and my sister Elena, I would sing in the Patriarchy Choir. Because our studies' duration was six years, unlike in other colleges where it lasted for only four years, we were classified as taking evening classes. Students in both the conservatory and the Theater Institute had only "evening classes." There was no regular study. That required us to find somewhere to work, to have a job—fictional or

*Romanian radio and TV journalist.

real—because only people who had jobs had the right to study at night school. It was certainly one of the many anomalies, as the Communist regime had not the slightest understanding of the concept of an artistic career. It put us in all sorts of bizarre situations such as the obligation to have employment, even though our classes were organized in daytime, like any other regular classes. Somehow, I think everybody knew what was actually going on, but these were the Communist ideas, these were the initiatives of the Ministry of Culture at the time.

In these circumstances, an employment contract with the Patriarchy Choir was really a very suitable solution. Gathering professional musicians from the radio, the philharmonic, and the opera choir, the Patriarchy Choir was a real musical elite team. We three—Mioara, Elena, and I—we were the youngest of all, and taking part in their concerts, in addition to a good working exercise, gave us the opportunity to go on international tours and, last but not least, earn a decent income.

My mother had already begun to take her shearling tailoring seriously—under the guidance of her brother, she was manufacturing and selling the materials successfully, and with this substantial help we managed, more or less, to get around in the capital, to have a reasonably good life. After many adventures in the conservatory's dorm, my sister and I grew tired of all the bullying, which added to the miserable living and accommodation conditions, so we decided to rent a room together in order to have peace.

Renting a room back then was very different from today. You would have to live with the host—you could not rent the whole house, could you?

Socialist Romania did not have the concept of "roommate." I could not simply rent together with a few friends or colleagues an entire apartment, so the only practical option was to live in a room in a private home and stay with a host. In addition, it was also a matter of money. Renting a room in a private house was usually more expensive than staying in the student dorm, but the living conditions were better.

During this period, the Patriarchy Choir concerts and broadcasts on television helped me gain a certain degree of independence, a feeling that I liked very much. My money went for mundane things—the kind of things that were very expensive back then or very difficult to obtain, although now we can find them on any street corner. I would often go downtown with Gladiola Nițulescu, who, although she didn't share my taste for cakes and sweets, accompanied me gladly to the sweet shops at lunchtime.

You were practically going back to the area of the High School of Art. . . .

Yes—from the rehearsal room of the Patriarchy, we would go straight to the sweet shop on Boulevard June 11, for which I had had a penchant ever since my high school years. Usually I would buy a bag of chocolate-coated peanuts. I would then go to Mia Barbu's study room, where I would sing and look in the mirror. There I could see myself growing up; I would study my facial expressions and look for new styles of makeup for the stage. I was trying to make sense of my transformations. I would admire myself in the mirror and sing.

As a student at the conservatory you could not go abroad to sing anywhere.

Yes, but I was able to do so with the choir—during my first year of college, I went to Finland, Austria, and Moscow on a collective visa. Group visas were yet another Communist Party method of preventing us from leaving the country. Finland, like Austria, was considered a tempting destination, and it was well known that artists sought every opportunity in international travels to escape the clutches of the Communist regime. So, just when we were about to leave, the choir sharply increased the number of members and became filled with new "priests," who, in fact, were all Securitate agents. We would notice this and understand, of course, that we were held prisoner in our own musical ensemble. To me, it all seemed ridiculous. At that point in time I had no thoughts of leaving the country, but there was no way to comment in any way. Without such "companions," we would never have been allowed to travel abroad.

From that first trip to Vienna, which was around Christmas, I have three memories that stayed with me all through my life. The first meeting with the Austrian capital—elegant, lavish, all bright and colorful, draped in genuine winter holiday decorations—placed me in a magical state. If regular tourists photographed the imperial buildings and museums, I was photographing, as well as all these, the shops filled with fruits and vegetables in the dead of winter, the fish and meat counters that I had never seen, the cake shops with windows full of wonders, the flower shops. . . .

Coming from a country where food stores were offering only canned fish, Vietnamese shrimp, and miserable compotes, all scattered on shelves to mask their scarcity, where bread either could not be found at all or was always cold and hard, and everything from butter and cheese to milk and yogurt was by necessity the cause of interminable queues, I wanted to share with my folks these heavenly images. At the time, Bucharest, the city in which I lived, was gray, sad, and humiliated—people just carried on with their days and all religious celebrations were held in *sotto voce.*

I was nineteen, I was still a kid, and my weakness for sweets acutely manifested in the capital of the Sachertorte. As part of the Patriarchy Choir, we had all been provided with accommodation at a monastery near the city. Patriarch Teoctist accompanied us.* Exactly opposite the gate of the monastery, there was a confectionary that we could see quite well, showcases and all, through the fence at the entrance. Imagine what it meant to me to see a display full of Viennese cakes and sweets. . . . Heaven on earth. . . . It was not more than twenty meters away from us—all you had to do was cross a small road up to it. Seeing it every day so close to me, I thought I'd melt with cravings.

Sure, I asked permission to cross the road to the confectionary shop to buy my cakes. I did not even care that one of the Securitate anointed priests would have had to accompany me. Quite the contrary. I did not want to stay behind, or run off to anywhere. I just wanted some cakes. And all I got were refusals.

Being a student and a soloist choir singer in whom they highly prided themselves, I conjured up all my courage one evening and went straight to the door of the patriarch, exasperated by the relentless and completely unjustified attitude of all the other priests. Arriving in front of Teoctist, I explained the situation and ended by asking him to at least send someone to pick us up a plate of cakes, since we did not seem to be trustworthy enough for him. With a smile which was more sardonic than devout, Teoctist replied dryly, "This cannot be, my daughter, good night!" I thought of shouting from the top of my lungs to make sure everyone in Vienna heard me from there, from those few kilometers away where we were, but everyone calmed me down and confirmed to

*Born Toader Arăpaşu, Teoctist was the patriarch of the Romanian Orthodox Church from 1986 to 2007. He served his first years as patriarch under the Romanian Communist regime.

me in every way possible that I would never get my cakes and all I had to do was go to sleep. After all, the good patriarch of Romania under Ceaușescu was in the service of the party and of the Securitate.

The second memory? More enjoyable than the first?

Fortunately, yes. In our free moments visiting the museums of Vienna, we reached the Hofburg and Schönbrunn Palaces and I saw the famous portrait of Empress Sissi in her white dress, with edelweiss flowers strewn all over it. The image struck me to such an extent that a few years later when I was asked how I would like to be dressed as Violetta in the first act of *La traviata*, when the atmosphere is more serene and "gioir" is the name of the game,* I remembered that dress in Vienna and I recommended it as an inspiration for the costume design. My Violetta, at Covent Garden, wears that dress in memory of my first trip abroad, to Vienna.

And the third?

Our concert, for which the entire journey to Vienna had been organized, was held at the Archdiocesan Cathedral, the Stephansdom. A choir concert offered by the Romanian Patriarchy was an unusual event, so it not only gathered choral and Byzantine church music lovers in the cathedral, but also many of the fugitive Romanians who lived in Vienna.

While I was actually singing, I saw behind a column a familiar face. And as the person kept moving between the columns of the cathedral and drawing my attention, I realized at some point who this was: Cristea Avram, a handsome, well-beloved Romanian actor who had chosen the path to exile a few years before. At the time when he was still filming in Romania, Cristea Avram played the role of Scarpia in *Darclée*, the biopic about the Romanian soprano Hariclea Darclée, the first Floria Tosca ever. As a dedicated moviegoer, of course I had seen the story of the woman who asked Puccini to write "Vissi d'arte." His presence in the audience that night inspired me, and after recognizing him I sang with even more pathos and emotion.

He surely made an impression on me, but I seem to have impressed him as well in my turn, since at the end of the concert Cristea Avram

*In Italian "gioir" means joyous, quoting Violetta's coloratura explosion in the recitative just before "Sempre libera."

came to me to congratulate me, in tears, and asked me to give him one of the first autographs of my life. Overly surprised by the meeting and remembering his role in *Darclée*, I managed to scribble just a few words on the evening's program: "With great admiration for Scarpia . . . from a future Tosca."

From then until today, I feel an intense surge of emotion whenever I meet the great artists I admire. Quite often I behave just like a fan, so I do understand very well how my fans feel.

One of the artists whom you met and admired at that time was Eugenia Moldoveanu, who would soon after become a good friend.

Eugenia Moldoveanu is a sublime soprano who had sung already on the great stages of the world and was, for our generation, an example of success. Along with Maria Slătinaru-Nistor, Ludovic Spiess, and Nicolae Herlea, Eugenia Moldoveanu was among the few truly world-class, valuable lyrical artists who had chosen to still live in Romania, but she had also managed the impossible: to have a valuable international career.

Because she was close to my style and voice, I had watched all her performances of *La traviata*, *Der Freischütz*, and *Madama Butterfly* since I had been in high school, and I continued to follow her presence on the stage of the Bucharest Opera because she was undoubtedly the best female voice at that hour. I admired her enormously, but because of my shyness, I had never dared tell her a few words after her performances. When I finally found the courage to go to her, knees trembling with emotion, it was 1985, I was already a student, and just the night before, the second edition of the gala *Do You Like Opera?* had been aired on TV. It was the one in which I had participated, and the TV producers included the enthusiastic applause I had received as well as the encore with "Addio del passato." Imagine my surprise when I saw that, from her dressing room, Eugenia Moldoveanu beckoned me over the crowd of admirers and came toward me with open arms. She already knew who I was and greeted me, at first glance, with the air of an old friend and colleague. It was an extraordinary moment of intense affection and mutual admiration. I was surprised to hear her compliments toward me and I, in my turn, kept telling her how I had never missed a show with her onstage in Romania.

She too came to Bucharest from a small town, and began singing opera and operetta at sixteen, without having studied classical singing before admission to the conservatory, but just mimicking what she had heard on radio and television. In the same generous, collegial spirit, Eugenia Moldoveanu opened her home to me and, at one time, gave me a lovely white concert dress, which I wore with great joy. Recordings with me wearing that dress have been kept until today. Her stories about the sacrifices she had to make and the way she had built her career were fantastic for me, and I would listen to them with all my heart and with infinite admiration.

That was not the only concert dress you had received in college. . . .

No. Ironically, Arta Florescu also gave me, around that time, a concert dress—a black velvet one—but the two gifts and their meanings could not be more different from each other. Arta was trying to impose a certain style of dressing and hairdo on us and we hated it because it made us look old. Her dress—neither short nor long—was a complete misfit, and as it came imposed by someone who did not inspire me in any way style-wise, it was just as nasty as the old Pioneer uniforms to me. Sure, some of her advice, which came from an era of severity and rigor, made sense.

On the only occasion when I and Gladiola Nițulescu were obliged to go to Arta's hairdresser for styling, we looked so ridiculous that we decided that we could not go onstage like that. We put the blame on the fact that we did not know how to sleep, masochistically, on cylinder pillows, so that overnight our exaggerated buns had been ruined. In truth, with the way we looked that morning, like two ruffled feathered ghosts, we could not go out on the street. So although we had been to a "stylist" that had come with "solid" recommendations, we had to redo our hair by ourselves, to the Homeric laughter of our colleagues, Alexandru Badea and Mihnea Lamatic.

Laughter was a kind of therapy for you back then. . . .

We would make fun of trouble, as we used to say in Romania, on all these trips. While we were on the tour buses, we would sing anything, at any time. I, for example, liked to perform the songs in *Snow White*, Disney's animated movie, all complete with the chirping of the birds, and I kept on singing them to the delight of my colleagues.

We used to take comfort in the fact that, being Arta's students, unlike the other classes of singing, we could at least go on tour and had good places where we ate. In a country where everyone had to "make do" and finding food was hard work (in the '80s, at least, this had become the national sport), a decent hot meal in a restaurant or a Communist cafeteria was a rarity. With Arta's blessing, we knew that we could die of cold during our tours, but not of hunger. . . .

Sure, we all understood the underlying threats. Artists were considered particularly high-risk people. After the defections of the early '80s, all the trips to international summer schools or superficial festivals were stopped, and even more so we were under constant surveillance in our own country. We would teach each other what to do to be considered inept in order to escape the vigilance of a mustachioed man who stood on guard every day for two years in front of our conservatory, watching us whenever we went in and out of classes. It did not matter to anyone how talented you were, how you could have contributed with your art to the world's culture—they were all obsessing themselves with finding ways to prevent us from fleeing the country. The pressure and the constant threat often brought me to tears, because I knew that in these conditions I could never escape, I could never get to where my voice could take me.

In our house, ever since I had been a baby, all we listened to was Radio Free Europe and Voice of America,* and we all lived with the hope that, at some point, the monarchy would be restored in the country and things would return to normal.

But any evasion came with consequences. Surely there were consequences for me as well. Arta Florescu was the only professor in Romania who was allowed to accept invitations to sit on the juries of international singing competitions, as a reward for her political dedication. We were not even allowed to participate.

I quickly understood how things were in the world of classical music competitions, but then, in that context, and just at the beginning of my career, any trip to another country was important. Looking back, I personally do not believe in such competitions. I think they are just lucrative businesses that work only for certain artists, theater directors, and managers, and they do not establish any real hierarchies:

*Romanians were officially forbidden to listen to these short-wave transmissions from Germany and the United States, but some people risked it.

some of them do not always reward a genuine performance. For some artists at the beginning, a prize can be helpful, but it can also be a false, short-lived victory. Prize or no prize, later on the artist must convince theater directors and managers that he or she can be a complete performer able to carry out an entire show. I know countless winners with an impressive portfolio who are not able to sing more than a few nice arias in concert format only. Judgment based only on concert performance, not the full show, is typical for contests, and it can often lead to misjudgments.

Going back to my student years, in all that time I was allowed to go only to the Moniuszko Festival, in Poland. Poland, a Socialist country, was considered a safe-enough destination for Arta to let me visit. Otherwise, any application form to an international singing contest had to go through her, and she, along with others that have remained in the concert and festival business until today, decided who would go and where. I did not want to flee the country, I was a diligent student, but that was the general policy. Leontina Văduva had recently emigrated and requested political asylum in Paris, so for us, all the others, the leash had become even tighter.

There was no solution for me to get out of Romania and see the world. I wrote application upon application, but I never received a response. For me, the continuing presence of the same administrative people in the cultural life of Romania up until today is a clear sign that the Ceaușescu regime still survives, that the tentacles of Communism are still alive, that we still have not become as free as we had wanted in the winter of 1989. This completely inappropriate and irreverent attitude toward Romanian artists is preserved until today in the great cultural events of the country. The management board of the Enescu Festival still claims that Romanian artists must participate in the festival free of charge or in some offensive and humiliating financial conditions, which have nothing to do with their value or stature, local or international. Meanwhile hundreds of foreign musicians are, of course, well respected and offered normal financial conditions, as befits their artistry.

Isn't this ironic?

The irony is that if during Ceaușescu's time the attitude of these people prevented me from leaving the country, it now prevents me from performing in my own country, and from participating in its great cultural events. And it's sad and bitter to me that although Communism officially died in Romania in 1989 together with Ceaușescu, its foibles and the people who thrived during that era of misery continue to keep the public away from the Romanian artists.

Unfortunately, Romania has a rich history of such incidents in which great artists—sculptors, painters, writers—have had to seek glory elsewhere to be finally valued in their own country. The great Constantin Brâncuși also received the same treatment until he was forced and obliged by sadness and bitterness to give up his Romanian citizenship. That is why his sculptures, which he wanted to donate to the Romanian people, must now be purchased by his fellow countrymen for huge prices, by public fundraising, and why Brâncuși foreign collections are richer than those in his home country.

In Romania, for the past three decades at least, since I became part of the art world, I have painfully realized that I was born in a country that does not respect its artists—on the contrary, it has always asked them to compromise or make undue concessions. In all festivals or other kinds of events, all world-class Romanian artists have forever been invited to participate without being remunerated, as a kind of patriotic duty, and many of them who no longer live in Romania have even agreed to come.

I do not wish to be misunderstood: I have always loved and I still love my country and have accepted numerous invitations to perform pro bono when I have been involved in a social cause in which I have believed, but I've never understood why commercial concerts, from which organizers derive profit, must be underwritten by Romanian artists just because they are Romanian.

Fortunately for you, with a rich international career, the interest or lack of interest of the Romanian authorities is far from being of any professional importance—but emotionally?

Despite everything, I enjoy a warm welcome whenever I return to a stage in Romania, along with the admiration of fans around the world, and this is sufficient consolation. Back then, I used to cherish the appreciation of wonderful people in the country, people whom I remember fondly to this day.

By the second or third year of study, all kinds of concerts were organized jointly by the conservatory and the Institute of Theater and Film, bringing together young actors and young singers, which is to say virtually all students of the performing arts. At such a gala, held in the Enescu Hall of the conservatory, the great Romanian actor Octavian Cotescu, rector of the IATC, had come along with his students. During the show I saw and recognized him in the audience. I respected and admired him enormously, but had never met him, and that gave me wings—I did not know how to sing any better. I finished the performance and was about to leave immediately. Back then I would have to come dressed pretty neatly directly from home, because we could not change from street clothes into stage clothes and vice versa, so I was in a pretty chic outfit. As I descended toward the exit, Cotescu was downstairs. He began to recite, emphatically—"Behold who descends, our goddess!"—and he started to pay me extraordinary compliments. I felt overwhelmed with delight and very privileged. We loved and respected each other from the first moment; he gave me courage and confidence.

From that time I have been the same—I love to sing to people I respect and love; they inspire me and lift me up and help me express, in my turn, even more emotion. I am a person who, the greater the public, the better I feel and the more I give back. Even today, when I sing in a rehearsal, I like to have people around me. The more important to me they are, the more they inspire me and the happier I am.

I continue to admire and love Octavian Cotescu as I love many actors of my time: Victor Rebengiuc and Mariana Mihuț, Leopoldina Bălănuță and George Constantin, Gheorghe Dinică, Marin Moraru, Gina Patrichi, Ileana Stana Ionescu, Olga Tudorache, Ilinca Tomoroveanu, Toma Caragiu, Amza Pellea, but also Horațiu Mălăele, Rodica Mandache, Tamara Buciuceanu, Draga Olteanu Matei, Ion Caramitru, Simona Bondoc, Dan Condurache, Claudiu Bleonț, Marcel Iureș, Florin Piersic, Medeea Marinescu, Marius Manole, Anamaria Marinca, Vlad Ivanov, or Florina Cercel, without forgetting the voice and the class of George Vraca, or our great comedian Grigore Vasiliu Birlic. They are some of the best actors of theater and film who ever lived in Romania. They are my idols, extraordinary artists and people with a strong backbone, who had the courage to say and do something even in the darkest times.

Aside from all these great actors, I have a very special friendship, based on a sincere and mutual admiration, with Nadia Comăneci,

NADIA COMĂNECI

Romanian Olympic gold medalist Nadia Comăneci and Angela Gheorghiu first met at the Metropolitan Opera in New York, and since then they have seen each other on many different occasions.

◆ ◆ ◆

Angela Gheorghiu is a symbol of the international opera scene. . . . Angela is more than a powerful voice and an accomplished talent. . . . Angela transmits elegance and grace with every step and word beyond the realm of classical music. . . . Angela is of undeniable worth and an extraordinary ambassador of our country. It is an honor and joy for me to befriend such a big soul and such a special person, an example of inner and outer beauty for all of us. I would like to congratulate her from the bottom of my heart for her accomplishments and I wish her eternal strength and inspiration in all her future endeavors. She will always find a huge admirer and a reliable supporter in me.

Romanian Olympic gold medalist, the first gymnast in history to be awarded a perfect score of 10.0. She was born very close to Adjud, only twenty-five miles away, and since I was little I wanted to be the best, like her, when she received the perfect 10! After some years, I met her at the Metropolitan Opera and in Los Angeles, where she came to see me.

But during my student holidays, in Adjudu Vechi, for years I had a different audience, an audience I loved with all my heart, at the house of my maternal grandmother, who lived long enough to hear me sing real opera.

Did she understand what you were singing—did she love opera?

Yes, my voice gave her great joy. Mamaia Sanda Sandu would ask me to sing to her on the porch, at a specific time, when she knew that the people would go to rest, so the whole street could hear me and she could brag about me later on. She had her favorite arias and I would sing them to her with much love, I would usually give her a full recital—although, truth be told, sometimes I would wait for her to ask me several times, "Come on, Gina, sing it to me," and only then would I sing. . . .

She would gather some of her neighbors, and they would all sit on benches and become my audience, all excited, all crying and sobbing. I would try to explain to them that some arias were not even sad, just their tone was a little melancholic, but they knew better and said, "But they are so heartwarming . . . and you sing so beautifully." I would pause and let them catch their breath, because from a certain point on their crying could prevent them from hearing me altogether, but I knew it was an uncontrollable reaction and, after all, I also loved to see them so excited. . . .

CHAPTER 4

Romance and Revolution

◆ ◆ ◆

*D*uring *your student years you also met the Gheorghiu family, and later on you became part of it.*

One of my uncles, Ionel, my mother's brother who had taught her to sew shearling coats, lived in Bucharest, on Tunari Street. While I was living in the dorm, I would go to visit his home quite often. One day, as I was heading to his house, I passed by a superb villa, located on the same street. There, in the garage, I saw a young guy with glasses who was fixing something. Our eyes made contact for just one second, and I noticed him. His face stayed in my mind because it seemed interesting that in that old and elegant house, where I would have expected to see elderly people, lived such a young man.

By the third year of study, I had become friends with a very talented lady, a violinist, who was also famous at the time, Cristina Anghelescu. At her wedding at the Intercontinental Hotel, several colleagues gathered, including a pal of mine from the first year of conservatory, of whom I knew only that her name was Irina. I did not know her surname. Cristina Anghelescu's wedding was the first time that I saw Irina accompanied by her family. And then I realized that they were the Gheorghiu family, the most famous family of musicians, well known and respected in all elite artistic circles in the capital. Her parents loved me very much from that very event, and although we were barely acquainted, they immediately invited me to visit them.

My mother had taught me to never go in someone's house if I did not know him or her very well—especially as I was little. Knowing that I was in Bucharest, in a big city, far away from her, she was afraid, quite understandably—and because of her words, I was left with a reticence. However, upon receiving Manuela Gheorghiu's invitation, I had no hesitation in accepting; I trusted her the moment I met her. She invited me to watch some recordings of opera performances at their home.

76

There were recordings that I could not have found anywhere else. All said and done, a few days later, I dressed in a beautiful red dress I had bought in Poland, when I had been at the Moniuszko Festival. In Poland I had sung an aria from *Halka*,* I had an encore, I was in a wonderful shape and state of mind, and with the money I had received for my performance I had bought a few things, including this red dress, which was a bit retro, tightly fitted to my waist, and looked gorgeous.

When I arrived at their address, I realized that I was just in front of the beautiful villa on Tunari Street, where I had seen the young man working in the garage. The building had several floors, but I still could not wrap my mind around the idea that he might actually live there.

Did the entire house still belong to them? I am asking because usually the Communists completely rejected any rights to ownership and most of the time owning a big house was rather a problem.

The entire building had been made by Manuela Gheorghiu's parents. Her father, a great doctor, had built it before the war, specifically to have a place to work and live with his wife and their two daughters. During the Second World War, the house was bombed by the Americans. Just like all the Romanians, they too had been waiting breathlessly for the Americans to come, but certainly not in that way. . . .

Once the house was repaired after the end of the war, Manuela continued to live there with her sister, who had married the Romanian historian and art critic Ion Frunzetti. Back then when I met them, only half of the building still belonged to them. With the coming to power of the Communists, their friends had advised them to take in tenants or sell part of the house, and so they sold, lest their home be nationalized and taken away from them completely.

The villa was beautiful, it had great style, and the couple living in it, Ștefan and Manuela Gheorghiu, were quite phenomenal. If there ever existed people endowed with all the qualities possible—well, it was them: they had education, culture, class, kindness. Manuela was always taking care of someone. Ștefan, the great violinist and mentor to many other great violinists, both Romanian and foreign, was really funny, well loved by all his students, full of anecdotes, a great character, and an accomplished musician with real education and culture, who I

*An opera by Stanisław Moniuszko.

always loved dearly. He thanked me very much for the fact that I kept the family name even after I was no longer part of it and brought so much honor to it. I have always remained on excellent terms with the Gheorghiu family to this day.

When did you first set foot in their home?

I was in the third year of conservatory. Sure, I was starting to appear in many concerts and performances, they had seen and heard me on the TV shows, they had already understood at that time that I was not just anyone. So I went to visit them, and when I was about to leave, the boy I had seen one year before in the garage came dashing into the house. He was Andrei Gheorghiu, the son of the family—and his mother said, "What are you doing, dear, aren't you going to see the girl home?"

He took me home—I was living quite nearby—and then he extended another invitation to me to come and see the family. There was no *coup de foudre*, but rather a beautiful romance that came to life slowly, as we got to know each other while I visited them time and time again for that extraordinary atmosphere. . . . After two or three months, Andrei asked me out for the first time: our first real date, and the rest is history.

Manuela Gheorghiu preferred to invite us to her home, as the city had nothing much to offer anyway. I think everyone loved me from the first moment they saw me. They adopted me immediately and, as they understood art and artistic values and appreciated my innocence, had a completely different life philosophy and a different vision of women's role in society compared with the traditional Romanian families. "Dear —everyone can wash and cook. You have other work to do. Haven't you got something to study? Here—take the piano, it's free," they said. Every night we would watch together an opera performance or a good movie. They were part of the rarefied elite in Bucharest, and through them I joined this exclusive circle.

Manuela and Ștefan Gheorghiu counted among their friends the best university professors, members of the Romanian Academy, the best surgeons, the most important musicians, the best actors. . . . They had friends in all categories, and in each category their friends were the *crème de la crème*. They had been well acquainted with George Enescu and David and Igor Oistrakh, they were friends with Yehudi Menuhin and many others. What great letters I read in the Gheorghiu house, from all these great musicians. . . .

Before the Communist regime, the Gheorghiu brothers—Ștefan, grand master of the violin, and Valentin, the legendary pianist—had received, just like George Enescu, scholarships from the Royal House of Romania. Their mother was still living with Valentin, who at that time was not married. We would all call her Nonna, for she had Italian and Greek roots. Nonna had a sister in Bacău and they both spoke Italian—their family had preserved their ancient language and Italian traditions.

Was a wish to preserve the traditions of pre-Communist Romania widespread?

A thin social layer—which included philosopher and writer Andrei Pleșu, piano player Dan Grigore, an aunt of director Andrei Șerban, with whom I was taking English lessons, and several other intellectuals—had very strong royalist convictions. All these people could dream about was to see the King return home. In those last years of Ceaușescu's regime, there was a fervor and a desire to restore the old order, the old structure of society, but people did not know how to make it happen. They were all personalities with an extraordinarily strong backbone, with very consistent and uniform views, which they would express without any care in the family home of the Gheorghius, even though in those days you did not know where a denunciation could come from, who could follow you and report you to the Securitate.

On the other hand, thanks to Iosif Sava, Luminița Constantinescu, and Liviu Tudor Samuilă, who produced the TV shows featuring classical music, you continued to receive invitations for TV appearances.

Thanks to their intense support, there was never something important going on in Romania artistically speaking that would not include me, violinist Gabriel Croitoru, and the Madrigal Choir. In addition to these performances that were a joy and were of course much more interesting artistically, I had continued to tour the country together with my colleagues and Arta Florescu singing our patriotic music or romance concerts. I remember our master of ceremonies was a young actor then—Radu Duda.*

---

*Now Prince Radu of Romania, the son-in-law of the late former King Michael I of Romania, having married the King's eldest daughter, Princess Margareta of Romania (m. 1996).

During one of these concerts, in Târgovişte, where everything had been surprisingly nice—because we had been allowed to choose our own repertoire and we had been able to sing Romanian romances without other political pieces—we were introduced by Radu Duda and another actress. By mistake, Radu introduced Arta as an Emeritus Artist —instead of a People's Artist, as her real title was. There was quite a difference, indeed, but anyway nobody had the slightest attention or appreciation for these titles awarded by the Communists, so this slip of the tongue was surely not a good reason for a public outburst from Arta. And yet, as she was in the back of the hall, she started screaming furiously at Duda, scolding him in front of everyone because he had dared to present her as an Emeritus Artist, instead of a People's one. . . .

It was at about this time that composer Mişu Iancu wrote a romance for me—"The Piano." In our repertoire we had to have patriotic songs written specifically for us, but not romances, as this song was. I do not recall how I got to him, but I do remember that he was a gentleman, a very handsome and talented man. He wrote this romance for me and every time I would sing it, he would come to listen to me and sit in the front row, crying with excitement. The emotions of those in front of me had become, in time, a kind of barometer, a kind of measure of mine which indicated to me if I had managed to go the extra mile, if I had been able to convince them. Whenever I saw a tear in the eyes of those who were listening to me, I could not ask for anything more. I was the happiest girl in the world. And still am!

It was around then that your very first recording was released.

My first LP was recorded by Electrecord, which was then the only company authorized in Romania to produce and distribute music discs. It was produced in 1988. Obviously I could not include opera arias on it, as this would not have pleased the party. I sang instead "A Country like a Rose" by dear Paul Urmuzescu,* who had followed the recording sessions very excitedly. I recorded it and sang it. Surely, it was a patriotic piece, but not quite. . . . I would bypass Communist propaganda any way I could, as much as I could. It was a beautiful song, which had some lyrics written specifically so that we could record it, because otherwise we had no chance to make a disc and have it distributed on the

*Romanian composer.

market. In this political, social, and cultural context, people like Arta felt so powerful in the country—before the moment of the big change —that nothing interested them. They had no scruples. Although her role was to train us, it was clear that she could neither understand her role as a teacher nor was able to practice it. Most of the time, as we could clearly see, all she could do was pretend, put up a show. . . .

Despite Arta's attitude, you were performing at prestigious events in Romania.

Indeed, I continued to be invited to take part in the most important events. These included one of Mikhail Gorbachev's visits. At his first official trip to Romania, in 1987, the show organized for him was staged at the National Theater in Bucharest, and on that occasion I sang several Russian arias, in Russian. It was surprising that although Ceaușescu was present in the theater, we did not sing any patriotic songs. This was a kind of a subtle signal . . . although I do not know how many of the people watching the show noticed it. The fact is, all of us, the musicians, knew what was going on.

How were you dealing with your emotions onstage during your early performances?

Despite intense concert experience at the highest level and TV appearances, all the while that I was a student I went through a tremendous emotional torment, the biggest of my life. When I sang on the set of the national TV or in the Radio Hall, I had attacks of spasmophilia, or failure of calcium. I do not know exactly what was wrong with me, but my cheeks and hands would just freeze, so I had to physically unclench my fingers, one by one, and move my mouth so I could make a sound. I was horribly nervous. However, when the moment to enter the stage came, I would suddenly go into some sort of a trance, as if commanded. I never wanted to understand what I went through, I did not want to talk about it, but it was happening to me really often in those years. With time, my extreme emotions were attenuated, but I never got rid of them. True artistry cannot be created without emotions.

How was your personal life evolving?

The love affair with Andrei Gheorghiu was the materialized dream of any teenager. Andrei was the first boy who kissed me and with whom I had my first romantic encounter in the true sense of the word. I was extremely innocent and dreamy and I was twenty-four when I got married. I had had a very strict upbringing. Until he came to my life, I had no boyfriends, no one had held my hand, and no one had kissed me, even though I had had my freedom, already, for so many years, as I was away from my family, in Bucharest, living at the dorm or in a rented room.

With Andrei, who in his turn was very well-bred and very good-natured, everything was perfect, as I thought it ought to be. He was capable of the most beautiful and sincere gestures. He made me understand what I was, he encouraged me to spread my wings, but he never challenged me; he was extremely careful not to impose on me or scare me in any way. He treated me with perfect delicacy and affection—he was a true gentleman, devoted, honest, as he is today with his current wife.

When did you get married?

In 1988 we first had an engagement ceremony at his family's home, with a priest. Then the civil marriage ceremony took place at the end of the year, and the religious ceremony in January the following year. We were married by Father Nicolae Bordașiu and Father Galeriu in the St. Sylvester Church. Both priests were real personalities and also quite some characters, and both were well known and respected in Bucharest. Our godmother was Eugenia Moldoveanu, with her husband, Iacob, who was an engineer. For the church wedding I remember wearing a gorgeous white feather cape, which I had received from Gita, as Eugenia Moldoveanu was called by her friends.

As we wanted to have the wedding celebrations at home, because the city at the beginning of 1989 was not providing us with any viable options, we ended up throwing a series of parties. We could not fit too many people at the table and so we invited our guests on separate days, by category. One day we celebrated with the doctors, another day with our families, another with the artists. . . . The parties were one after another, but we wanted to celebrate the event with everyone who was close to us and we had no other choice.

How was the atmosphere of the Gheorghiu home at that time?

Extremely pleasant and beautiful. Ștefan was able to invite and receive friends, former students and colleagues from all over the world, as he was allowed to leave the country every year to teach master classes in Switzerland, Germany, or Italy and judge international competitions wherever he was invited. He enjoyed special treatment from the Communists because he was a very good friend, as I said, with Oistrakh, Menuhin, basically with all the greatest musicians of the world. And, in some cases, with some people, the party was trying to save face and create an illusion of "normalcy." This is why just a very few musicians could have some sort of freedom. Of course the party would take the lion's share out of all the fees they received abroad, but this was a given —there was no way you could have left the country if you refused to pay them.

All the world's great artists who came to Bucharest were sure to visit Ștefan, always. Oistrakh's son came to see him more often after his father's death. They would frequently meet outside Romania too, as they were both judges in international competitions. From their conversations and from the discussions I had with them, there was very much that I learned from the very beginning about what an international career really entailed, about artistic opportunities, but also about unorthodox things that were going on in the music industry. These were invaluable lessons and I got them just at the right time to prepare me for what was to follow.

In Ștefan and Manuela's house, the great baritone David Ohanesian once told me, "Little doll, don't ever try to sing too high or too loud— always try to sing from 'the inside.' Don't give me all you've got, that is too much. Don't try to sell me everything you have." He taught me how to make it all sound natural, effortless—"I want you to make sure that you always have additional resources, that you can always do more. And always look in the mirror, see how you look, see how you look to your audience." Simple words, priceless lessons.

In that family home, watching countless recordings from all times and all artists, I began to take the temperature of the world of opera. I remember Ileana Cotrubaș came to visit once—she listened to me and congratulated me. I liked her very much, and sometime later, when she heard that I was preparing for *La traviata*, she offered to help me study. She was hard to turn down, but I still said no to her, because I was used to studying on my own and I was quite happy with my own way—and any peculiarities that I might want to add to the interpretation, be they good or bad, were my own contributions to the role; they reflected how I wanted to build it, how I wanted to define myself as an artist by means of the score. I wanted to do whatever I felt was right, not what others had felt or had learned before me.

You were sensitive about interference?

I would ask anyone, anyway, "If you care about me, please do not give me any advice, unless I ask you to. I do not want it, really—I know what I can do and what I want to do and do not even need you to criticize me. If I ask for your opinion, I am happy to receive criticism. But if I don't, I won't be." I did not want to be influenced by anything. That is why I refused to read reviews—it is the subjective opinion of a handful of people, most of them with no musical studies whatsoever, but only opera admirers hired by some publications; that is why I never asked anybody anything like, "What do you think? What could I have done differently?" I had had my training with Mia Barbu, and she had instructed me to be very careful with the roles that I do—what I have to sing before them, what I have to sing after them, what breaks I need to have between performances, so that I do not push too hard. She told me to take care if the orchestra plays too loudly, and try as much as I can not to get tired. Her exact words were, "Do not let anyone mess with your voice: you must hold on to that voice for your entire life"—and I listened.

Did you see many different kinds of opera productions at this time?

It was about that time that I saw *La traviata* staged at the Craiova Opera*—with all characters wearing blue jeans. Much has been said about this production and probably this was just what the director wanted, but I thought it was an eyesore and a horror show, an act of unsubstantiated presumption. I felt it was completely unjustified for a man to alter the meaning of the libretto and the novel and transpose the score into a period and an environment that were completely inappropriate. I said to myself then that in my life I will never do something like this, participating in such weird productions, regardless of what happens and how much noise they are able to make. That is to say that even before I had started my international career, I had a clear opinion of what I should and what I should not do.

A true artist will always stay true to the composer, to his musical score, to the libretto. . . . What would anybody say if I would take a paintbrush and paint on a Rembrandt, Monet, Picasso, Van Gogh, et

---

*Craiova is the capital of Dolj County and the sixth-largest city in Romania.

ANGELA GHEORGHIU

cetera. It is the exact same thing when opera directors nowadays do all sorts of horrendous experiments. . . . Maybe the new generation—directors, company managers, and singers alike—can make fun of the great composers. . . . I respect them!

What was your sister doing at this time?

My sister was also attending the conservatory in the class of Maria Slătinaru-Nistor, a great voice and a great artist. She too had gotten married shortly after me, to a surgeon, Andrei Dan. So each of us had an Andrei of her own. Hers was an utterly erudite person, an incredibly intelligent man, with a keen sense of humor. We got along very well and we felt good when we were together. Their great desire was to have a child together, and several months after the wedding, my sister became pregnant.

We are toward the end of 1989—and revolution was around the corner in Romania.

Yes, and in those months, we all knew that something big would happen, but we just did not know what and when. It all began with the meeting in Timișoara, the first public meeting in years, where people had the courage to stand up and tell the truth. But until things spread to Bucharest, nobody could believe that something would really happen, much less to anticipate the scale of the events.

I still had classes at the conservatory, the winter vacation had not started yet, and I remember Arta—on December 17, when in Timișoara things had already escalated—coming to our classroom and putting a finger to her lips, to indicate to us to keep quiet. "Sssshhhh!!!" She simply forbade us to talk about what was happening around us.

Ultimately you did experience the Romanian Revolution as it happened, in Bucharest.

On December 21, I was out with Irina Gheorghiu, my sister-in-law. We were looking for some gloves to buy, just as Ceaușescu convened a meeting in the Palace Square to rally the people against the Timișoara uprising and scold the protesters from the balcony. I was close by, in a commercial area, when I left the store and started hearing loud noises and gunshots popping, some of them very loud. I saw more and more people running away with placards and flags, and with whatever they had been equipped with by the factories' management for the staged demonstration organized by Ceaușescu.

It was the dead of winter, it was cold, and chaos ensued. Suddenly cars no longer had anywhere they could go, among the thousands of people who ran all over the streets. All those who had attended the "meeting" came pouring in, in waves, tossing down their banners and pictures of Ceaușescu and stamping on each other's feet. Seeing these demonstrators, we returned home immediately, Irina and I. We walked hastily to the Gheorghiu family home, which was not far off. As we arrived there, we learned that the national TV station had already stopped airing, which was most unusual. As the hours passed and we were starting to understand that we were free, our first reaction was to weep with emotion, joy, surprise. Millions of Romanians were pretty much in the same state as we were.

In the coming days, my sister Nina and Andrei Dan, her husband, were on the barricades, at the Bucharest University. She was pregnant. We were wild with fear for them, because there were chaotic shootings going on in the city, there was great confusion, and the risk of being caught in the line of fire was enormous. I would bring them food and they kept camping at the university, dodging bullets but understanding that there was no going back until the change finally took place.

Only much later did we make sense of what happened then in Bucharest, and even then not in full.

At one point, a helicopter flew over our heads. It might well have been the one taking Ceaușescu to Târgoviște. It distributed fliers that urged us to take care, not to heed the people fighting against the Communist values . . . but those were "values" that nobody ever believed anyway. . . . At that stage of the events, such propaganda was already terribly childish . . . there were already tens of thousands of people in the streets, there was nothing to be done, you had to be downright crazy not to get it. . . . We were all watching with our own eyes history in the making.

Nina and Andrei occasionally would come back home to tell us what was going on. They would come on foot, because nothing was working in town anymore, no public transportation, no taxis. I would see them scared, bruised, tired, but also with all kinds of stories. I confess, I was very scared—I was locked in the house the whole time, and, putting things in the context of all the discussions that had been held in the Gheorghiu house for so long, we were beginning to understand what had happened from what we were seeing on TV.

When we realized that, following a brief moment of authentic freedom, the power had been seized by a group of second-rank Communists, we drew our own conclusions and backed off, even though the
new leaders had brought with them several artists to gain sympathy
and popularity through their endorsements. . . . Classic. . . .

There were, however, in those days, people who honestly believed in
change. . . .

There were two great idealists in those days—the actor Ion Caramitru and the poet Mircea Dinescu. Dinescu was well known as a dissi-
dent; he had been ostracized, somewhere in a remote neighborhood
of Bucharest. Caramitru hitherto had not been outspoken against the
party, but he did not hesitate to engage in that very important moment.
Their presence did a lot of good, brought credibility, and gave courage
to people to resist to the end. In our family, however, we soon realized
that although the change was good, it was not as good as we had all
expected.

As for the murder of the Ceaușescus in 1989—with all the justifi-
cations that have been made in the meantime, it still seems cruel to
me. For years I felt very embarrassed to talk about this barbaric gesture
outside Romania. It would have been preferable for the two dictators to
be taken to a panel of judges, although in a purely Communist country
the notion of authentic justice was quite debatable back then. It was
a complicated situation, and I leave it all to history to make sense of
these atrocities.

Otherwise, the entire 1989 winter holiday season, from Christmas to
New Year's Eve, was a time of sheer happiness. We all lived in a continuous state of elation. For a full week, no one was able to sleep. All our
eyes were simply glued to the TV set. Everything that happened seemed
great; we were completely overwhelmed. . . .

In my artistic career, the days of the revolution marked another important event. While I was in the Gheorghiu family home standing
near the TV, I answered the phone when Luisa Petrov, an opera impresario of Romanian origin who had an artists' agency in Germany,
called. Luisa had already heard about me from two of my colleagues
who had managed to leave Romania and earn their fame on the big
opera stages—Leontina Văduva and Alexandru Agache. Both of them
had spoken about me in very laudatory terms and had encouraged her

to look for me. For this gesture of comradeship and generosity in a time when it really counted, I will always be grateful to them.

There were gunshots around the house as we were speaking, Luisa heard them, so we interrupted our conversation and I let her listen into the receiver. There were the sounds of a full-fledged civil war, there were demonstrators passing in front of the house, and from the living room I could also see the tracers and hear fire weapons of all kinds.

With that phone call came an invitation and I said yes on the spot. I was a student, but I already knew I was no longer depending on the approval or disapproval of Arta. Luisa Petrov had invited me to take part in a concert in the Netherlands, a televised concert with a mezzo-soprano and a tenor. The television studios were in a town near Amsterdam, called Hilversum. There was a superb concert hall there. I went, we sang, the show was televised. It was very nice; I felt splendid.*

Meanwhile, in March 1990, my sister gave birth to a baby girl. Together with Nina, I decided that she would be called Ioana, like our mother. We both liked the name, both adored our mother, and we agreed it was the best choice for the little angel. In those days I felt incredibly close to my sister. I remember that we solemnly declared, "We have a child, we have a little girl." Ioana was, right from her first day on earth, my baby too, and my feelings about her have remained as strong as ever. My Ioana, our Ioana . . .

*The concert took place on October 6, 1990.

CHAPTER 5

Falling in Love with Covent Garden

◆ ◆ ◆

*I*n your last months of study at the conservatory, although you were *finally able to sing abroad, things in Romania were still not yet really chang-ing much?*

As we were now free, we had a meeting with all the colleagues—just as had happened in many other educational institutions—and de-manded the dismissal of all those without any professional value who had been forced upon us by the party. So we managed to remove almost all the professors, because we all wanted to make room for better ones, and we realized that change had to happen quickly, if it were to hap-pen at all.

Of all the teachers, the only ones kept by us, the students, through an open vote, were Georgeta Stoleriu, Maria Slătinaru-Nistor, and . . . Arta Florescu, the latter only for the master class. She remained in the con-servatory, in spite of everything she had done before 1989, as head of department in singing, because she was the only one who had been al-lowed to travel outside Romania for forty years, and as such she was the only one to feel the pulse of international competitions. Never again was she in a position to give singing lessons to anyone. In time, she fell into disgrace and slowly disappeared completely from public life. . . .

Of course, in the meantime, the Bucharest conservatory also had some great professors and valuable artists, such as Ionel Voineag, Iulia Isaev, Silvia Voinea, or Eleonora Enăchescu, but many inappropriate things are still happening there. People of great professional mod-esty and exceptional human quality are still suffocated by impostors who have continued to thrive, while those who could and should in-tervene and make things right seem to be content to just watch this masquerade. . . .

When was your first professional appearance on the stage of an opera house?

Before graduating, in the summer of 1990, I sang for the first time at the National Opera in Bucharest,* because there Arta Florescu had organized a tribute concert for herself. She called it "Arta Florescu and Her Students" and had me sing there, together with Maria Slătinaru-Nistor, Eugenia Moldoveanu, Mioara Manea, and Iulia Isaev. To some extent, I was still depending on her further along until my graduation, there was no way to say no to her, and the opportunity to sing on the stage of the Bucharest Opera in the company of my colleagues was good.

There she did something I did not notice at the time, but saw later, on video. When my time came to go onstage and Arta was supposed to introduce me, she avoided mentioning my name, presenting the aria I was about to sing with the words, "Such and such . . . will be interpreted by 'a voice.'" This was not a flattering metonymy. I sang the aria from *Madama Butterfly*, the church scene from *Faust* in semiscenic, with Dan Zancu, and "Muzica" by George Grigoriu. I first heard this piece of Grigoriu sung by Leontina Văduva and I liked it so much—the melody and lyrics altogether. It seemed that it suited me so well that it became a sort of personal anthem. The aria itself is a tenor aria, drawn from an operetta written by George Grigoriu, *Valurile Dunării* (Waves of the Danube), but the melody and lyrics, taken out of context, are able to express some innocent feelings, the true emotions of a lyrical artist.

As for the church scene from *Faust*—I performed it again twenty-five years later, on the same stage of the Bucharest Opera, in a gala concert celebrating my former colleague and my great friend, Mihnea Lamatic. During the gala, Mihnea took me by the hand for a second, so we could go together onstage. I hear that he got scared when he felt how nervous I was and how wildly I was shaking. Fortunately, my emotions were good that night and all the shaking was more of a vibration. That entire performance was an evening of joy for me, reuniting with my good friends and my home country audience.

*At that time the Bucharest National Opera was called the Romanian Opera (Opera Română).

Weren't you supposed to have your graduation performance there too?

Yes, we wanted to return to the Bucharest Opera with the conservatory graduation—a full performance of *La bohème*. This was how it should have been, but we were turned down for no reason, at least none that I know of. At that point in time, however, it no longer mattered to me, it no longer made any difference. The graduation was just a necessary step in the new conditions, and I had already started thinking about my international career. We moved without further ado to an opera house we were not familiar with, to a stage that we did not know, the National Opera in Cluj-Napoca.* The people there welcomed us with open arms.

I had sung in concerts and recitals before, but I had never been in a full opera. For our training sessions, we were accompanied by a pianist from the Bucharest Opera—Marietta Leonte, who was the same person who had helped us with the admission exam, so somehow we came full circle. She was with us from the beginning to the end. Together with Doina Micu, Mrs. Leonte was my support, and my singing teacher. Working with them—watching their reactions to my interpretation, my pronunciation, my phrasing—was extremely important to me.

Did you sing the opera in the original Italian or in your native Romanian?

I talked extensively with Mr. Anghel Ionescu-Arbore, the opera professor in Cluj, trying to persuade him and the company to let us sing *La bohème* in Italian, just as it was composed by Puccini, but there was no way to change his mind. As most of the Communist officials barely knew their own language, an Italian opera libretto was considered "elitist," and therefore all the singing on all the stages in the country had to be done in Romanian. I was thinking that, being free, we would soon get to sing these roles abroad and I wanted somehow to get ready. But Arbore would not give us permission: we had to sing in Romanian, following the tradition of those times. Eventually, the freshness, the pathos, and the credibility of the interpretation prevailed, and we were able to deliver a very nice performance.

Did you have any personal support in the audience that evening?

The night of the performance, my dad and the Gheorghius were present in the audience. We had been lucky to cover the entire cast with

*Commonly known as Cluj, located in central Transylvania.

graduates of our year—for the tenor role of Rodolfo we had Alexandru Badea, for Musetta we had Adriana Urechescu, and for Marcello the baritone Dorin Mara. Later, in 1994, with the latter and Iulia Isaev, I sang the quartet in a concert, together with Plácido Domingo, in Bucharest.

The performance-exam was sensational. We had the costumes leased from Cluj, where they had their own production of *La bohème*, so we had been able to give a professional performance, with rehearsals, with stage direction and everything. I did not know then that this would be the only opera performance I would sing in my country until today.

And this was also your farewell to the conservatory?

Yes, and immediately after graduation we went to a competition in Austria, to be heard by an international audience and to enjoy the freedom that had just been given to us. I, as you know already, disliked contests, but as I was pushed by everyone around me to go, I eventually went.

We arrived in Vienna at the Belvedere Competition, which was organized on rather lucrative principles, as, indeed, is the case today for many competitions. Instead of being a place of validation and talent-based ranking, it was more of a commercial vehicle for the early discovery and contracting of young artists. That is why, before going into rehearsal rooms, we were all supposed to go through an office, where the best of us were seen and selected, with the intention of being offered contracts with the Vienna opera companies. We were all singers from Eastern Europe, so presumably we would have enjoyed the opportunity and would have agreed to sing for lower fees. The prizes that were awarded were designed to the same effect, to provide concert opportunities, with the condition of signing a long-term contract, for at least a year or two. Although it must have seemed unusual for a young debutante recently graduated from the conservatory, I did not really like that.

In the audience, during the competition, a journalist from the British newspaper the *Times* noticed me and wrote in his report, "The most interesting singer of the competition, a young Romanian, Angela Gheorghiu. . . . Her account of 'Addio del passato' from *Traviata* was easily the most compulsive piece of singing in the final round." Orbiting around the competition were Ioan Holender, then secretary-general of the Vienna State Opera, and conductor Claudio Abbado, the artistic director of the same institution, a fantastic, eclectic, and passionate maestro. With Claudio I got to sing later in Berlin, with the Berliner Philharmoniker, the *Requiem* by Verdi, which was broadcast throughout Europe via Eurovision.* Also with Claudio and the Berliner Philharmoniker I recorded a wonderful disc of duets by Verdi, with Roberto Alagna—*Verdi per due.*

I won seven awards at the Belvedere Competition, all consisting of various commitments in various places, but of the seven, I took advantage of only one. Of course, after the contest, Ioan Holender contacted Luisa Petrov and tried through her to offer me a fest contract—that's a contract stipulating that I would be hired in the permanent ensemble of the theater. This was a standard offer that Holender was extending to all singers coming from Central and Eastern Europe, and Romania in particular. I explained then to both of them, quite clearly, that my wish regarding my artistic evolution was not to walk the same path or do like all the other Romanians had done before me. I was confident that I could and I would have a great career ahead of me and that I could safely rely on some honest audition sessions and the great gift God had given me. Sure, back then, at that moment, neither of the two was enthusiastic about my decision, but they soon understood where my faith came from, and I followed my path steadfastly and did exactly the way I felt was good for me.

Which of the seven award commitments did you take on?

The only opportunity "award" that I took advantage of following the Belvedere Competition was a concert in Wexford. I had been offered a performance there in the company of a baritone, and knowing that I was going to Ireland, Luisa Petrov and other managers recommended that I stop by in London on my return and do an audition at the Royal Opera House, Covent Garden. This all happened in the fall of 1990.

Luisa was a friend of Peter Katona, the ROH director of casting, so she arranged for the Royal Opera to pay my hotel so that I could get to the audition. Normally, as Luisa explained to me, such things did not happen, but I was a special case, in a special time. Somehow, my luck showed me the way; all the right stars aligned and helped me to pursue my destiny.

*It was also issued on CD and DVD (see discography).

This audition became famous.

Yes — it was quite cold in the city, so I was wearing a red wool cape made by my mother. Knowing almost no English, I was alone on the streets with a sheet of paper that read, "Where is the Royal Opera House? Where is the stage door on Floral Street? Which way do I go?" The opera house was near the hotel, and my accommodation was chosen specifically so that I would not get lost, but for me everything was intoxicating and I felt like I was anesthetized, a state from which I do not think I have ever woken up, even today. All I knew was that I must get to the audition; I knew that I should be heard by those people at Covent Garden.

As I was looking for the artists' entrance, I stumbled upon a nice gentleman, stopped him, and putting my sheet of paper in front of his eyes, I stuttered the text I had learned by heart. Who knows what else I said — my accent and my attitude must have given me away — but the fact is that he was none other than Peter Katona and he understood immediately that I would be his two o'clock audition in the Chorus Rehearsal Room of the Royal Opera House. But for the moment, he did not say anything about this: he merely showed me the way — there it is, just ten meters away, thirty-three feet!

When I reached the rehearsal room, I did a rehearsal with the pianist, and when the audition was about to begin, I saw the gentleman who had given me directions on the street coming through the upper door of the hall, accompanied by another member of the staff. We saw each other, we recognized each other, I began to laugh, and the entire audition was a beautiful dream. Of German origin, but with some Hungarian-Romanian-born relatives, Peter Mario Katona, a true citizen of the world, had always felt a bit of nostalgia for our country, or so I think. . . . The pianist who was onstage with me is to this day in Covent Garden and is a member of my extended "family" there.

I began to sing, something that was not very hard, because I wanted to leave a perfect impression. I chose two arias from *La bohème* — I had already learned to be very careful and calculated, even back then, indeed especially then, when there was no room for error. I sang the arias, and after I finished the second one, I heard Peter Katona telling me, "Would you like to sing *La bohème* with us?"

"Of course!"

PETER KATONA

Peter Katona was the director of casting at the Royal Opera House when Angela Gheorghiu sang her first and only audition for the company in 1990. He is still the director of casting today.

◆ ◆ ◆

At her audition Angela sang arias of Mimì, Louise, and something else, and at once I realized, "This is the real thing, one doesn't have to give any thought what to do with this voice, it is immediately certain," and that doesn't happen very often in auditions. It was very clear that we had to arrange something straight away. The voice had this wonderful unique beauty and a marvelous ease of technique and delivery. There was no question of, "First she needs to do this or that"—I engaged her for Mimì on the spot, to take place in June 1992.

"In a year or two—would it be okay?"

"Yes, for sure."

"Do you know your role?"

"Yes, of course."

"What else can you sing?"

"*Louise*, by Charpentier."* All said and done.

At the end of the audition, Peter Katona came down toward me, hugged me, and told me he would call Luisa Petrov. The audition had been organized with both the Irish agent from Wexford and Luisa, and so he asked me whom I preferred him to speak to. I chose Luisa then, because it seemed the right thing to do, as she had been the first agent who contacted me, while I was still a student.

And did Luisa draw up a contract?

A few weeks later, I received the contract, my first real agreement—from the very opera house where I most wanted to sing—directly into a leading role, in a very important production. I could not believe everything was happening to me exactly as Mia Barbu had predicted and

---

*"Depuis le jour," Louise's aria.

I was entering Covent Garden through the front door, just like she had advised me. As the stakes were so high and I was so nervous, being unsure of my stage experience, after receiving the contract for *La bohème* I kept thinking, how could I possibly straight away sing Mimì in *La bohème*—wouldn't it be wiser to first take on a smaller role, perhaps something else. . . . And so I proposed to them that they cast me in another role before Mimì, so that I could have some time to get used to the stage.

Peter Katona understood and gave me Zerlina in *Don Giovanni*. I started in this role at the Royal Opera House,* in a cast that included another artist who was at the beginning of his career—the Welsh baritone Bryn Terfel. We were both two supercharged racing engines that were revving, both willing and able to do much, much more, but waiting at the same time, to accumulate some experience first. We both wanted to do that, to begin with this work when we each had important roles ahead of us, with already signed contracts.

In that *Don Giovanni* production Bryn Terfel was making his debut with Masetto. From the outset, our relationship was great, and since then we got to sing many times together. Today, we know each other so well that most of the time we no longer need to talk, we understand each other right away from a single look, a single gesture—we know exactly how good we feel, how excited we are, what we have in mind. Bryn is and will remain one of my closest colleagues and friends, and one of the most talented.

Meanwhile, your concert appearance in Wexford in the summer of 1990 had prompted a number of international organizations to approach you.

Back at the Gheorghiu house, the phone kept ringing and draft contracts of all kinds kept on coming. . . . Toward the end of the year, I got a call from Silvia Marcovici,[†] who told me that I would be contacted again by Luisa Petrov, who was her friend and agent, this time for an opera in Basel, *L'elisir d'amore*. Luisa Petrov, who had listened to me and had already seen recordings of me and with whom I had already worked for the concert in the Netherlands, proposed to me that I sing Adina. I started to study the role because I felt the need to do this before Mimì.

---

*On March 3, 1992.
[†]Distinguished Romanian violinist and teacher.

ANGELA GHEORGHIU

SIR BRYN TERFEL

Angela Gheorghiu and the bass-baritone Sir Bryn Terfel both made their first appearances at the Royal Opera House in Johannes Schaaf's production of Mozart's *Don Giovanni*, conducted by Bernard Haitink in 1992. Angela sang Zerlina to Sir Bryn's Masetto.

◆ ◆ ◆

How can I ever forget that first encounter. This gorgeous wafer-like creature with jet-black flowing hair walking timidly into a dark, dusty Royal Opera House rehearsal room. Both of us having our debut that season at such an auspicious iconic opera house. Both of us young, naive, nervous. Not knowing what to expect. A memory I will never ever forget. Maybe that is why we have always had that bond of friendship. That collegial understanding of what had to be done. Heads down, dedication, hard work. No matter how shy, no matter how nervous, we had to get those Masetto-Zerlina scenes done for the run of shows and for our first-ever visit to Tokyo on the ROH tour. Thankfully we got over the line. The management liked us. The conductor loved us. Not sure about the director. He had no patience for these young singers and fobbed us off to the assistant director. Naughty Mr. Schaaf!! Strange silly man. His loss.

My new best mate was my Zerlina. I adored her, her singing, her acting, her gentle quiet persona. I still do. Fast-forward twenty-five years and she still makes me smile. So unpredictable. Who can forget the first time she sang "Vissi d'arte" in the rehearsal room, having just returned from her jaunt during the rehearsal period to the Cannes Film Festival, nudge nudge wink wink!! The whole room descended to quiet sobbing. Who can forget those three *Tosca* performances with Jonas [Kaufmann] and Tony [Pappano] where everything seemed to fall into place and an opera house that was buzzing. Not a ticket in town.

Bloody marvelous!!

I even persuaded her to come and sing in Wales. In my festival. In a field surrounded by sheep! Now that was an invitation. Mind you, she did get to meet Dame Shirley Bassey. Sparks must have flown when they met. Two of the most amazing singers in the world meeting in a caravan!! Unrepeatable.

Angela. Love you and adore you.

Sir Bryn. Your Masetto.

In Basel, I was told that once Montserrat Caballé had been hired on a fest contract, during the early years of her career. That was the fashion of the day, people kept telling me . . . but I remained firm in my beliefs and said no to any long-term commitments. I have never accepted this type of agreement—I was open to any guest-type contract, but nothing else.

From the very beginning of your career you knew what you had to do.

Well, yes! I had heard the theory that at first one had to do *la gamelle* —get a contract with a smaller theater and build some repertoire—but right from the outset I was completely against this. I believed I had no time to lose; I was ready to debut in the big houses, to get in through the front door, as Mia Barbu had told me, and I intended to do just that. Indeed, in 1991 Holender finally understood and sent me a first guest contract. For the 1992 season, he offered me *L'elisir d'amore* at the Wiener Staatsoper.* So this is how it happened that, in 1992, I made my debut both at Covent Garden, with *Don Giovanni* and *La bohème*, and at the Vienna State Opera, with *L'elisir d'amore*.

From early in my career, I would only sing in the biggest houses—if I was singing, I was singing for Covent Garden, Vienna, and, just a bit later, for the Metropolitan. When I had no performances there, I would make records, but I did not go anywhere else for a long time, keeping this relentless faith that I must sing only in the best places, together with the best stage partners.

Which was of course how the finest artists of the time came to know you.

The destiny indeed was that in these great theaters, where I had these important debuts, I would also meet the people who would be so important to my personal and my professional life. In London, at the Royal Opera House stage door, I met Plácido Domingo. There, with *La bohème*, I made my debut alongside a young tenor, Roberto Alagna, and in Vienna in *L'elisir d'amore* I ended up also singing with him. We were both very talented newcomers and we had been cast after we had gone through the auditions.

During the same period—1991 to '92—I met Dmitri Hvorostovsky, one of the most extraordinary artistic personalities, a magnificent baritone voice. We developed a great mutual admiration from that time

*The Wiener Staatsoper is the Vienna State Opera House.

because Dima was a charming Don Juan, from head to toe—whatever he did, his singing was extremely well studied. That always struck me about him, how well prepared he was, both lyrically and stylistically, how rarely you realized that he was of Russian origin. His pronunciation was extraordinary and his style—unmistakable. Until the end of his life we were great family friends.

It was in 1992 that I met Georg Solti. The great conductor heard me onstage, alongside Roberto Alagna, in *La bohème*. After those performances, Solti immediately thought of me for the new production of *La traviata*. Alfredo was Frank Lopardo and baritone Leo Nucci had a done deal, as everybody wanted him in *Traviata*; he was by far the best in the role of Germont. Alagna came to sing in *Traviata* sometime later, in a revival of the production in 1996.

So this is how you met Roberto Alagna?

The first meeting with Roberto was during the rehearsals for *La bohème*. I had come there, to London, accompanied by Andrei. I was married to my first boyfriend, the first man who had held my hand and kissed me. I had kick-started a big international music career, but I had not the slightest life experience. All I knew was that I had an exceptional husband in a family that loved me, I had been first his girlfriend and then his wife, and for all his folks I was an adored artist they treasured and treated with exceptional care. In his turn, Roberto was also married, but although he was only two years older than me, he had a completely different view on life and a completely different attitude. The first day we had rehearsals, he was late. I began to sing, probably the first aria, so at first he listened to me behind the door without knowing who I was and how I looked. He had probably imagined someone bigger and not as young as I was, and when he came in and saw me dressed in the female version of a kilt, all Scottish from head to toe, he had a surprise.

Were you attracted to each other then?

Sure, we liked each other from the first moment and we impressed each other with the way we were both singing, but because he had more life experience, he had the courage to take the first step, right from the very first meeting. After the first day of rehearsals we went out the stage door and then he asked if I wanted to go with him for a coffee. Andrei was waiting for me at the hotel, so I said no. Roberto was shocked by my reaction, he did not know how to interpret it, but

perhaps my refusal attracted him even more. In the days that followed,
he began to pursue me relentlessly, we started talking, we held hands,
he kissed me, and I slowly melted. . . . But in 1992 everything was limited to a mere flirtation, nothing more.

Did it feel awkward, with Andrei being there?

Well, Roberto tried to befriend him too. They were speaking French
together, Roberto started to invite us out, we would eat together, spend
evenings together, watch French movies together, have fun. I saw him
just as a nice young man who had a great voice, a great personality, and
with whom rehearsals were magnificent. Incidentally, these rehearsals
for our performances took place somewhere else, not at Covent Garden but across town.* In 1992 the theater was not so big, and it did not
look as it does now—by the way, when it reopened after its expansion,
the opening performance included Roberto and myself. Back then in
1992 we rehearsed in another area of town, and from our hotels, which
were close to the opera house, we had quite a long way to go by taxi.
We would either split our cab fare or Roberto would take the bill, and
we would travel together, back and forth, for nearly an hour. This was
the best opportunity for Roberto to charm me with beautiful words, to
court me persistently.

---

*The rehearsals were held at the Troxy Cinema, which had many years earlier been
the venue of the London Opera Centre, an opera training school under the aegis of
the Royal Opera House.

ANGELA GHEORGHIU

PAUL FINDLAY

The late Paul Findlay was the Royal Opera House's director of opera when Angela Gheorghiu sang her first Mimì in the house in 1992.

◆ ◆ ◆

We realized immediately that she was an instinctive singer and an instinctive actress and she commanded the stage. She was also hardworking beyond belief and a perfectionist. I remember how impeccably dressed she always was—it was a lesson to everyone at the Royal Opera House as to how to dress perfectly. The public were absolutely enthralled by her as Mimì because she gave a very measured performance, she was very fragile and delicate onstage and the role suited her perfectly. It was an enormous success and it gave us the confidence to know that we had picked a winner.

Roberto's wife, Florence, had just given birth, and therefore had not been able to come with him to all the performances. I think that she did eventually come to one of them and so I met her. With all the performances of *La bohème* we had a huge success, so big that, as I said, I drew the attention of Georg Solti and received offers for other productions. The most important of all was that for the new production of *La traviata*.

You had sung Mimì for your stage debut in Cluj-Napoca and now it was your main debut role at Covent Garden!

Yes, *La bohème* was the real debut at the Royal Opera House. And the opera felt very real in my life, again. In a way *La bohème* had been my young life in the conservatory of music, because in that period I had a completely bohemian style of life, quite *la vie de bohème*.* I was in love with music, in love with life, and I had the passion and talent to start to make my dream come true—like Mimì does. Then of course *La bohème* had been the very first opera I sang onstage, at Cluj-Napoca —and in Romanian! As I mentioned before, I had asked if I could sing

*Puccini's opera *La bohème* is based on *Scènes de la vie de bohème* (1851), by Henri Murger.

it in Italian, but there was no way because of the mentality at that time. The director of the Bucharest Opera, conductor Cornel Trăilescu, had told me then that Mimì was not suitable for me. I won't elaborate any further on that. . . . Although we had just said goodbye to the Ceauşescu regime, the old mentality was still there. But the Cluj Opera performance had been a wonderful experience. Even when I had been preparing the opera, I was very clear in my head that wherever my debut on the international stage would be at that time, Mimì would be my role, and my dream came true after two years, because in 1990 I sang *La bohème* at Cluj-Napoca, and in 1992 I performed it at Covent Garden. I was living my dream—and I am still doing that!

This is a perfect debut opera and in fact it was perfect for my entire career. Throughout the years, I sang it in New York, Vienna, San Francisco, Paris, London, Barcelona, Milan, et cetera, all together hundreds of times, along with *La traviata* and *Tosca*.

Although Mimì is young and fragile, sometimes it is overlooked that she is not an ingénue—and so maybe it's tricky to balance her delicacy and womanliness?

She is not a girl! She's vulnerable and sensitive, but she also knows what she wants. She has the courage to knock on the door of her neighbors, probably on Christmas Eve, looking for company with a cute pretext—she wants to get a light for her candle. At the same time, she has the courage to see the man that really she knows is there for her. In that epoch we know she was called Mimì as a lady who was helped by other men to have a wonderful life—in other words she was a kept woman! On that particular evening she was free, and she feels, "This is my moment—now or never." Don't forget she is ill—and that kind of malady in that period was very serious. So, when you are in love and you know you are not going to live for long, and you want to conquer something, you are not thinking about anything: you just want it and that's all.

I remember you once said that the third act is the key to Mimì because although she is physically so much weaker than Rodolfo, she is mentally stronger there—so that in the aria "Donde lieta uscì" you bring a calm strength to the color of the voice, which is so much more powerful than the rather tearful way in which this is sometimes sung.

But it must be like that. Both Mimì and Rodolfo know that really she is dying, but while he is so upset that they have to say goodbye, she is

Mother Ioana Sandu and her friend, Tănțica, posing for the Russian magazine. (Unless otherwise specified, all photographs are from the author's personal archive.)

Family picture, at a typical Romanian wedding in those years. To the groom's left and right are Ion Burlacu and Ioana Burlacu (Sandu), respectively. To the bride's left and right are Angela and Elena, respectively.

Angela Gheorghiu and her mother, Ioana Sandu, at the Royal Opera House, Covent Garden, February 27, 2017. Neil Gillespie

With Mia Barbu and
Angela's mother, Ioana
Sandu, in London.

With colleagues from the
music conservatory, 1986/1987:
Paul Basacopol, Nicu Raiciu,
George Martin, Gladiola
Niţulescu, Iulia Isaev, Cristina
Iordăchescu, Mihnea Lamatic,
Angela Burlacu, violinist Gabriel
Croitoru, Mioara Manea.

Angela with her sister, Elena Dan. Vivienne Purdom

With Peter Katona, on the set of act 3 of *La traviata*,
Royal Opera House, 2010.

In Puccini's *La bohème*, with Ramón Vargas, Metropolitan Opera, 2008. Marty Sohl

The cast of *Pagliacci* at the Royal Opera House, 2003: Daniil Sthoda, Dmitri Hvorovstovsy, Antonio Pappano, Angela Gheorghiu, Plácido Domingo, Lado Ataneli.

With Sir Georg Solti,
in his London home.

As Violetta Valéry in *La traviata*,
Royal Opera House, December
1994. © Catherine Ashmore

With Princess
Diana, after *La
bohème*, Royal
Opera House,
1992.

With Anthony Hopkins,
Jennifer Lynton, and Sir
Richard Eyre, Royal Opera
House, 1994.

With Pier Luigi Pizzi
and Nello Santi,
in Venice, 1996.

Angela at her signing with
Decca, Paris, January 1996.
From left to right: Roland
Kommerell, president; agent
Luisa Petrov; Didier de
Cottignies, head of marketing;
Angela Gheorghiu; Michael
Haas, executive producer; Evans
Mirageas, senior vice president
A&R. Mary Robert

As Liu in Puccini's *Turandot*, Royal Opera House, 1993.
Clive Barda / Arena Pal

Angela with Ioana and Angela's father, Ion Burlacu, backstage at Covent Garden's *Turandot*, December 1996.

With Ioana at the Teatro Colon, Buenos Aires, 2012.

With Peter Gelb, Rollando Villazón, and Joe Volpe, 2006.

With Franco Zeffirelli, rehearsing for *Pagliacci*, Royal Opera House, 2003.

Angela as Micaëla and
Plácido Domingo as Don José
in Bizet's *Carmen*, Metropolitan
Opera, 1996. Winnie Klotz,
Metropolitan Opera

With Jonas
Kaufmann in
La traviata,
La Scala,
2006.

With Toscan du
Plantier, on the set
of the *Tosca* movie,
2000.

With Luciano Pavarotti, on the "Porta a porta" television show on Rai 1, Modena, Italy, 2001. Daniele Venturelli

With Sting and his wife, Trudie Styler, Petra, Jordan, 2008.

Curtain call for *Roméo et Juliette*, with Roberto Alagna, Royal Opera House. 2000.

As Marguerite at the Metropolitan Opera's 125th anniversary gala, March 25, 2009. © Ken Howard

With Alexander Gerdanovits, Florentina Bucos, and Mihai Ciortea, Regensburg, Germany, 2014.

With Virginia Zeani, West Palm Beach, 2014.

With Prince Charles, Plácido Domingo, and Roberto Alagna, at the Gold and Silver Gala at the Royal Opera House, December 12, 1996. © Bill Cooper / Arena PAL

As Tosca, Royal Opera House,
2006. © Catherine Ashmore

As Magda in *La rondine*,
San Francisco Opera, 2007.
Terrence McCarthy

As Adriana Lecouvreur,
Vienna State Opera, 2014.
Wiener Staatsoper /
Michael Poehn

With Vangelis,
in the recording studio
in Paris, 2011.

With Jeremy Irons, Royal Albert Hall, May 13, 2010.

With Mihai Ciortea, after a recital at La Scala, May 16, 2014.

stronger and calmer than him—which is how it is in real life when you don't want someone you love to be upset about your death. So you must not sing "Donde lieta uscì" with a lot of intense emotion as though you are afraid. She is just saying it how it is: "Addio, senza rancor"—let's say goodbye; no hard feelings. We shall see each other again in the flower season—"alla stagion dei fior," sing both Mimì and Rodolfo, at the end of act 3.

From that debut with *La bohème* I made friends with many people at the Royal Opera House—from the orchestra, the chorus, the machinists, the hairstylists, to the makeup artists and ushers. With each of them I have a little story—from each of them I have received, over the years, a small gift or token of their appreciation.

What kind of stories?

In 2000, for example, I stayed on beyond my contract to do another performance with Offenbach's *Les contes d'Hoffmann*, singing Antonia. As a way to say thank you, the ushers chipped in and got me a gift, because I had not gone after I had done my performances. I never forget these gestures. At Covent Garden the ushers and the security people are my friends—I hug them every time I go there, we're very close, they are the first people I encounter, and they are able to put a smile on my face whenever I step through the door.

But these are not the only people who are dear to me at the Royal Opera House. A machinist once gave me a pair of uniform pants with the ROH branding simply because I noticed them and I told him I liked them. Choristers keep in their dressing room my life-size poster and dress me up in various fashions, depending on the occasion. For Christmas I wear red, obviously—they always find glamorous outfits for my poster. In 2003, when I was doing *Pagliacci* with my dear friends Plácido Domingo and Dmitri Hvorostovsky, directed by Franco Zeffirelli, the choristers blindfolded me and led me into their dressing room to show me the poster and take pictures of me standing next to it. It was proof of their creativity and the love from them, one of those priceless little gestures, which you never forget.

Also in London, makeup artist Babett Weber is the one who knows me best and she does my hair every time. A consummate professional with great artistic sensitivity, Babett gives me courage and ensures that each and every wig as well as the makeup looks flawless. Fay Fullerton, head of costumes, has always made me feel beautiful and protected, regardless of the difficulties that usually ensue with dress rehearsals and costume fittings, especially for the new productions.

It is essential to have around a very good and dedicated team to help you get over your emotions and excel onstage every time. From this perspective, I was spoiled and pampered and lucky to work with the Covent Garden team, I must admit. And in turn, I can only hope I have not disappointed anyone. I don't know if Peter Katona and the musicians and staff of the Royal Opera House really know that I consider them family. I'll love them my entire life and I will never be able to thank them enough. . . . It's been twenty-six years since my debut on this stage and I just celebrated my 150th performance with the Royal Opera House in 2017.

They are all members of the house where both you and Alagna really began your careers.

True, both Roberto and I began our whirlwind careers in London. We had six performances together then. Typically, a series of four to six performances at Covent Garden is just perfect. To have fewer performances in one season you have to be a big name. On the other hand, even if you're a big draw, it's still not good to have fewer performances, as the rehearsal time is the same and the preparation work is the same. It's a shame to waste it on just a couple of performances.

But this is not how all the opera houses operate, is it?

Indeed not. Vienna does not have the same system; it does not provide grand rehearsals with a full orchestra for productions which are already in repertoire. The rehearsals take up fewer resources and less effort. It sometimes might happen that you go onstage after just one rehearsal. This can create really interesting and rather thrilling situations. In the end, the final result is the one that counts, and it's not rare for us to discover that more rehearsals do not necessarily mean a better performance. Ideally, though, you do need at least two weeks of rehearsals, in my opinion. The ROH system is the best, as far as I am concerned, but of course it all depends on the way an opera theater is managed.

What happened with Roberto after the performances in London had finished?

Roberto and I went each on our own way. We were both married, he had a small child, I had a husband I cared about very much. We met

SIR ANTONIO PAPPANO

In 1993 Angela Gheorghiu sang Micaëla in Bizet's *Carmen* as her first collaboration with the conductor Sir Antonio Pappano, who later was to be the conductor
for many of her most acclaimed recordings and performances at the Royal Opera
House and elsewhere.

♦ ♦ ♦

I first heard Angela in the autumn of 1993 when she came to the Théâtre de
la Monnaie in Brussels to sing Micaëla in *Carmen*. If the role is sung really
well indeed, because the aria is placed quite late on in the evening, she can
steal the show, and that is exactly what happened every single night. The
beauty of the voice, and not only the beauty but the individuality, just sent
people into raptures. Also it was a voice that made the orchestra prick up
their ears, and that makes orchestras play differently. She was lovely — always dressed to the nines, even for rehearsals!

again shortly after in Vienna, for the performances of *L'elisir d'amore* for
which I had received the contract from Ioan Holender.* Roberto's wife
was there too. And this time the onstage chemistry between us was
amazing, because we were both trying to add a theatrical component,
some dramatic interpretation, and this made the roles come to life. But
we did all this guided by our natural instincts — otherwise, we were just
two young artists doing their job and nothing more.

Were you now singing in a large number of countries?

The following year, in 1993, I continued with new roles in London
and Vienna, I went on tour in Japan with the production of *Don Giovanni*
from Covent Garden, I gave a concert in Germany, I was Micaëla in the
Royal Opera House production of *Carmen* alongside Plácido Domingo,
and in December I debuted at the Metropolitan Opera, as predicted by
Iosif Sava.

The Japanese tour of the Royal Opera House enjoyed an extraordi-

---

*This production of *L'elisir d'amore* was Angela Gheorghiu's debut at the Vienna
State Opera on October 27, 1992.

nary array of artists—Karita Mattila was Donna Elvira, Carol Vaness sang Donna Anna, and Thomas Allen was a perfect, sensational Don Giovanni. Claudio Desderi, Bryn Terfel, and I completed the team. I enjoyed the whole trip and the experience enormously, except for the food, which was to me extremely hard to get used to and at first made me suffer horribly. As I was never able to sleep after a performance, thus accumulating hundreds of sleepless nights, the fact that I could not eat either was just terrible. In time, of course, I got used to Japanese cuisine, and now I really like it a lot, but the accommodating period took me quite a while.

It was in London's Covent Garden that you also started to have true admirers and very soon-to-be "close followers" of your career.

Yes, that's true! Among them is Barbara Sims, a wonderful lady who was present at my debut in *La bohème* at the Royal Opera, in 1992. We share quite a funny story together: I used to watch many performances of my colleagues at that time, and I was usually sitting in the Stalls Circle area, close to the stage. There was a curtain there and I must have been moving it a lot or making some sort of noise with it. Then, suddenly, there was this lady hushing me up, telling me to be quiet during the performance. In the intermission, she saw me in the foyer, and when she realized who I was, this woman began staring at me and walking quickly up to me, when she finally asked me, in a cold sweat, "Are you Angela Gheorghiu?!" I told her, "That's me," and then she suddenly started crying and told me how sorry she was, because she loves me and already she had seen every performance I had given at Covent Garden. She couldn't believe she had hushed *me* up and was very upset about this. From then on, all through the last twenty-six years, Barbara has not missed any performance I have sung at the Royal Opera House and she has come to see and hear me all over the world: in Europe, America, and even Australia. And she continues to do so, even now, at seventy-nine years old!

Among my true and very faithful admirers are Anne Detain, whom I had also known since my debut at Covent Garden, Claudia and Beate Peters, Martine Chiron, Tracey Claire Dodd, Victoria Pniel, Cedomir and Eva Bogoszavliev, and Susie Leff. I developed a wonderful relationship with them over the years, I am always happy to see them in the audience or after a performance, and they are all very close to my heart.

CHAPTER 6

A Star Is Born

• • •

ow did your debut at the Metropolitan Opera come about?
In 1993, in spring, after several performances of Liu in *Turandot* at
Covent Garden, I sang Nanetta in *Falstaff* in Vienna. Falstaff was Benjamin Luxon, and the role of Ford was sung by the Russian baritone
Vladimir Chernov. He was an absolutely sensational Ford, and all the
directors of the major opera houses were crazy about him. He was a big
draw with the audiences, and the cheers and the ovations he received
after his arias were incredible.

Singing right next to him, I remember that we had our rehearsals
with orchestra for these performances in the hall of the Musikverein,
because the rehearsal rooms of the opera in Vienna are mainly smaller.
There, above the organ and directly above the orchestra as you look
from the hall, there was a small balcony. We all got up there in the tiny
balcony to sing our roles. Our voices sounded truly heavenly—Ramón
Vargas was Fenton, Vesselina Kasarova was Meg Page, Nancy Gustafson
was Alice, the entire cast was sublime. We were all excited and transported by the miracle of the music, and the conductor was Seiji Ozawa,
an extraordinary man who gave me one of the most beautiful musical
experiences.

What did you think of Seiji Ozawa?
Seiji had an extremely subtle and elegant way of requesting something of you, and he would always get you to agree with the suggestions
or recommendations he was making as if they had been your own. He
never used a commanding voice, none of his requirements was subjective or whimsical, and everything was justified and well substantiated. For us musicians, all nuances, details, and in particular the tone
of voice in a conductor or director are essential. They make the difference between feeling good and giving your best, or feeling constrained
and then limited.

RAMÓN VARGAS

Tenor Ramón Vargas first sang with Angela Gheorghiu in 1993 when they appeared at the Vienna State Opera in Verdi's *Falstaff*, with Benjamin Luxon in the title role, Angela singing Nanetta, and Ramon singing Fenton. They were to partner onstage many times and were the Mimì and Rodolfo when the Metropolitan Opera filmed their production of Puccini's *La bohème* in 2008.

◆ ◆ ◆

Angela Gheorghiu and I met in 1993 in Vienna for the centenary of Verdi's *Falstaff*. We were two youngsters full of expectations. She had just left her native Romania and I was also starting my international career. Since then we have maintained a beautiful friendship and an artistic collaboration that has taken us to sing together in important productions around the world. When I listen to Angela or when I sing with Angela is always a special experience and a privilege. I have always believed that individuality in an artist is one of the keys to success.

Angela is a unique artist!

They can have a negative effect!

Even today, if someone asks me something using an inquisitorial or dictatorial tone, as if I should feel guilty about something, I feel a lump in the throat and I could as well go home. Many colleagues react like me, especially early in their career, and some conductors take advantage of this sensitivity to assert their authority. This seems completely wrong to me because, after all, we all want to have a successful performance, and in order for everything to work smoothly, we'd better behave like a family, supporting and stimulating each other rather than constantly flaunting our superiority and authority.

Now, coming back to your debut at the Metropolitan . . .

During these rehearsals for *Falstaff* in Vienna and after hours we were all together and we would go out together. The vibe of the entire team was very good, and one day after rehearsals Vladimir Chernov came up to me and said, "Angela, I have decided: you need to be heard by James Levine." I was of course thrilled by his proposal—I was sure that the time would come for my debut at the Met, but I was rather thinking I would have to have a bit more patience. Moreover, I knew that there was a legend that no one could be hired by the New York Metropolitan Opera unless he or she gave an audition in front of Jimmy, in the very theater where they would later be supposed to sing. It was very important for him to hear the singers there, in that very hall, to see whether their voices were big enough to fill the space's requirements. True, the Metropolitan Opera is very large, but it also has very good acoustics, so this practice wasn't really necessary, in my opinion. With the passage of time and experience, looking back, I realize that in fact Jimmy had underestimated the quality of his hall, so he may have misjudged other artists. The acoustics of the Metropolitan are much better than in other, smaller European houses, and there the architecture effectively compensates for its enormous size.

So did you travel to New York for your audition?

For my audition, Vladimir Chernov had thought of everything. He had already spoken with Jimmy Levine and had already told him that I would not have time to travel to New York, as I was "too busy." But he also told him it was a must to bring me to the Met for a performance, that very year. Chernov had many new productions in New York, he was very much *en vogue*, and he simply and generously used his influence over Levine to promote me. As he also knew that Levine was supposed to come to Europe from time to time, he used one of these visits —the Bayreuth Festival—to bring us to the same place.

So I went to Bayreuth and started my audition with Jimmy. I sang an aria and saw him begin to sob. His face turned red and he burst into tears. I was very impressed by his reaction, and he was the first very important person in my life who was so moved by my voice. He asked me to sing a second aria, I gladly obliged, and as I sang, I saw him seriously beginning to cry, tears streaming down his face.

After the second aria he hugged me, kissed me, and told me, "Vladimir was right. Our season is already planned, but I'll see what I can do, I got it. What would you like to sing, what else have you been singing?" I suggested *La bohème*. He accepted immediately, and there and then we agreed that I should come to New York in December. We both knew the audition was over, but in the end Levine had another request: to sing him something else, only for the pleasure of his soul. That moment was so awesome, even endearing, that I could not have refused him anyway. I just teased him and said, "Okay, but this is the last aria"— then I sang *Butterfly* or *Louise*, I don't remember exactly.

So you were making your Met debut only a few months later!

This audition happened during the summer, and soon after I got the contract through Vladimir's manager, who was working for Columbia Artists, so in December I already was making my debut at the Metropolitan Opera with *La bohème*. For this collegial gesture, which was invaluable to me and completely selfless, I leave all my gratitude to Vladimir Chernov. Spasiba, Vladimir!

Before the show at the Met, I remember that I had an interview with a journalist who looked at me with enough curiosity and a certain amount of suspicion. Sure, I was very young in opera, where anyone under thirty is a junior. He asked me something along the lines of, "How on earth did you get to sing there?" I explained to him, very seriously, that I had previous singing experience in my home country, that I had already made debuts in London and Vienna. To me it was just natural, whereas to him it just sounded unbelievable. . . .

The performance was a great success; it was great to get standing ovations when I went alone in front of the curtain, right from my first performance. I must admit, I was not really shocked, but rather my expectations had been confirmed. From a mere dream, from just aspiration and impetus, there is a long way to actually achieve something, so the fact that I was able to live my dream was wonderful for me.

After the first performance, I had already prepared my postcards to send to my parents, to the Gheorghius, and, of course, to Mr. Iosif Sava. I could not wait to tell him that he was right and that his prophecy was fulfilled. Somehow I felt him by my side, both spiritually and professionally. This man was a big help to me. He gave me the confidence I needed, precisely when I needed it.

What was it like for you being in New York?

With the first performances at the Met, I got to meet a very popular and very special New Yorker, Sissy Strauss, who worked as an artist liaison for the opera. She was the perfect hostess, who opened the doors of her superb apartment next to Lincoln Center to all the artists singing or directing there. For forty years or so she had been the artist liaison for the Metropolitan, which for her was not so much a kind of job,

CAROL NEBLETT

The late soprano Carol Neblett was Musetta in Angela Gheorghiu's Metropolitan Opera debut in 1993, when she sang Mimì in Puccini's *La bohème*.

◆ ◆ ◆

The first time I heard Angela Gheorghiu I was so impressed with her personality, her vibrancy, her vulnerability—her ability to put across the emotions to all of us. Not only does she have a really remarkable voice, really beautiful and remarkable—she is a great interpreter, and she loves the music: she absolutely loves the music; and she loves the audience. And because she truly loves the audience and truly loves the music, she gets this enormous applause—which she deserves, greatly. She is simply a superb, superb singer, with all the wonderful attributes that I have not seen in a very, very long time.

but rather a vocation. Three to four times a month she would throw a party at her home, which gathered everyone in town, the entire New York high society. We would all meet, talk, and make music together. I was staying near the Metropolitan Opera, in the vicinity of where Sissy Strauss lived, so I could come to her events quite easily.

Who exactly did you meet there?

The first time I was in that beautiful house, I met the fantastic Birgit Nilsson, full of humor and with an unmistakable laughter; the divine mezzo-soprano Marilyn Horne was coming very often and was always ready with a joke; also a guest of Sissy's was baritone Hermann Prey, a gorgeous man with the manners of a noble gentleman and a very beautiful voice; conductor Valery Gergiev was also there, having recently become famous—later on, he was to become a truly fabulous conductor; Renée Fleming, an American artist who was extremely open and friendly—she had the voice of an angel and had recently made her debut at the Metropolitan; and Plácido Domingo, whom I had already known from the Royal Opera House. In the years to come, there was not a single colleague or artist to miss from Sissy's soirees, the so-called "goulash parties."

MARILYN HORNE

Mezzo-soprano Marilyn Horne and Angela Gheorghiu met for the first time after Angela's debut at the Metropolitan Opera in 1993.

♦ ♦ ♦

It's such a beautiful voice with a tremendous sense of legato, which I think is just fantastic. One doesn't hear a lot of that, and I think the combination of the beautiful voice and the beautiful person as well as the very strong focus on what she is doing is very special. I am a great admirer of hers.

What was Sissy's background?

Of Austrian origin, Sissy was a true aristocrat, and her apartment looked accordingly. It was sumptuous, bright, and decorated with true museum-quality pieces. At the soirees she organized, we would either sit around the table if there were a few of us, or we would scatter about in all rooms if we were many. Apart from the guests, the hosts would usually call one great jazzman, and so, one by one, we would all start singing. It was a fabulous atmosphere and a tremendous star power . . . just like in the movies.

Together with her husband, Max Strauss, from whom she was inseparable, Sissy never missed any of my performances at the Metropolitan, even though there were many. . . . They always impressed me with their passion for opera, the infinite patience with which they listened to and supported all the artists, and the beautiful words they were able to find for each of the dozens of stars that paraded through their home in New York for over forty years. . . . After Sissy's contract with the Metropolitan ended, in 2014, she returned to Vienna, where she continues the good tradition.

Among the colleagues whom I met at the soirees there was Natalie Dessay. One of those evenings, at the end of 1993, I saw Natalie coming over to me. We had already met on the premises of the theater, as the Metropolitan has this policy of actively encouraging artists to get acquainted, to talk together, to create a family. "Écoute, I must tell you something," she said. "Do you remember Roberto Alagna?"

"Yeah, sure, we sang together."

"He asked me to ask you to call him. His wife has died recently, he is quite down, please call him when you can."

And did you?

I did call him, not while I was in America, but when I returned to Europe, a few days later. Of course he was receiving calls from everybody. It was a difficult time for him; everyone liked him and he liked everybody. I called him too and we picked up our conversations from where we had left them. As he was a free man, he started to become insistent just at this time when there was a certain distance between Andrei and me. Surely, I had nothing to reproach Andrei for, nor he me; it was just that he no longer enjoyed traveling the world to be with me wherever I was singing. He also wanted to do something in Bucharest, so he got a job with the Romanian television and I could feel that my schedule was way too much for him.

Can you recall when this distance between you and Andrei started?

By 1993 we had started to see each other quite briefly and not very often. Sure, he would come to the premieres and most of the performances, and Ștefan Gheorghiu would come too. At Covent Garden I was also able to see Ștefan's wife Manuela when I did *Chérubin* by Massenet, or when I sang Liu in *Turandot*, or in *Carmen*, or *La bohème*, or countless others. They would come for a few days, but when you are away for a full year, a few days here and there seem never enough. . . . It was a big and steep change for everyone, and that happened although everyone understood clearly that there was no way I would not go wherever I was called, there was no question that I would follow my destiny.

Which ordained that you were about to travel the world.

Yes. In 1993 and 1994, in addition to the very heavy agenda of performances in Vienna, London, and New York, I started a beautiful friendship with Plácido Domingo, who had an international concert tour and wanted to take me with him wherever he went. Very few great artists have this habit of taking young singers on tour and introducing them to the biggest audiences. In my case, things were a little different, as I had already made my debut in all the big houses that interested me and I had already begun to have my own audience, but of course I could not and had no reason to say no to the opportunity of going on tour with one of the greatest tenors of the time, a consummate professional and a great artist, especially since his invitation was extremely gracious.

You were, though, already a much more celebrated and acclaimed artist than the sopranos in this position usually were.

Of course, that was all well, although perhaps not *very* well. I had sung at the Met, I had made my debuts at Covent Garden and Vienna, I had important commitments for the coming years, therefore such tours were not really promotional tools for me, and financially they were, of course, quite modest at that time.

In fact, you now sang many concerts with Plácido Domingo.

Yes, and this is how we arrived at doing a concert in Romania, my home country, at my insistence, after a televised concert in Prague. In 1994, for Romania, the concert of one of the greatest tenors in the world singing together with a young Romanian soprano was a major event. It was nice that we could organize everything quickly so that we included the concert in the tour, and it was also nice that our fees got redirected to a children's hospital in Timișoara. It was a great gesture of humanity from Plácido and it was not to be the only one.

Years later, in 2011, when we were by now at the same level in our careers, we met again for a concert event at the London O2 Arena. There were posters of us all over the city, and seeing them made me think about the progress we had both made over the previous two decades. I enjoyed very much thinking that years have passed in our favor and that the music brought us back together in a highly professional way.

You mentioned before that in the same year that you had met Plácido Domingo and Roberto Alagna, which was 1992, you had also met Sir Georg Solti for the first time, when he came to see you in La bohème. *How did that lead to your famous* La traviata *performances with him at Covent Garden?*

As I said, after seeing *La bohème*, Maestro Solti proposed to me a new production of *La traviata*. Because everything happened very quickly and Maestro Solti had made me the original proposal only relying on my interpretation of *La bohème*, but also because *La traviata* was a new production that required both a large financial investment and a vote of confidence, the maestro asked me to perform an audition. He was quite a character, with a special brand of humor; he knew how to ask one to do things for him with great elegance and delicacy and was always able to create a very pleasant atmosphere, so there was no question I would

PLÁCIDO DOMINGO

Tenor, baritone, and conductor Plácido Domingo was in the audience when Angela Gheorghiu sang Mimì at the Royal Opera House for the first time in 1992, and he subsequently partnered with her onstage many times.

◆ ◆ ◆

I first saw Angela in *La bohème* when she made her debut at Covent Garden in 1992. Of course I was very impressed. Without any doubt here was a singer of quality, a very young artist with great possibilities to become one of the really great sopranos. I realized that here we had the lyric soprano who was the perfect Mimì. [. . .]

I was so impressed with Angela that I invited her to join me on a concert tour of several countries. She was already very busy by then, but we found some dates. I have been doing concerts with several generations of sopranos, as I have been around so long, and I can say that Angela was an artist with a personality and a variety of repertoire that was ideal for these concerts. They were a great success and I enjoyed them very much.

I had already then recognized the beauty of the voice, the ease with which she sang, and also the pathos in the voice — there is a very vocal pathos there in her performing. It is a voice that acts by itself, and as well as being a fine stage actress there is a special performing quality in her voice. Sometimes you hear a beautiful voice but you don't feel the performer in it. In Angela's voice you hear the performing actress. [. . .]

do it. Quite to the contrary, I considered his request to be a natural one and I gladly obliged.

So—what was it like auditioning for Sir Georg Solti?

There were two auditions. One was in Covent Garden, in a large rehearsal room, and I remember I also sang the high note at the end of "Sempre libera"—an E-flat. Maestro Solti was very excited about the audition, but when I got to my E-flat he said, "Are you sure that Verdi wrote that note?"

And I replied, "No, but you know how it is the tradition."

"Yes, yes, I know, but we must stage *Traviata* here, not something else, and so I want to follow the score exactly as Verdi wrote it."

LADY VALERIE SOLTI

Lady Valerie Solti, widow of the conductor Sir Georg Solti, was at the Soltis' home in 1992 when Sir Georg auditioned Angela Gheorghiu there for the part of Violetta in Verdi's *La traviata*, which he was to conduct at the Royal Opera House in 1994.

❖ ❖ ❖

Georg was very concerned to have a Violetta that in her voice and her acting could portray the purity that he saw in this simple girl who, because of the circumstances of her life, had to keep herself by entering into this uncompromising but very grand lifestyle in which she had to adopt the "persona of a grand dame" in her position as the paramour of the high-ranking Baron Douphol.

When Angela Gheorghiu gave her audition to Georg he was struck by how her voice and musicality were exceptional. She was a natural and she had clearly received an outstanding vocal training in Romania. Also she looked ideal for the part. Even so, he wanted to hear her one more time, and then see what Richard Eyre would think. After that, history was made.

Truth be told, the score did not require a final E-flat, but it did include two stanzas in both the great aria "Ah, fors'è lui" and the little aria, "Addio del passato," and the maestro wanted to stick to the score completely, although often people were used to singing just one stanza.* "That final note does not interest me much," he said, "but practically you have to play both arias twice because there are two stanzas for each of them, making the scene a whole lot harder and much longer. So next time sing the great aria to me with both stanzas."

For the second audition I learned both stanzas; I went to his house and I sang the whole aria.

And Sir Georg Solti decisively engaged you for La traviata—*with a handpicked team!*

Yes. Besides Frank Lopardo, who was Alfredo, and Leo Nucci, who was Germont, the team was completed by theater director Richard

---

*Indeed, usually in both these arias the second stanza is cut.

Eyre, who back then was the director of the National Theatre in London. From the moment he learned he would direct the new *La traviata* in London, for about a year and a half Richard came to my performances in Europe and I think New York to see me, get a sense of how I worked, and prepare, perhaps, for when we were going to work together. I do not know if it was his idea or whether the Royal Opera House encouraged him to do so, but the fact is that it was a very good idea. Whenever he came to see me, we would have dinner together; we were gladly getting to know each other and have discussions at length, and all this was very useful later, when we started the work for my debut as Violetta.

And how did the preparations for that evolve?

Well—the first days of rehearsals were quite unique for me, and I don't know if this preparation process for a new performance has ever been used anywhere else. It may have been caused by Richard Eyre's theater background: the fact is that in the early rehearsal days we just read the score, sitting around a table, all of us together, just like actors do at their first reading. The text was, of course, in Italian, and as the director did not know the language, he would ask for Leo Nucci's opinion whenever he was unsure about one detail or another. We would read the lines and the lyrics of the arias just like actors would, but also with some musical intention: speaking the words instead of singing, but thinking of the musical phrase. Only later on did we switch to full music rehearsals.

The first music rehearsal was from act 1. We were all together, all the cast, including the chorus, which appears in the beginning of the opera, all accompanied by a pianist. We would stand in a circle, as the stage was round, a bit higher than the chorus. Although theoretically once they had rehearsed their part they had no other job to do, none of the chorus members left; they all stayed on to listen to me. They did not know whether I would sing full-voice or not, this was only a rehearsal after all, but they were all curious and probably wanted to listen to me because they had never heard me sing Violetta before.

When we were just about to begin, they were frozen, and I was frozen stiff . . . but I still began to sing, full-voice, both stanzas of "Ah, fors'è lui," à la carte. Solti had not yet arrived, but all the other colleagues were present, the whole team, a lot of people. As I was looking around, I had the same feeling as when I was little, when I sang

SIR RICHARD EYRE CH

The film, theater, television, and opera director Sir Richard Eyre was the stage director of the new production of Verdi's *La traviata* at the Royal Opera House in 1994,
when Angela Gheorghiu sang Violetta and Sir Georg Solti conducted. Her Violetta
brought her international stardom.

◆ ◆ ◆

I went to Vienna to hear her sing Mimì. The production of *La bohème* at
the Vienna State Opera was twenty years old but given new life by Angela
who was only a handful of years older than the production. I knew as soon
as she came onstage that I wanted her to play Violetta. She had wit, beauty,
a defiant energy, no self-pity, an outstanding and unaffected voice—light
but with a strong core—a real innocence, an expressive strength, and a tiny
waist. And she was a natural actress.

As she started the aria ["Ah, fors'è lui," in the first musical rehearsal for
La traviata], the low susurration which passes for silence in a rehearsal room
containing a hundred-odd people stopped, and there was an absolute purity of concentration, unbroken even by the movement of the chorus from
the back of the room to the front where they could see Angela more clearly.
The complete aria, and the one that follows—"Sempre libera"—lasts perhaps ten minutes, and for ten minutes we watched with breathless awe as
she climbed, like an unroped climber on a vertical rock face, from note to
note, phrase to phrase, verse to verse. When she finished there was a silence, followed by an earthquake of applause. Lorca talks about being pos-
sessed by *duende*, the essence of great performance—"whoever beholds
it is baptized by dark water." We drowned in the dark water and as the applause went on and on and on, Angela stood motionless, saturated by tears
and astonished at her own genius.

"Sara pe deal" to my parents, my grandparents, and in school for my
classmates. The effect my voice had directly on my loved ones, be they
colleagues or family, was quite unique. I've experienced it many times
since then; it reflects strongly upon me, it's very difficult to explain. I
can still remember everyone's faces, some with tears, some with smiles,
some laughing, some weeping, others stunned, some amazed, each per-

son with his or her own reaction but always one of extraordinary emotional intensity. It was a fascinating moment. I finished the aria and everyone burst into applause, on and on and on, they would not stop, there was *delirium totalis*. From that moment on, I began to live.

Next came the rehearsals with the orchestra. . . .

To this day I am very fond of the *sitzprobe*, or *l'Italiana*, when we all sing with the orchestra, in front of the curtain. The reaction of the colleagues who are watching us matters most to me because that reaction is my first exam before any performance. At Covent Garden, in the first *Traviata* music rehearsal, that reaction was crazy, and the story was repeated after two weeks at the sitzprobe when Maestro Solti was there too. At the first rehearsal with him, I started with act 3 and I think I began almost directly with the scene where Violetta has her aria. Before starting the aria, I have that letter to read—"Teneste la promessa"—it is the letter Violetta had received from Germont, a very emotional moment. I began to read, to act, and then to sing the two stanzas of "Addio del passato," and then I suddenly saw Georg Solti, who was no longer conducting but was somehow crouched in his chair weeping, his face all red. He was listening to me, sobbing, tears streaming down his cheeks. All he could say then was, "I cannot stay here any longer, I must go." Richard Eyre told him, amused, "It's been two weeks since we've been in the same condition as you are now . . ."

That general emotion brought me much good then. Everyone I worked for in that production, in one way or another, helped me become who I am today, helped me have more faith in myself; they all boosted my confidence. All my colleagues, the entire theater. . . . I remember the general director of the Royal Opera House, Jeremy Isaacs, would shout, "Trăiască România!"* whenever he met me on the street, whenever he saw me from afar. He had probably learned these words from Leontina Văduva, Alexandru Agache, or Ileana Cotrubaș, who had sung there before me. He would effectively greet me in my mother tongue, to make me feel good. These may seem like small details, but they meant a lot to me back then.

Already at this early stage in the proceedings, there was an unusual frisson.

---

*"Long live Romania!"

LEO NUCCI

Baritone Leo Nucci first sang with Angela Gheorghiu when he performed the role of Giorgio Germont alongside Angela's Violetta in the legendary run of *La traviata* performances at the Royal Opera House in 1994, and he subsequently appeared with her on many occasions.

◆ ◆ ◆

I have a great respect for this singer. She is a true artist. I remember when we did *La traviata* together at La Scala in 2007, with Lorin Maazel conducting, she received a really huge acclamation from the public. We did an incredible *La traviata* together. She had been wonderful in this role in London in 1994, with a great success of course, but at La Scala she had a really incredible exit.

Angela found in me a stage partner who was very simpatico with her, and I say that because she needs a real acting interaction on the stage. She needs a kind of acting expression from the other singers that is not easy to find in opera today when—and I am so sorry to say this—so many singers go onstage just for singing. This for me is not enough, but with Angela everything is a real dialogue of life when she performs.

There was indeed. From the moment when Solti left the rehearsal in tears, things moved quickly on several fronts. Until the time of the premiere, Leo Nucci and Frank Lopardo would always say, "This is history, we are living historic moments, where is Verdi, if only he could see us. . . ." Everything seemed so unusual, so unprecedented, that they did not want to miss anything, to fail in any way; they wanted to make everything superlative, so that the magic could take full effect. Georg Solti, in his turn, would come to the rehearsal with a metronome to keep the pace and make sure he did not depart from the score. Yes, even for—or especially for—magic, you need the precision of a metronome.

I was just a rookie, but from the beginning everybody treated me as a colleague. Georg Solti spoke to me exactly the same way he spoke to Leo Nucci; he never made any difference between us. We were all on a first-name basis and were all a very united group.

When the rehearsals with orchestra began, Solti would let his assistant conduct, and for the duration of a scene, he would go to all the corners of the theater hall, from the first row to the last, all the way to the last balcony, everywhere, in all angles; he would go there and listen to ensure that all sounded well and good and the orchestra was playing well with my voice, not too loud nor too quiet. He wanted to achieve the perfect balance for our new *Traviata*, to make sure that we were all in agreement with each other. This was quite a unique attitude in the world of opera. The whole experience was great, and made me feel like the luckiest artist.

Even the costume design team asked me how I thought I would have to look, how I felt about the part, how I wanted my dresses to be, what fabric I preferred. They gave me confidence, and I them. This is how I got to wear a gown inspired by the iconic dress of the Empress Sissi—the one that had impressed me so strongly as a student, during my Viennese tour, the one dotted with white stars, like the edelweiss flowers.

That new production—a first for me, as well as for Maestro Solti, who had never before conducted *La traviata**—was and remains the golden standard in terms of production process. But as I was to discover later, it was really a very happy set of circumstances, about which I had a lot to learn, and not necessarily the standard way that things were running in the opera world.

Well yes, but altogether this was an exceptional situation—so much so that on very short notice your performance was recorded live in the opera house by Decca Classics, filmed by BBC television, and produced for home video. In fact it was the first time in its history that the BBC suddenly canceled its scheduled television programs in order to transmit an opera performance live from the theater.

Immediately after the rehearsals had begun, Georg Solti approached Decca and the BBC. The BBC was supposed to televise and record a later performance, after the premiere, with another cast of the production. But Solti went to them personally and to the people at Decca and told them he wanted them to film and record the disc earlier, live, whether they had the facilities at hand to do it or not. He felt that the moment

---

*Solti had indeed never conducted *La traviata* in any theater: he had only conducted the score once in a radio studio performance in Munich, in 1951.

that was about to happen was so beautiful and ineffable that on no account must it be lost. People at the BBC and Decca agreed with Solti's requests, and this is how I came to meet the television producer Peter Maniura, who later on would make a movie in Romania about me, my years in the conservatory, my experience with the Patriarchy Choir, and about Byzantine church music, when we recorded the Decca CD called *Mysterium* together with the Madrigal Choir and Ion Marin conducting.*

All the people involved in that *Traviata* became my friends and admirers, and they and everything that was connected with that project contributed to one of the greatest moments of my professional life.

And one of the greatest occasions in the Royal Opera House's history. "A Star Is Born" was one of the headlines in a swath of accolades that appeared in the press.†

Georg Solti did everything in his power to get these things for me, and for his tremendous commitment I will be forever grateful to him. It was a truly historic performance. One month after the live telecast, thanks to the promotion campaign and the CD and video that were in preparation, everyone knew about me, everyone wanted to work with me, every door opened wide for me, exactly as I had dreamed since I was a child. The promotion was global in all countries that had partnerships with the BBC and in all record stores all over the world. The PR campaign was also extremely strong, both short term and long term. My media session for *La traviata* included thirty-eight meetings with the press. The last journalist that I met then and with whom I had a long conversation because I liked it and I liked him, although I was by then dead tired, is one of my two interlocutors for this book, Jon Tolansky. My life changed dramatically from then, and a whole whirlwind of offers started to appear.

Even with those singers who have been faithful to Verdi's written score, not so many have been able to convey just what he wanted in terms of characterization—that with the highly volatile and emotional character of Violetta there are some elements that cannot exactly be notated, but can only be suggested by the notes. For instance, the first two bars alone of "Ah, fors'è

---

*Angela Gheorghiu's Romanian Journey (BBC documentary).
†"A Star Is Born" was the headline in the *Spectator*.

PETER MANIURA

Television producer and director Peter Maniura was the executive producer and co-director when BBC Television relayed the 1994 Royal Opera House production of *La traviata* in which Angela sang Violetta.

◆ ◆ ◆

My first experience of Angela was encountering her Violetta when I and Humphrey Burton started to prepare our television relay of *La traviata* from the Royal Opera House, Covent Garden, in the momentous opening run of Richard Eyre's production conducted by Sir Georg Solti in 1994. I was bowled over first of all by her freshness and by what a magnificent actress she was. Then, as over the next very intense days I started to learn the opera, I was struck by how she made the most demanding parts sound easy to sing, such as the famously difficult "Sempre libera" cabaletta at the end of act 1. Her technique was superb, there was not a trace of any strain, and the notes were all absolutely there, bang in tune. But also, after I had been listening to recordings of several different Violettas, Angela's performance was musically revelatory. Everything was beautifully shaded, and I will never forget her range of color and expression in the duets with Frank Lopardo's Alfredo and Leo Nucci's Giorgio Germont.

I realized that Angela was affecting me on two levels simultaneously. One was seeing the artist in the flesh and being captivated by the truthfulness, intensity, and freshness of her performance. The other was listening to her as I had my head in the score and realizing that there was this extraordinary technical facility and musicality coexisting as a completeness that we so rarely encounter. Added to that was her wonderful tenderness and sensitivity coupled with her incredible beauty and stage persona, and the entire experience made a tremendously exciting impact.

After all that, it was a wonderful delight to discover, as I began to get to know her toward the end of the run of performances, that the effervescent, sparkling, fun-loving, amusing person is also Angela. She has within herself actual characteristics of Violetta's appeal, and although of course she is not *La traviata*, she is endowed with special personal qualities that can be amplified to make a wholly convincing and touching tragic stage being. That is a touchstone of a great artist: obviously they are not playing themselves in a simplistic way, but they do have the ability to draw out those facets of their own character and magnify them to create credible stage personas.

lui": *you ideally fulfill Verdi's wishes by, in the first bar, totally observing the short and detached note lengths and the dynamic and accented markings, but also give a feverishly nervous quality that implies a very subtle rubato—and then change the color and character strikingly in bar 2 where Verdi writes, "Dolcissimo."*

The story gives you what to do with the voice. It's like—I was asking to myself, "Ah, fors'è lui—maybe this is him!" Alfredo has left the room, and the guests have all left, and now Violetta is alone in her home. Now at last she is free to think—she is free to think about him. And when you are thinking about someone you are in love with, your heart and everything else in your body goes faster. You cannot sing that passage like a machine! You are breathless. You do not want to go to your bed and sleep. When you are in love, your stomach and all your senses are anxious. You are really agitated: "Oh my God! It's him! What's happening?" Imagine it! She is astonished by her own feelings. She has never expected this: she has had a lot of men in her time, and she has seen in her short life how many men and even some women have been in love with her, but she—she has never been able to feel any love. She is shocked that she is in love. "Wow," she says to herself. "I—am—in love. Maybe—just perhaps, this is the right man." But then there is the duality: "But no—what am I saying—no, I must be free—always free." You must understand what this experience has meant to her when you sing Violetta, that she is going to give up all her freedom because something very deep has happened to her. And then of course later she is going to lose everything because of Alfredo's father. She will die abandoned by the world that used to fete her. If you know this, you know what Verdi means when he writes the music in "Ah, fors'è lui."

Also there is maybe significance about an aspect of Violetta in the instructions Verdi has written for her in "Sempre libera," because they are more to do with color, tone, and character than dynamics—as though he is avoiding too much weight and fortissimo because she is physically fragile even when she is so excited at the thought of her freedom and her glittering lifestyle?

Particularly in this role too many singers are worried about volume. They want to sing with a lot of decibels. But in this opera, and not just in this opera, what matters is not the power of the volume but the power of the quality of sound and the quality of the emotions. I have always been careful about this. Maybe my colleagues can argue with me, but I always say, "Please, do not sing so high and so loud so often, because you lose your quality. You lose the healthiness of your voice. Nothing can replace this if you lose it. Of course there are places where you need a lot of volume, but you must only sing like this at the biggest climaxes." And not only so as to keep your voice: it becomes unmusical and boring if you do this all the time. But there is a problem today for the audience. People are hearing a lot of volume and they have become used to it. And it is a kind of volume that excites the body—not the soul and mind and heart. I trust more in the feelings of the emotions. If I want music for gymnastics or for dancing, of course I need volume, but for intelligent music I do not want volume, except when it is necessary. What is most important is that the voice can express many different colors.

Surely a very wide range of colors is so important for the role of Violetta, who is so emotional—so that you almost have to have a range of different voices?

You are right about the colors but not about the voices! People sometimes say that for Violetta Valery you need two, three, I don't know how many voices. Not at all! You have to give a very wide range of different colors with the same voice—the same Violetta. What is so demanding is that she changes so much and sometimes so quickly, so you have to give those changes many, many different shades and kinds of color and sometimes quite suddenly. You have to be able to change your colors during every role that you sing, but with Violetta the changes are really extreme. Again I have to say this: the word gives you the color, and Violetta's words are so expressive, so emotional—there are your colors. But not with different kinds of voices for the different acts, no—very many different colors, yes: sparkle and coloratura at the end of the first act, often very dramatic and tragic in the second act, then of course she is dying and abandoned in the third act, but all with the same voice singing. And something else as well: this is such a famous opera and we hear it so much that sometimes people think now it is an easy opera. But I think *La traviata* is still one of the most complex operas and Violetta is one of the most complex characters, because she changes so much in a very short time.

CHAPTER 7

New Beginnings

♦ ♦ ♦

*Y*our life changed dramatically after this exceptional success in La traviata—but it was also different on a personal level.

I was still married to Andrei, but I was about to break up with him.
While I was still in rehearsals with the new production of *La traviata*,
Roberto Alagna was also in London. I was torn between Roberto and
Andrei and I did not know what to do. But with all the demands of
my work, most of the time my private life did not matter. I was completely dedicated to what I was doing—even though it was hard for me
at home, even though I had to go through some very bitter moments.
All that mattered was that I be well onstage, in front of my colleagues
and the public, and to move on professionally.

The distance between my personal life and my professional life was
enormous, but then, just like at many other times, I let my work take
precedence. Sure, over time, I paid dearly for this, but I could not do it
any other way. It seemed to me that nothing could be more important
than my work and the performance I was supposed to prepare. Apart
from that, all that mattered was just to have a comfortable little place
where I could study.

How did matters develop after that?

In that year of 1994 Roberto had a series of performances of *Roméo
et Juliette* in which he sang together with Leontina Văduva, while I was
rehearsing Violetta. I was in very good relations with both of them. Leontina invited us to eat together—her mother often came with goodies
from Romania, and she would make traditional meals for all of us. We
were all having a good time together, singing, telling stories; there was
a very nice atmosphere. Leontina had always been very friendly to me
and I admired her very much. She was the first person to invite me to
an afternoon tea. Colleagues rarely make such friendly gestures toward
other colleagues. I appreciated that a lot back then and I will never

forget her kindness. In turn, I kept encouraging her to go and sing at the Metropolitan, where I had already debuted, as Leontina had an extremely beautiful voice and great artistic sensitivity.

Against this background, Roberto began to insist more, and gradually the feelings between us became stronger. He was about to finish his performances in *Roméo et Juliette* as I was just starting my work in *La traviata*. He came once to meet me at a rehearsal, and then he saw how everyone was literally ecstatic about what they knew was going to happen in the upcoming performances. I was gradually becoming quite an important person, so to speak. . . .

The day he was supposed to leave London, I could not sleep. I had received from him a very gallant and flattering letter, so I went to his apartment in the morning. The first thing I did, once I got there, realizing that this was my moment of decision, was to pick up the phone with him and call Andrei, who had remained behind in the house where I lived during my stay in London. Andrei asked me simply to the point if I was at Roberto's apartment. I told him I was.

Andrei reacted very calmly and told me later that everything might just be coming to me on the spur of the moment amidst the enormous success with *La traviata*. True, neither as an artist nor as a mere human being had I ever been swamped with so much proof of love from the public, nor had I had so many admirers—from artists and singers to conductors and directors. But Roberto's persistence was another story, and as I was also in love with him in my turn, I just wanted to believe it.

It is true, however, that during that very time, I met a "friend" of his from France several times in his apartment. He told me not to worry, as she had other love interests. It is true also that after a while, I discovered that this was not the case at all. But by then, I had already made up my mind and there was no turning back, although I understood well that I was leaving behind a kind man with a broken heart and a great family, and I began to realize that I needed to prepare myself for the same thing to happen to me.

But that day, after Roberto's departure, you returned to the Gheorghiu family?

Yes. Immediately after the departure of Roberto, I continued to speak with Andrei and with his sister, Irina. I told them everything, trying to make sense of what was happening to me. She told me the same thing—that this is not uncommon, things happen. . . . They told me, "Yes, it's okay to want to go out one evening with someone else, it's absolutely normal for you. You've never had such an experience before; now, suddenly, the whole world is discovering you, it is natural for something like this to happen—but try to understand, to move on, because otherwise, in the future you will suffer." And I told them all, in tears, that I was aware of that. I told my family and their family and everybody close around me, "All of you are right, but at the moment I cannot do otherwise." I thought this was a mere gesture of fairness toward Andrei—I'm not a deceiving person, I cannot lie. Even if it hurts, I have to tell you the truth, exactly as it is.

And, of course, as a performing artist, you can be in a particularly vulnerable personal position?

Incidentally, as I was to learn afterward, artists do have an unusually intense emotional life. As the years passed by and I got used to it, I allowed people to flirt with me, there were times when my dressing room was full of flowers, of letters, but of course I never led them on. I'm happy with all the attention that I get, I sincerely thank all those who write to me and send me flowers, their gestures make me feel splendid, but to me these are just tokens of admiration and nothing more. Things that go past a certain line can no longer be controlled, especially between professional colleagues. I did not want any colleague of mine to look differently at me when we were together onstage, as I knew it could happen and have often seen it happening around me.

In the context of this mentality, everyone behaves as he or she feels. At the end of the day, I have seen artists of all calibers that have no problem with that and act like nothing had ever happened, but I cannot, I could never. Things can move very quickly in our world because the great majority of us are single people and we lead extremely difficult lives: we always go from one place to another, always creating around us this state of adulation, which takes all possible shapes and sizes and comes from all types of people, regardless of gender or age.

How serious do you think this adulation is?

Most opera lovers would do anything for you, and it is difficult to distinguish between real feelings and a certain sense of momentary infatuation. Some artists perhaps go along with this and take advantage of this euphoria, but most of them go straight to their hotel room or their apartment after a performance, always sleeping in an unfamiliar bed, always living among strangers, in another place, with other food, preparing for another show with other colleagues, away from their family and, most tragically, away from their children.

Colleagues create a temporary group. But when this temporary bond goes further, it usually ends with the breaking of hearts, with double lives or dissolutions of marriages—in short it always ends in many problems. And that's a choice you have to make—whoever can do it, however he or she can take responsibility for it, each according to his or her way of being, each according to his or her own principles. I never judged this, I could never judge. I didn't even judge Roberto, only way later, even though I was aware by then of all the stories he would tell me about all his escapades, especially when he had, in his turn, his fits of sick jealousy. Sometimes people tend to boast with such stories, but I never wanted to read too much into them or analyze whether any story was true or not. For me, they had no significance.

I know full well it is precisely because of this interior turmoil and extreme sensitivity that all real artists have, that they are able to create a magical atmosphere once they get onstage; that ineffable emotion that gets the audience to believe what they see. Onstage, artists play love stories and sometimes they get to live them for real. They hug, they kiss, they breathe the same air, feel the same thing at the same time. For the public to enjoy a genuine artistic vibration, artists have to accept right from the beginning the fact that the scene is like a mine-field. If you have a stronger character, if you have a family or a fresher romance going on in your life, you can get over it, get over the moment, but otherwise most of the time you are emotionally exposed.

And with Roberto?

I went to Roberto's apartment and I decided then and there that we would be together. Of course that was a very difficult decision—I was married, and he had a small child of three and a wife who had been deceased for only one month, after two long years of suffering from a ruthless disease.

All that experience with *Traviata*, everything that happened to me then, took place against this emotional backdrop. It was very stressful, not pleasant at all—after most of the performances I would come home and cry. Andrei was with me during all this time. He never said a harsh word to me, never bothered me, never reproached me for anything, never made a scene. At one time, Ștefan also came to see the performance, but even he did not say anything. They all hoped everything would go away. . . .

Altogether your life was dramatically changing.

The success of the opera and the live broadcast was absolutely incredible and propelled me into an area where I had never dreamed to get so fast. It gave me the opportunity to meet people whose company I had never dreamed of being in.

One of them was Princess Diana, who had come to see *La bohème* before she saw my *Traviata*, and who would often come to the opera unofficially, as she was very moved by the music. On one of the *Traviata* evenings, after the performance was over, I was on the stage. The house rule said that when special guest spectators were in the hall, they were allowed to come directly onto the stage to greet me, after the curtain had come down. We would say hi and hug, and I was being very familiar and cordial with all of them, but at some point I saw Valerie Solti bowing in front of someone. It was . . . "just" Her Majesty Queen Margrethe II of Denmark, who I did not recognize and with whom I had talked very closely and also taken photographs. I started apologizing for not recognizing her, and she apologized in her turn, but it all seemed surreal to me that a crowned head would stand in line to greet me, just like everyone else, without announcing her presence in any way, not even when she was in front of me. This was a very nice, very beautiful and noble scene, one of those beautiful stories that were weaved into the legend of that *Traviata*.

As was your meeting with Anthony Hopkins, a family friend of Maestro Solti.

Anthony Hopkins was the first great actor that I met, in 1994. I treasure the memories of those encounters in Maestro Solti's family home, with some unforgettable meetings and conversations. From that moment I have been following everything he does and all that is related to him. Anthony Hopkins is not only a great actor but also an accomplished painter and composer. Over the years, he has sent me recordings of his compositions and asked me to sing them. I'm seriously considering doing so in the future, because Hopkins writes very romantic music, extremely beautiful, of great sensitivity and depth.

So what happened next, after this now-legendary La traviata?

In 1995, I returned to Bucharest. From there I had to leave for Vienna, still accompanied by Andrei. It was okay, but the vibe was strange. I would run briefly from the hotel room every now and then to call Roberto. . . . I was still very confused. Andrei did not appear jealous; he tried his best to keep things under control, because it was something so serious. . . . He had a lot of faith in me, as we had come to love each other very much. I do not believe in love stories that end in hatred —hatred shows you that maybe at the beginning there was not a true love, but something else, a spark and fizzle, a competition, a flirt. Besides, I had reached a very close relationship with everyone in his family and they were all trying to bring things back to the old normal; they were treating me like I was an innocent, ignorant girl. Which, I have to admit, was probably true. . . .

Did Roberto show any signs of jealousy?

No, as he was probably pretty sure of himself and my feelings toward him. The entire responsibility of the decision remained on my shoulders. There were many who begged me to open my eyes and advised me not to take any chances and make such a major change in my personal life, particularly at that crucial moment in my career. But I was in love. . . .

In the first year after the decision I made regarding Roberto, in 1995, our performing contracts had already been signed long before, so each had our own business. In order to see each other, we had to travel one after another, according to the schedule each of us had. In a moment of respite for us both, Roberto took me and introduced me to his family.

What was your first impression?

I don't know how much they really liked me. Roberto's first wife had been dead for just a few months, in 1994, after two years of severe illness. The memory of her suffering was still fresh. I was coming from Romania to the home of some very ordinary people. Roberto told me that neither he nor his family had ever heard of my country before. He, at least, had known nothing about Romania until he met Leontina Văduva.

I was in full career, with widespread international success, but Roberto's family continued to believe for many years that of the two of us, only he was a great artist. . . . Maybe they even had the impression that I was trying to take advantage of him. . . . I do not know and no longer care, but at the time it was very difficult for me. In fact, things were just the opposite of what I had known in my life until then. I had sacrificed a family of elite society and a circle of select intellectuals and artists for love, and I was entering another family, very different, with different rules and a completely different opinion on life and whatever it was that I was doing. . . . I discovered very quickly that, out of my own naiveté and a very strong emotional impulse, I had joined a traditionally Sicilian house, amidst people who had just lost their daughter-in-law and needed to make sure that there was someone to take care of Roberto and his daughter, Ornella. It was an already very complicated family picture, from which only I was missing. . . .

I had no intention of permanently leaving Romania and settling down anywhere else. In addition, I had already discussed this with Roberto, and for both professional and sentimental reasons, we had decided that the best option for us was to buy a home in London, the city where we had met, near Covent Garden, each independent of our families. His relatives all smiled when I told them this. I was young and very naive.

So did you not move to London?

After the marriage, I was obliged to accept taking a house together in Paris, right next to Roberto's family. The pretext that made me give in was his proximity to Ornella—the girl was an angel to whom I had already grown very attached, and she had already started to call me "Mommy."

In this year of 1995 you continued with your schedule, singing in London and Salzburg, among many other cities.

Yes. Besides this family intermezzo that predicted nothing good and which I overlooked at the time, I went to sing, as had been scheduled, in Salzburg. In August, when I was in a series of performances of *La traviata*, I had a sudden meeting with a famous conductor, whom I had heard of for a long time but with whom I had previously avoided meeting. Personally, I have always had a tendency to keep away from conflicts that seemed waiting to happen, from discussions with people who were either too inflexible or too haughty. Even if that meant not going to a particular house or not doing a certain show, it still seemed a good price for me if that meant avoiding a potential collision. Singing at Covent Garden, Vienna, and the Metropolitan, I had so far been able to stay away from Riccardo Muti and La Scala. I had thought we might not be able to work well together because it was well known that he wanted to run everything, leaving little freedom to the singers. I had very good contracts with all the houses that I wanted to sing in, doing exactly what I was sure I could do well. Moreover, early in my career, I had this fixed idea that I should sing only in the best theaters and enter only through the front door, as Mia Barbu had told me when I was a teenager.

From La Scala I did not like the latest footage I had seen with Riccardo Muti. Of course, I liked their productions and artists, but not the parts of the shows where the singers were musically placed into a corner. For me, conducting is not supposed to be a power play—if that was the way it was supposed to be in one opera house or another, I tried to keep away from it. I was telling myself I had lived through twenty-five sufficient years of Communism, in which I had been constantly told what to do and how to do it and where I had no freedom of opinion. In music, as far as I was concerned, totalitarianism had no place whatsoever. I still cannot call a performance successful if I feel it has been sung with a lump in the throat or with a fist in the mouth of the artists. I prefer to disappear, not to be involved at all with anything like this.

La Scala was pretty famous for its loggionisti. . . .*

The nasty stories about the audience's attitudes in Milan had already surfaced—apparently they scorned and booed many great artists. Three years earlier, in 1992, the incident with Luciano Pavarotti had happened, on his debut in *Don Carlo.*† I decided I did not want any stress. I was not interested in such vulgar and aggressive gestures against an artistic effort. In addition, career-wise, no one had ever asked me whether or not I was singing or had sung at La Scala. The Milanese opera house was no longer a measure of performance or talent after 1990. Major international careers no longer required singing at La Scala, and being hired by them did not necessarily mean you were doing too well.

---

*The Milanese opera fans who flock to the upper reaches of the theater and make their presence known by shouting and catcalling. Some of the loggionisti groups would even be paid to cheer and boo to order.
†In 1992, Luciano Pavarotti sang his first Don Carlo in a rare, late-career return to La Scala and suffered the wrath of the loggionisti.

How had La Scala ended up in this situation?

Things had changed a lot since the days of Renata Tebaldi, Maria Callas, Virginia Zeani, or even the time of Mirella Freni. It is possible that much of the negative impact on the prestige scale had just come from their loggionisti. Initially, they were considered authentic music lovers, brave enough to challenge any vocal performance that was below the standards of excellence of the theater, but then there had been many instances where it had become apparent that their increasingly violent cries had been without good reason or had been downright paid for, in some sort of mafia style. So why, as an artist, would you subject yourself to moments of pure hatred or, worse, paid-for hatred hired by God knows who?

Please believe me that this impression I had about La Scala was not just a personal opinion, because I did not debut in this theater until 2006, but a fact lived and felt directly by all my colleagues. And it was a real shame, because the theater had spectacular artists, very good professionals who had nothing to do with what was going on around them. But since these bad habits did not cease and the administration had not taken any action against them, things had escalated and people began to avoid the theater altogether.

The brilliance of the Milan ensemble can be heard in their recordings. Because I appreciated them very much as artists, I insisted on them for Decca's recording of Puccini's *La bohème*. The conductor for this recording, made in 1999, was Riccardo Chailly. The experience was unforgettable—we had an extraordinary cast. Roberto was Rodolfo, and other roles were played by two great artists with whom I have remained friends for life—Simon Keenlyside and Ildebrando D'Arcangelo. Roberto was then in great shape, and all together, with the chorus and orchestra of Milan's opera house, we created a dream team.

Now coming back to Salzburg's Traviata . . .

I had just finished with huge success the series of *Traviata* performances in London and had agreed to make a new production of the same opera in Salzburg, but I had expressly requested that the performances should not be conducted by Riccardo Muti. Instinctively, I was trying to protect myself; I did not want to get into any altercation with him.

When I got to Salzburg, I was surprised to discover that Muti had arranged that he was replacing the originally contracted conductor. The rehearsals with piano were completed in a very tense atmosphere, culminating with the conductor firing the pianist and playing the piano himself. I did, however, rehearse all of *La traviata*, from beginning to end, and, finally, Muti seemed very happy and everything seemed to be fine. That is, until toward the end of rehearsal when Roberto showed up, although he had not been involved at all in the shows. He did not sing Alfredo, Frank Lopardo did, but he had come with me to Salzburg. Riccardo and Roberto knew each other well, they had worked together in *La traviata* and *Rigoletto* at La Scala, so on the arrival of Roberto, Riccardo Muti greeted him with, "Roberto—you're here! Because I love you as my son, I let you attend my rehearsals, otherwise you wouldn't be allowed here." To which Roberto answers, "Because I love you as my father, Angela sings here."

I looked at both of them. I was not accustomed to such banter, and I reminded both, "I have to sing *La traviata*—you were not supposed to conduct, you have no business here, so quiet, please. I have a performance with a new production in Salzburg—mi lasciate fare?" It was the first of a long series of conflicts with one, and especially with the other. . . .

In Vienna, during the same period, you met Alexander Gerdanovits, who was to become your private secretary.

I met Alexander Gerdanovits at the Staatsoper, because he came very often to see me sing; he was a true fan. I had made my debut in Vienna in 1992 and up until 1995–96 we kept on meeting. At one point, after a performance, I had a Romanian evening in the house of our mutual friend, soprano Simina Ivan. Periodically, all Romanian singers in Vienna used to meet somewhere to talk and taste our traditional dishes because there were many who lived there and who were feeling homesick.

That there were so many Romanians at the Staatsoper was, of course, to the credit of Ioan Holender, who was following them and hiring them. The not-so-good part was that through the contracts he was offering them, he was paying them very poorly. I was really upset about this with Holender and I still am to this day. Sure, he had helped many, but to others he just closed many other doors, because he would just keep them there and not let them do anything, even when they were of a higher level. I could never approve of something like this.

Returning to the night when I had the discussion with Alexander Gerdanovits, we were both guests of Simina Ivan, my friend who had been hired by the Staatsoper on a fest contract about the same time that I had made my debut. As she was married to my former colleague Alexandru Badea, every time I went to Vienna I would stop by her house and have a Romanian evening. At this dinner I questioned Alex a little bit—what are you doing here, what do you study? He studied in Klagenfurt and Cambridge and then settled in Klagenfurt. He was and still is a scholar, a cheerful and friendly person. I made him an offer to work for me and Roberto at the time, but after two years he started working only for me and today we are as close friends as ever.

Alex is my right hand and he has always been a big help. He has a great sense of humor, he is a first-class fan of opera, and that night he had entered the operatic world. For over two decades, he has been my secretary and the person I trust completely.

And now in this year you made a major decision.

In 1996, right at the beginning of the year, I had to go to the Metropolitan, and when we set out for New York, I packed my suitcases, Andrei took me to the airport, and we both knew it was over. I left without anything; everything I had earned till then remained there at home, I took only two suitcases with me and started everything from scratch.

A new beginning in your life?

Roberto still lived in the same apartment and for the moment I agreed to move in with him next to his parents and the rest of his family, although I did not feel at all at "home." However, we were both so busy and traveled so much that we would just occasionally see each other in various places. Most of the time we would meet in hotels in the countries where we were singing.

I was already feeling that Roberto's family tolerated me rather than appreciated me. For our home in Paris, which we had ended up buying just to be around the family, I had bought a major painting signed by Nicolae Tonitza, a famous Romanian painter, that I loved immensely. It was both a beautiful and valuable work, and since it was made by one of the greatest artists of my country, I wanted to have it displayed in our new home in France. From where I first placed, in plain view, my Tonitza painting, I saw at one point how it got put away in a hallway,

ALEXANDER GERDANOVITS

Alexander Gerdanovits, a connoisseur of opera, first met Angela Gheorghiu at the stage door of the Vienna State Opera. A few years later he started to work for her.

◆ ◆ ◆

While I was a student at the University of Klagenfurt, I had the opportunity of being in Vienna almost every time Angela Gheorghiu was performing there, as I organized my trips to Romania and back to Austria in accordance with her Wiener Staatsoper performance schedule. In those years I used to queue up for standing tickets at the Staatsoper, being one of those true "fans" of the Wiener Staatsoper and first of all a very passionate fan of Angela. I waited for her many times at the stage door entrance, offering her flowers and wishing her "In bocca al lupo." One evening, however, was different from all the others. After one of those touching *Bohème* performances in January 1996, I was suddenly invited by her to join her for a visit she and Roberto Alagna were making to the apartment of a good Romanian friend, the soprano Simina Ivan, whom I also knew from my Timișoara years. I will never forget that evening: it was wintertime and as the party went on, Angela and Simina sang Romanian carols and other Christmas songs. I was living as though in a fairy tale. I was almost speechless the whole evening given the great honor of being present there.

That night proved to change my destiny. After returning to their hotel, Angela and Roberto asked me whether I could consider working for them as their secretary. I said immediately "Yes" with the greatest joy. As the years passed by, my work concentrated more and more on Angela, and as their careers (and later their private lives as well) parted ways, it was Angela to whom I dedicated my whole attention.

Angela has that unique timbre that makes you recognize her voice out of thousands. Her voice also possesses this morbidezza, a quality that is so much appreciated by opera lovers. Angela feels what she is singing, her voice comes from her soul. It is an ample, generous voice with an irresistible timbre like velvet, with wonderful pianissimi and a consummate middle range. Even though I have heard many *Traviatas* and *Bohèmes* with her, every time Angela interprets "Addio del passato" or "Si, mi chiamano Mimì" I have tears in my eyes. And is there anyone who can sing "Un bel di vedremo" more touchingly and at the same time more accurately than her? I doubt it.

hidden behind a door. It's just a small gesture, perhaps insignificant to some, but to others it had enormous symbolic meaning.

This year 1996 was a busy one for you at the Metropolitan Opera.

Yes, I was very busy and very much in love. I sang several operas at the Met during that season, and early that year I was on a plane from Paris to New York, on my way to my performances of Liu in *Turandot*, where I was to be conducted by Nello Santi. He was also on the same plane, sitting next to me on the journey, when we both saw on the news images of Teatro La Fenice in Venice, which was on fire. We were both supposed to go there to do *La traviata* in just a few months. We both froze in our seats on the plane when we saw those images, after which we started screaming at each other, "Oooh, our theater—where are we going to do *Traviata* in Venice now?"

We did do it, eventually, at PalaFenice, in a much larger space, and with Nello Santi was also Ramón Vargas, one of the most talented artists and dearest stage partners. Also during this *Traviata*, I met another dear friend, one of the most beautiful tenor voices, Marcelo Álvarez, freshly arrived in Europe from Argentina.

Were you planning to marry Roberto at this time?

During one of my free days in between performances in *Turandot*, I went to the opera to see another show and sat in Joe Volpe's box. Joe, who was the general manager of the Met then, was a good friend of the mayor of New York, Rudolph Giuliani—and that day I shared his box with both him and Giuliani. I told them then that Roberto and I intended to get married and that we wanted to go through with our ceremony during the time Roberto was making his Metropolitan Opera debut singing with me in *La bohème*.

This was how things had come together: finally both of us were free at the same time, we had arranged our schedules to sing together, and since the performances we were to do in New York were of *La bohème* —the opera that had brought us together for the first time—we decided that we would get married during the *Bohème* performances. Hearing that, Rudy Giuliani immediately told me, "Well then, I will marry you." I gave Roberto the news that Giuliani wanted to marry us —both for the Met and for Giuliani this was a very beautiful opportunity that they could capitalize on, and I liked it: I thought it was a kind of idyllic transposition of the opera love story in reality. I was thinking

Angela Gheorghiu is one of the most important icons of the opera world of the last decades. She is a bastion of the operatic tradition worldwide not just for her impeccable vocal technique, her exquisite musicality, or her accomplished scenic instinct, but also because she has known how to put all these virtues at the service of her musical interpretation.

The world of opera opened up to modernity with the figure of Enrico Caruso, who was probably the first modern divo of the twentieth century. Later on, other artists followed his steps, from Maria Callas to figures of our time like Luciano Pavarotti and Plácido Domingo. Angela with no doubt belongs to that select group of singers who have managed to bring the artist beyond the scenarios. She has known how to move the emotions and the dreams of many people, generations already, in the whole planet.

with the mind of an artist. Besides all this, I had not been able to plan anything else, so I was fine with Giuliani's proposal.

Naturally, being in New York, we had to go first to the embassies of our respective countries. Giuliani received our documents and set the date of our marriage ceremony. It so happened that the next day was very long and important to us—we had a matinee of *La bohème* at 1 p.m. and the Levine gala in the evening: that was a special show celebrating twenty-five years since the debut of Jimmy Levine in New York. All this was to happen on the twenty-seventh of April. On the twenty-sixth, we went to the beautiful town hall and when we were asked to present our documents, we said that we had left them with the secretary—except the secretary was not at her desk and no one else could find our papers. Rudy Giuliani had already put his ribbon on, everyone was ready for the ceremony, so we went through half of it and for the other half we decided to leave it for the next day, April 27. Rudy assured us that everything would be fine and he would come to our *La bohème* performance in the afternoon.

We also called Joe Volpe and explained the situation to him—that we had completed only half of the civil wedding ceremony and that

New Beginnings   139

we still needed to sign the papers the following day. We had prepared everything well, all of Roberto's brothers had come following the invitation of Lucienne Tell, a fan of ours, and we had taken our formal marriage photo, but in fact we were still not married, as we had not had a chance to sign anything because we had no papers.

The next day we did the *Bohème* in question, and during the interval after the second act, we walked into Joe Volpe's office, in the theater, our costumes still on, and we said, "Da, da, yes, yes," signed, and went straight back onto the stage. Nothing was premeditated. Joe Volpe immediately seized the moment, came out in front of the curtain, and said, "I am not often seen in front of the curtain, and usually whenever I am, the reasons are not very happy. This time, however, it is an exceptionally happy occasion, as Mimì and Rodolfo have just gotten married."

Almost like a fairy tale.

This is how it all happened—though, I repeat, nothing was premeditated. Simply because of a clerical error, we came to complete our civil ceremony inside the opera house, and that night it was clear we could not do anything to celebrate it, because we had the Jimmy Levine gala, which lasted for about four or five hours, and we finished at about three in the morning with all the celebrations afterward. We both worked continuously until the show, then both fell flat with fatigue and stayed in a box in the hall, to listen to our other colleagues. We could not move —we were both dead tired—so from the opera house we went straight to the hotel toward the morning. And so we got married.

CHAPTER 8

Dramas and Traumas

◆ ◆ ◆

The public was captivated by your marriage, and you were headlined as
an idyllic artistic couple. How long did it really stay like that for you?

Soon after our marriage, difficult incidents began to reappear. The
problem was that some of them risked affecting my professional relationship with Maestro Solti as well as other important relationships for
my career. After the *La traviata* performances I remained in very good
relations with the entire Solti family. They would ask me over to their
home, where they were preparing superb dinners and invited extraordinary personalities. In their house I met Anthony Hopkins, Prince
Charles, and the best of London high society that I greatly admired
and in whose presence I felt extraordinarily well. Obviously I treasured
enormously Maestro Solti's friendship and I always appreciated his professional advice.

Therefore, when I had to decide on a record label, I was hesitating
between Decca, which Maestro Solti had recommended, and EMI,*
which was where Roberto was and which he insisted I come to. A third
major label to woo me then was Sony Classical—and their recently
appointed director with whom I had a meeting was to become later on
the general manager of the Metropolitan Opera.

Peter Gelb—who had been appointed to head Sony Classical just a little
while before.

Yes, he was in search of new and very good artists and in this context we met at the Maison du Caviar in Paris, the go-to place when you
want to impress or pamper someone. I went to see him and listen to
the terms he had to offer so I could make the best possible choice. Peter
Gelb was waiting for me with a humongous caviar dish.

Because this was a business conversation on a sensitive issue that

---

*The EMI Classics label has now been absorbed into Warner Classics.

was very important to me from a professional perspective, I specifically asked Roberto not to come. The tensions relating to choosing one label over another had already become so great that I could no longer have a normal conversation on this topic with him or in his presence. After a quarter of an hour of discussion, Gelb spotted Alagna coming toward us, despite my request. To avoid a scene, I slowly got up and left, leaving Peter alone with the glorious caviar bowl.

I knew exactly what I could expect from Roberto, as pretty much around the same time Sir Georg Solti called once to plead in favor of the Decca people, with whom he was recording, and then Roberto snatched the phone from my hand to talk to him and explain why I absolutely had to be at EMI with him. . . . This was yet another outburst that shocked me. Plus there was another distressing moment, when I started working together with Maestro Solti on a disc of Verdi arias. Roberto suddenly had a fit of jealousy for no reason, right in the Solti family home, so the maestro promptly invited him to leave. . . . An exchange of letters followed, filled with pathetic excuses, and the conflict finally died out.

Which recording company did you sign with?

In the end, I signed up with Decca. I had two recital discs planned and one opera—*Pelléas et Mélisande*—and I had started working on the first disc, with arias by Verdi. But Roberto came to the studio from the very first sessions and quarreled again with Sir Georg. I just watched them, completely powerless.

Finally, out of the entire track list, we barely managed to record three or four arias that Decca kept, and when I tried to reschedule and resume our recordings together, Solti—as delicately as he could —clearly said to me, "OK, we go back to the studio, ma senza tenore."* Later, I made that disc of arias from Verdi operas with Ricardo Chailly. It was called *Verdi Heroines* and was still produced by Decca, with the Giuseppe Verdi Symphony Orchestra of Milan.

Did you stay with Decca for long?

My contract with Decca lasted from 1995 to 1998, when I finally had to sign with EMI Classics to keep my family at peace. At Decca I had managed to record my first disc of arias, which drew the attention of

*"But without the tenor" in Italian.

PETER GELB

Peter Gelb, the general manager of the Metropolitan Opera, first met Angela Gheorghiu when he was president of Sony Classical Records.

❖ ❖ ❖

I first heard Angela shortly after I started my work at Sony Classical. I went to see her in *La bohème* in Zurich, in 1994, and I thought she was one of the most remarkable talents I had ever experienced. I was immediately enchanted by the extraordinary beauty of her singing and the way she inhabited the role that she performed, and I very much wanted to sign her up for Sony, which I failed to achieve. Later, in 2006, she sang *La traviata* shortly after I had become general manager of the Metropolitan Opera, and to this day she is for me one of the greatest Violettas I have experienced.

When we put on *La rondine* in 2009, this was mounted specifically for Angela. I doubt that we would have presented the opera if it were not for Angela. In the case of an opera that was not in the mainstream repertory, the only reason for putting it on was the presence of an extraordinary artist in a role that would delight the public in a way they were not necessarily expecting. She brought a greater range of emotion to Magda than anyone could have ever hoped for from the role—she really made the opera a discovery for the Met public. And of course she made it a discovery far and wide beyond the theater, because we broadcast the performance in cinemas live in HD, and there must have been at least two hundred thousand people watching it around the world—and several million more listening live on radio. And in the tradition of the greatest artists, she rose to the occasion of that Saturday matinee with one of the most wonderful performances of the entire run.

Renata Tebaldi. Following the launch of this disc, I received a photo with a signed dedication and a wonderful letter from her. It totally surprised me and I was impressed beyond measure because we had never met, of course, but I had listened to her recordings so many times and I had tremendous respect for her as an artist. It was the kind of gesture that came out of nowhere and that just gave me wings. To receive a

Dramas and Traumas 143

letter from one of the greatest sopranos in the history of opera, for her to congratulate you . . . on your first disc of arias . . . was just huge. . . . I appreciated her gesture enormously.

What was the second CD with Georg Solti supposed to include?

There were arias from operettas composed in the Austro-Hungarian Empire. We agreed to include on the disc fragments from operettas composed in Romania, as I had already put them in my repertoire. But in the meantime, Maestro became ill and left for the angels. He had a very turbulent life, but also a very lucky one. He was a great conductor, a brilliant scholar who left his mark on the world of music and on the artistic biographies of many musicians and performers. Just like Carlos Kleiber and Herbert von Karajan, from his conductor's lectern Maestro Solti was a great creator, with a very strong personality.

I continued to be good friends with the Solti family. In 1998, I participated in the gala held at the Royal Albert Hall in his honor;* years later, we made a short film for the BBC, which featured the master class I gave at the Georg Solti Accademia in Tuscany. Generally I am not a big fan of short master classes—neither short nor filmed ones—but this was an exception and I wanted to do it specifically in memory of Maestro Solti. I will never forget how much he meant to me, what an enormous opportunity he gave me when *La traviata* was broadcast live and immediately became a worldwide success.

In 1996, among all these events and incidents, you managed to complete more recordings—a disc of duets and arias with Roberto, which appeared just a few days before your marriage, and a DVD recording of L'elisir d'amore, *together with both Nina and Roberto.*

Yes, in the meantime, my sister had also graduated from the conservatory and was at the beginning of her career. She had worked with Maria Slătinaru, whom she adored. Once she had gotten married and become pregnant, during the days of the revolution in Romania, naturally she discontinued her classes briefly, to take care of the baby. Unlike me, she had quite a difficult time. She did not get all the support she would have needed from her in-laws and for a while she had to be a

*The gala was held on October 18, 1998, and also included Anne Sofie von Otter, Maxim Vengerov, and Mstislav Rostropovich, with the London Philharmonic Orchestra, conducted by Zubin Mehta.

wife and a mother and a student, all at the same time. The last years of the conservatory were a very demanding period for Nina.

So, in 1996, as soon as I had the first opportunity, I asked her to sing with us. The actual idea to have Nina on the recording together with us for *L'elisir d'amore* at the Opéra de Lyon came from my impresario at the time, Luisa Petrov. She was the one who asked me after a performance if Nina could also be part of the cast because she was interested in working with her as well, and I agreed. Afterward, of course, everyone embraced the idea.

How were you feeling, knowing you would share the stage with both your sister and your husband?

I loved Nina greatly and I wanted her to enjoy the same success as I had. So I had no hesitation when I heard Luisa's proposal, but I knew that her presence on the same stage with me would enormously amplify my emotions. All my life I had been terribly emotional, she was the same, maybe even worse than me, and in a situation where we would all sing in the same production—she, my husband, and I—we knew it would be awfully difficult for both of us. I never even got to enjoy our childhood dream coming true for both of us and for our parents. I was instantly consumed with worry. My only concern was how to make it work best for everyone, with everyone. I don't know if anyone

EVELINO PIDÒ

Since conductor Evelino Pidò's first collaboration with Angela Gheorghiu, the two of them have appeared together many times in various operas and productions.

◆ ◆ ◆

From the first time that I conducted a performance with Angela, which was *L'elisir d'amore* in Lyon in 1996, there was immediately a rapport between her and me. We had an incredible esteem for each other, and ever since then it has been a joy to make music with her. I particularly have special memories doing *L'amico Fritz* with her in Monte Carlo in 1999, also *La bohème* in my hometown Torino in 2003, *Faust* at the Royal Opera House, Covent Garden, in 2011, and *Adriana Lecouvreur* in Vienna in 2014. She also made a marvelous studio recording called *Diva* which I conducted with the London Symphony Orchestra in 2001. These were all different styles and every time it was my real joy to make music with her because Angela is an incredible artist: she is so musical and such a great professional. She is absolutely one of my favorite artists in the world. And she is also a wonderful lady and person.

Angela is a really very strong artist onstage, with great character, and she looks so wonderful. I also want to underline that she sings the text in a special way. In each syllable, in each word there is a color, and this means she deeply knows and interprets the text. For me as a conductor this is so important in opera. It is essential to find exactly the right relationship of the music to the text, and with Angela this combination is on the very top level.

Some people have said that Angela is very volatile, but that is because she is a diva in the real sense of the word—a passionate artist. And because there is really a huge esteem between Angela and myself, she trusts me, and if I ask or give her a suggestion, she is able to accept it. With Angela, it depends on whether she trusts a conductor's idea, and for me I have never had a single problem with her.

Let me say this: Angela is Angela. She is unique!

else has lived through something like this—the fact is, it was not exactly ideal.

Roberto did not have the same emotions when he had the whole family around him. He was able to study in their presence, able to do anything—it was just normal for him to have them around, but I was different. I needed my space, my quiet time. The emotions I was experiencing were so great that it was harder for me to concentrate knowing I had people I knew sharing the stage with me. . . . My emotions were amplified, tripled in this case for me, with Nina and Roberto.

But we all did—Nina, myself, and Roberto—*L'elisir d'amore* together, a DVD recording with Decca at the Opéra de Lyon. It was the first time that Nina was able to leave Ioana with her family for a little while and come with us. I remember we all arrived at Lyon and filmed the opera, and then we were on holiday in southern France, on the Riviera. Ileana Cotrubaș was also in the area; she came to greet us in her splendid car, a Rolls-Royce, and then she invited us all to her home. During this holiday when Nina was with us, we all had a really good time.

But life suddenly took a tragic turn. . . .

After only a month, toward the end of 1996, we lost Nina in an accident. She had been a wonderful artist, for whom we all had high hopes and great thoughts; she was just ready to start a career, but this was fate. At twenty-nine, her life was lost.

Where were you at the time?

I was in Bucharest together with Roberto, looking for a house for Nina in Romania, when the news struck us like a thunderbolt. I went through some terrible shock, as I had been brutally separated from the only human being that had been closest to me for three decades. My beautiful sister, cheerful, intelligent, with almond-shaped green eyes, was no longer with me. After the death of Nina I remember going through two stages. I cried every night for two or three years, every time I remembered her. Crying hurt me, but also helped me heal. I would cry and then the pain would go away.

Then immediately afterward, I had a new production of *Carmen* singing Micaëla at the Met, so I had to be reasonably well and able to go to work, to go to rehearsals every day. It was good that I had to sing in a new and interesting environment, which helped me greatly.

But the strongest emotional backlash I had was in relation to my hometown. For seven years, I absolutely had to stay away from it. Surely, I saw my parents, they followed me wherever I was singing, but they had to come after me; I was incapable of going to them. I remember that in the same year—in December 1996—they joined me in London and we all had Christmas and New Year together. Then Ioana, my sister's little daughter, came too, along with my father and mother —and the whole family reunited.

How was Ioana? And how were your parents coping with the loss of Nina?

I was singing in *Turandot* and I remember they came to Covent Garden directly from the airport. I was waiting for them quite eagerly, they came to see me right on the stage during an interval in the performance, and after the second act I saw Ioana backstage. She had short hair and was high-spirited, and she was talking to everybody. From the stage, I could not hear what language she was using, but I was amazed to see her interact with everyone. I then asked her, "How come you are able to talk to everyone?"

"I speak English."

"But where did you learn to speak English?"

"From Cartoon Network." She was only six.

In my family, the impact of my sister's death was very strong and far-reaching. My parents split up, and my father decided to become a monk. As he was already retired, he joined an Orthodox monastery where only men were allowed, and there he stayed. He made a decision which I respected, but to this day I do not agree with it. Retreat in a monastery does not seem much like a mere withdrawal, but rather a fleeing from the hardships of life. An act of cowardice. What would the world become if we all found it best to retreat when life hits us hard? What would happen to all those whom we would leave behind? How could we help each other and move forward if we all ran away?

So how did you face up to the situation?

I took Nina's little girl with me later and I raised her with all the love I was capable of, together with Roberto's daughter, Ornella. At her mother's death, Ioana was six, and Ornella was one year younger. If it were just for me, I would have wanted to adopt them both. I had always considered Ornella as my baby, implicitly, without anyone asking me to feel that way. When I caressed them, I caressed them both; when I gave one of them a kiss, I would also kiss the other even though neither of them was my natural daughter. All my life, everywhere I went I would get them something—I could never say no to them, because I was trying desperately to make up for the lack of maternal figures in their lives. The grandparents always scolded me, from all sides, saying I was exaggerating with my spoiling and pampering of them. . . . They had a different mentality, one that even today I do not agree with, particularly in the case of my two girls whose situation was totally special. I did not have my own children, but I loved them unconditionally and I missed them constantly. For years I have lived with insecurities and longings, thinking about what more I can do for them and how to bring them joy of all sorts.

I could not adopt Ioana back then, although I really wanted to, because Roberto said no. When it came to Ornella, I never had any hesitation, I never thought about inheritances, fortunes, money. But he thought of all these issues and raised them when we discussed Ioana's adoption, although he had lived with me since the day that my sister died and he knew very well how a child without a parent feels. . . .

Bizarrely, about the same time, Ornella told me something I would never forget: "Oh, you know what I'm thinking—it's going to be very difficult for you from now on, as you are going to have to work more now that you have two girls." She was tiny and I was dressing her up; she was only five. Whatever she may have thought, whatever she may have heard in her family, I had chills down my spine when I heard that sentence. . . . Such a little child was already so wise for her age and completely understood me. And indeed, a few years later, Ioana lost her father too: Andrei Dan died in an accident and the dramas were amplified.

When did this happen?

In 2001. I was at home in Paris when I received a call from Andrei's brother, Octavian Dan, my brother-in-law who was living in London. Ioana's father and Nina's widowed husband had had a heart attack while he was driving and had a fatal accident. So, at only eleven, Ioana was left without any of her parents. Andrei Dan was a surgeon with a great personality and belonged to the Romanian elite. He was extremely well educated and of impressive spirituality and intellect, but this was his destiny and Ioana was left alone at a very young age.

It was a huge shock for the entire family. Words cannot describe it.

IOANA DAN-HOLUBAȘ

Angela Gheorghiu has always considered her niece Ioana Dan-Holubaș like her very own child, since her birth in 1990. Ioana brings Angela strength, happiness, and support on every occasion.

◆ ◆ ◆

Everyone knows her as Angela Gheorghiu, the world's greatest opera star, but for me she is much more than that. She is Angela the person, Angela the mother.

For as long as I can remember, I have considered I have two mothers —my biological one, Nina, and Mama Angela. The childhood memories I have of Nina are quite blurry as I was very young when she passed, thus I am not even certain that the memories I have of her are real or ones I have with Mama Angela. As a young child, I called her "Mama Gela" since I could not pronounce her full name, but now I feel lucky to simply refer to her as "Mama" and she encompasses all that this word means.

Our relationship is an atypical one. Setting aside the differences of opinion that exist in all mother-daughter relationships, we complete each other and we are accomplices in everything. I like to believe that I have found in her the mother I so needed and that she has found in me a daughter, but also a sort of sister, a part of her Nina, a unique bond, honest and unconditional, stronger than any feeling in the world.

When I was little, we used to see each other mostly on holidays so I automatically associate her with joy, freedom, and delight. As she often reminds me, she never said "no" to me, never denied me anything, constantly offering me everything I needed and desired. I have always been able to talk to her openly about any mischief or adolescent little nothings, without ever feeling judged or scolded. She also confides in me as I confide in her to this day. She has supported, encouraged, and guided me throughout all my life choices and decisions and she has unfailingly been there for me, all of which have only made our bond stronger.

Life alongside her has been surreal. I grew up backstage, at rehearsals, in dressing rooms, on planes, in hotels all around the world but I always felt as though everywhere was "home" because "home" is wherever she is. She taught me everything I know including jokes, music, films, everything about art and culture, the importance of having an education as well as working hard for everything you want in life. She is a beautiful person, generous, open minded, curious, funny, and she taught me how to laugh in the face of tragedy and turn it into something good, learn from whatever life throws at you and always stay a child at heart. I could go on forever with this list and it still wouldn't be enough.

I know for a fact that I have an Angel in Heaven and one here on Earth and there are not enough pages in the world I could write to thank and honor her. She is an extraordinary artist, worthy of all the praise in the world, as everyone knows, but only I know the kind of mother that she is. I love her and I am overwhelmed with pride for the work she has done so far and has yet to do, as well as the amazing person that she is.

Life gives and takes from you, yet it has given me her, Angela Gheor-ghiu, the one everyone admires and applauds, as the most important person in one's life: Mama.

When we all met at Andrei's funeral, I decided to adopt and take care of Ioana, not as I had before, but much more than that, from all points of view. I wanted to take care of her education. Together with Otto—Octavian—I decided to let her stay at his home in London but to provide for her in every aspect of her life, and so Otto and his wife agreed to take her with them.

You took on the full responsibility for her life.

From that time, I took care that Ioana should not be deprived of anything. I paid for all her schooling, and all that she needed. We all tried to shelter Ioana, to alleviate her trauma in every possible way. Whether we succeeded or not is a very hard thing to tell. Only she knows in her heart how she feels and how she goes on with her life. But I did whatever was possible to appease her after all the tragedy she went through, to help her find a new world of dreams and help her to fulfill every wish. We all love her wholeheartedly to this day, of course.

With neither of the girls, Ornella or Ioana, did we talk about their mothers—I would mention them only very vaguely and in passing, telling them how they would approve of them and how they would love

FRANCO ZEFFIRELLI

Some of the most famous productions in which Angela Gheorghiu has appeared were directed by the opera, film, and television director Franco Zeffirelli.

◆ ◆ ◆

An instant blaze of vitality, talent, and beauty—like lightning! And she has extraordinary professionalism. You cannot reach that position that is so high unless you work hard. She started with a wonderful voice, of course, but the talent has to be developed by discipline and intelligence, and she has that. This is why—and I must say this with respect to all the other singers—she is unique today. There is one Angela Gheorghiu.

them. I would speak about them in an educational context, so to speak. And every time I bought something, I would buy something for each of them; whenever I comforted them, one would sit to my left, the other to my right. Every gesture, everything I did was in double for years.

Despite the trauma, life went on. . . .

Yes, indeed, and the show had to go on too. My schedule, which had been set up years before, was not taking into consideration the emotional turmoil I was going through. On the contrary, it threw yet another share of thrills and unexpected incidents my way, some pleasant, some others less so. After the spring of 1997, when I had several performances of *Carmen* at the Metropolitan singing Micaëla, in the summer we started a tour in Japan with this production. Plácido Domingo sang Don José, Carmen was Waltraud Meier, and Jimmy Levine was conducting, alternating with Plácido. It was a production of Franco Zeffirelli, the greatest opera legend, a man who was always and will remain forever a dear friend. To me, Zeffirelli has reached the Everest, the highest point an artist can ever achieve in terms of directing. He made the most legendary productions in opera, theater, and film. I adore him and I feel really fortunate that I was able to work with him.

As Micaëla you were a blonde.

Yes, for all performances at the Metropolitan where Micaëla had to be a blonde ingénue, I had a nice wig, with long, golden locks, and I felt perfect. When we arrived in Japan, however, I put my wig on and realized it was a different one, a bit reddish, very ugly—something that could not work well at all. I did not know what to do. To me, whenever I develop an opera character I am supposed to play, I always understand terms like simple, candid, sensitive, vulnerable, but not ugly. This does not sit well with me.

The wig for Waltraud's Carmen was a different color too. Who knows what a mess was created when the costumes were packed; the fact is that it was a big issue with the wigs then.

This was the moment when you had the famous argument with Joe Volpe —this was how the "legend of the blonde wig" came to be, right?

It all started as a joke, after a conversation that was half serious and half not, and a very calm one too. While I was trying my costume on in my dressing room, Joe came to the door and I got to tell him what was bothering me: "This is a really ugly wig—don't you have any other one here, like the one I had back in New York? I can't wear this one, it looks silly." He said soothingly, "Oh, but you can," without even glancing at it—"It's very good, it's very good." I explained once again that it looked ugly: "Please give me any other wig—I know we're on tour and resources are limited, it does not have to be a certain hair color, I just want it to look good."

With all my characters I used to say, "I can be poor, but never ugly." Onstage, I may turn into the most humble and the most insignificant character, I can play anything, I crawl, I cry, I do whatever the director wants or the role requires, I can understand the nuances of any character, but ugly I cannot be, especially if it goes against the character. The woman in me does not accept this. Finally, Volpe took me seriously, but in the same condescending tone he told me, "No, it is all going to be all right, you'll see." . . . And then I jokingly asked, "You don't mean to tell me the wig is more important than the voice." To which he felt provoked and responded, "Oh, but it is."

"Are you kidding?" I went on, without believing what I was hearing. "No," came the reply.

So, suddenly, a small issue became a big one. . . .

Yes, he absolutely insisted I wear the wig, and I replied, "If you force me to put on the wig, I will not sing." His reply: "The wig will be on the stage with you or without you." He chose the wig and I chose not to sing. Nevertheless, I joined the audience for the performance. I had enjoyed great success in Japan and with the recording of *La traviata* in London, and also with my first CD; I had come to Tokyo in January of that year to sing Violetta, the *Carmen* production had also been aired worldwide from the States, and everybody knew that I was to sing Micaëla. The audience and the organizers in particular expected to see me onstage. So, because of Volpe's decision to not let me sing onstage, I went into the hall as a mere spectator. As I was about to see, this was considered a very bold gesture!

That evening I went backstage and I remember that my colleagues who had heard of my "rebellion" would not even say hi to me, as if I were a pariah. Of all of them, only an American baritone spoke to me. The rest of the cast did not address a single word to me, staring at me as if I were a renegade, for fear that Volpe might see them. . . . But in the audience, everyone saw I had come together with the whole assembly, that in fact I was there, so a small revolution started and this eventually made things right for me and also pleased me a little, I must admit. If my absence had just gone unnoticed, I would have felt like an object.

In fact, though, you only missed one performance.

The promoters of our tour in Japan came to Volpe and told him that they wanted me onstage for the next performance, and then they found some creative solutions. . . . In the following performances, Micaëla had her wig on, but in the first act I wore a big scarf covering my head to my chin, so that no hair was coming out. Joe Volpe was backstage, biting his hands, and I was serene, singing. In the third act I wore a hooded cape and put my hood up, so no one saw, either onstage or during breaks, any bit of wig.

How did the director of the Metropolitan react after this?

For a while, Volpe was very upset, he did not want to hear about me, but later he probably reconsidered, because, in fact, nothing serious had happened; it was a mere childish quarrel. If the story had happened to someone else, certainly it would not have had this magnitude, it would have been just a trifle, but as such, it turned into a real story.

Finally, he came back to me the next year and gave me many important things to do. We had superb performances of Gounod's *Roméo et Juliette* in a production of old, from the days of Mirella Freni and Franco

Corelli, but we loved the opera and I loved to sing it alongside Roberto, who is by far the ideal Roméo, both stylistically and vocally, as well as in terms of stage presence. In addition, as he is native French, he could sing the role with a rolled *r*, something few people had done before, and none as well as him. To be able to melodically utter a consonant which has a particular pronunciation is a tricky thing, but to him this was as natural as drinking a glass of water. In the same year, Roberto and I had recording albums and recitals singing together, and we recorded the complete opera *Roméo et Juliette*.

What followed at the Met after Roméo et Juliette?

A new production of *La traviata* was being planned. When Joe Volpe presented me with the intention of making a new production of *La traviata*, to replace the Metropolitan's old Franco Zeffirelli production, I was very excited. Surely, I recommended to him that I should sing together with Roberto. Volpe agreed with me to hire a certain conductor and also showed me the sketches for productions he had already received from two directors. He was not convinced by either of them, and I also did not think that they were suitable to replace the existing production, so finally Volpe asked me, "Even if the old production was Zeffirelli's, wouldn't you like to have Zeffirelli do the new one as well?"

I said, "Yes, why not?" I always considered Franco Zeffirelli as one of the leading directors in opera's entire history, so I was glad to have him do this.

And yet, this was a project that did not materialize in the end—on the contrary, a whole story developed around it. . . .

One day, at that time, Joe Volpe asked us to come to his office. I went there with the lady who had witnessed our marriage, Lucienne Tell, an old friend of Maria Callas, with whom she had extensively corresponded, and a friend of Plácido Domingo, Mario del Monaco, José Carreras, Mirella Freni, and Nicolai Ghiaurov. She loved opera and its great artists with a fierce devotion: this was a woman for whom, essentially, the opera was everything.

I went, therefore, accompanied by Roberto and Lucienne Tell, to Joe Volpe's office. When I left home, I saw that Roberto had taken something with him and I had a hunch then what it might be, but I thought that maybe he would not have the courage to say anything. When all three of us came into Volpe's office, he showed us the new production of *La traviata* that Franco had prepared: "Look, we even have some boz-zetti—the miniature decor for all the acts."

And how did that look?

It was very beautiful and elaborate. It looked a little like the production they were having at that moment, but it also had some extraordinary technical movements, using two overlapping plateaus that created a gorgeous effect. In short, it was very beautiful and very well suited for the staging capacity of the Metropolitan Opera. It was among the last of the classic stage interpretations, in good compliance with the score. I always preferred the classic way and I continue to like this style because, after all, the classic is merely a sum of modernities.

You have indeed made public over time your opinions about various modernist stagings, and some of them you have refused outright. Were you ever afraid that you might acquire a reputation for being too conservative?

No. In many situations, the productions that I kept away from or have downright refused proved to have quite a short life in front of the audiences. They did not add anything to the scores; they were displays of the director's ego rather than genuine manifestations of creativity. There are things the artists see and know from their first discussions with directors. The difference between others and me is that I have never been docile enough with the directors to accept that they destroy, distort, or alter the meaning of a score. I sign a contract for the score. For me, the composer is the only one who can give us the key to interpret an opera. In the contracts I sign, there is never any other name except that of the composer who had written the score.

But in this case, that was not the problem.

Not at all. We had a superb score, a situation where we could mount a complex production, a great director to lead us all, and so I said, "Joe, it would be good to also meet with Franco, to talk with him. Maybe we could come up with something new in terms of costumes and direction as well; let's meet with him"—just the way we had met with the other two directors on whom, in the meantime, Volpe had given up.

Roberto was agitated and at one point we all saw him slam a folder on Volpe's table. The folder was filled with production drawings, and he said, "Look, this is a new production of *La traviata*, not what you had just showed us here!" From the folder, he took out the drawings made by his brothers, David and Federico, who had been aware of our meeting at the Metropolitan and had prepared them for him behind my back. I had recommended him to be my partner in *Traviata*, just to see him turn down Franco Zeffirelli's production like this.

When I saw that he did this in front of me, I thought I would just die with shame. Of course Joe Volpe could not have imagined that I had no prior knowledge of any of that. . . . He very well could have had the feeling that we had planned everything together. From the outside, it looked like a classic case of lack of gratitude, so I can easily imagine that when Volpe judged Roberto's attitude, he in fact judged both of us. I suddenly had a lump in my throat, and all I could say was, "In this case we'll talk tomorrow," and I left.

Did you talk to anyone then? Did you not try to explain?

I did not wish to, nor did I have time. The next day at breakfast, I read the *New York Times* headline — "Hesitating Celebrity Couple Loses a Met Opera Contract" — and the article telling of Angela Gheorghiu and Roberto Alagna refusing director Franco Zeffirelli's new *La traviata*.

The truth of that meeting came out very late and I could not say anything for so many years so as not to have arguments at home. It was not the first time Roberto had tried to push me into doing something produced by his brothers — they insisted for years and wanted me to do *Cyrano de Bergerac* and *Pagliacci* with them directing; eventually, in 1999, I sang *L'Amico Fritz* at the Salle Garnier of the Opéra de Monte-Carlo, where they did the sets for the production. Even so, back then, in April 1998, I never imagined Roberto would have as much courage as to interfere by bringing his family's proposals over a new production and a new direction of Zeffirelli, particularly at the Metropolitan. What can I say — I was supremely disappointed. . . .

I immediately received a lot of phone calls with invitations to appear on television shows to tell the story from our perspective, but I did not accept any of them because I knew I could not tell the truth. My career may have suffered because of all those situations when, due to family circumstances, I could not speak up.

Of course, today Joe Volpe and everyone in the theater knows what happened: in the end even Joe realized that the problem was not me, so after a few years he told me, "You are Violetta, the production Zeffirelli made is yours, please come and sing it." And I did.

When did this happen, more specifically?

In 2006—so the production was no longer new when I got to sing it eventually. It was Volpe's last year at the Metropolitan, he was still at the helm, but we had discussed my return to that role three to four years before, and then he gave me the freedom to come up with proposals for any amendments I needed so that I could feel good. I said, "If I come and sing in this production, you must trust me. We need to have other costumes, and I will come with a new tenor. Let me look for him."

The costumes were now designed by Raimonda Gaetani, a very good friend of Franco Zeffirelli, an extremely talented and intelligent woman whom I admire enormously.

I was in Switzerland, at home, when I received from my agent at that time, Jack Mastroianni, a recording of Cecilia Bartoli in *Nina, o sia La pazza per l'amore*, the baroque opera of Paisiello. Beside her was a younger tenor employed by the opera theater in Zurich—Jonas Kaufmann. I watched the recording and then I sent my proposal to Volpe: "Look, this is a tenor for *Traviata*. He has the colors, he has the physical profile, he is just the right one. Please, look at this video recording with Cecilia Bartoli, and pay attention to the tenor: he will be Alfredo."

I had no doubt that Jonas Kaufmann would be excellent. As I often say in interviews, I can be wrong about mediocre performers, but with those who are very good, I never fail. Coming from Zurich, Jonas sang with me in *La traviata* in 2006, and his international career took off from that point. A headline review after those performances was "Brangelina Sings!" Moreover, before this *La traviata*, in 2004, Roberto had canceled a number of performances of *La rondine* at the Royal Opera House, and knowing that I would sing with Kaufmann in New York, I immediately proposed him as a replacement. The success of the shows in London was considerable, although the tenor role in *La rondine* is not as flattering as is that of Alfredo in *La traviata*.

With Jonas I also sang *La traviata* at La Scala, and I recorded a much-awarded CD of *Madama Butterfly* with him for EMI Classics, together with Tony Pappano conducting. I opened doors for him as Maestro Solti had opened doors for me, and, as it turns out, he was totally deserving. Jonas is now an artist admired worldwide, one of the best tenors of his generation.

Tenor Vittorio Grigolo has sung with Angela Gheorghiu many times since he first appeared with her in Franco Zeffirelli's production of Verdi's *La traviata* in Rome, in 2007.

◆ ◆ ◆

Angela — The Soul Aloft the Voice

It all started with a not-so-easy audition that saw me become involved with a *La traviata* production at the Rome Opera in 2007. I was the third tenor on the list. For sure I was going to have a performance, but the chance to share the scene with Angela at the premiere was more of a dream than a reality really. Furthermore, rehearsals were cut down to a minimum. Nevertheless, as we say, "Hope is the last to die," and as if by magic, without having poisoned anyone—I swear!—I found myself at her side. To guide us through, we had the best director there ever was: Franco Zeffirelli. During the whole run of the production he spoiled and supported us, putting us at ease, getting the best we could offer as a result.

The first time Angela and I saw each other at rehearsal and I met her gaze, I understood there and then that we would be making music, and the sounds we would be producing together would go beyond the words and transcend any spaces for breathing. I just knew it would be pure magic. At the same time, the Queen of this role, Angela, knew exactly how to manage everything, she knew every single detail—that is how it was! The premiere at the Rome Opera with Angela was an absolute triumph and it remains an indelible souvenir in my heart. Her voice echoes again in me as if it were happening now. Her strong, special, and determined character, so out of the ordinary, has certainly made her the sublime artist that today everyone wishes to emulate.

Angela knows exactly when to rest her intellect and allow only her heart to speak when she is singing. One immediately feels at ease—but, attention: this happens only if she recognizes in her partner a similar soul. There have to be two animals of the same breed.

After that wonderful debut, our musical story together continued, and we have since then shared other exhilarating successes. I particularly have to mention the production in London of *Faust* at the Royal Opera House, Covent Garden, under the direction of the maestro and our dear friend Evelino Pidò. It was a production in which I nearly left my head in a trunk! With Angela, when the moment of the love duet came it was pure magic. . . . I felt as if I was walking on clouds. . . . I have so many lovely memories and sheer joy remembering every single note!

Then came our trip to Korea with the dear Maestro Myung-whun Chung! We really had a lot of fun bringing to the stage a very singular *La bohème* drowned by torrential monsoon rains at a time of year not really suited for outdoor performance, but once again made so memorable by sharing the stage with Angela, which invariably means electrifying emotions.

Such a shame that all these heroic women are always doomed to die!!! A real pity! But, thank goodness, Angela herself is alive and flourishing, and I hope we'll share some more premieres and debuts, some more travels, but most of all a lot more of that unforgettable musical magic!

Grazie, Angela.

Another artist who has had notable success singing La traviata *with you is Vittorio Grigolo.*

Yes, he too is one of today's great tenors, a "burning" artist onstage, a wonderful partner, with an unusual charisma. We sang *La traviata* in Rome together, in Franco Zeffirelli's new production in 2007; he was then a debutante. Then followed *La bohème* at La Scala, Vienna, and at the Royal Opera House, where we also sang in Gounod's *Faust*, alongside René Pape as Méphistophélès and Dmitri Hvorostovsky as Valentin—a dream cast.

CHAPTER 9

Royal Encounters

✦ ✦ ✦

n 1998, you sang La traviata *at the Opéra National de Paris, along with Ramón Vargas and Alexandru Agache. It was a new production by Jonathan Miller.*

Yes—I was singing Violetta, and in the second act I was wearing a red dress. After one of these performances a gentleman came to my dressing room. He was a Frenchman, Daniel Toscan du Plantier, and he told me bluntly, "You're Tosca." I laughed, I thought he was joking —that night I had been as much Violetta as possible. But he continued: "No, no, no, I mean it, my name is Daniel Toscan du Plantier, I am a film producer, and thanks to you, I decided this evening that I will make a film of *Tosca.*"

Eventually, I came to believe he was indeed serious because he told me he had a long personal history with *Tosca,* indeed his own name came from Tosca's, but before meeting me he had not found the perfect soprano to fulfill his vision. The other person he had in mind for the cast was Ruggero Raimondi, in the role of Scarpia, and he asked me how I felt about him, if I wanted him to sing with me. I said "Sure!" on the spot—and so the idea of the *Tosca* film came to life. Subsequently, the team was joined by Benoît Jacquot as director, and I proposed Roberto for the role of Cavaradossi.

The only rather challenging discussion referred to the conductor. Toscan du Plantier was thinking of a famous name, Lorin Maazel or Zubin Mehta, but I said, "Let's go with Antonio Pappano."

"But he is not a celebrity," he retorted, to which I replied, "He will be a celebrity after this film." I insisted on Antonio Pappano not only in my conversations with Toscan du Plantier, but also with the people of EMI who wanted to release a CD with the soundtrack of the film, and, naturally, they also wanted a very famous conductor. But I stood my ground very firmly: "Pappano is the best conductor for this work." Eventually, everyone agreed with me.

The film was a very big success for you, Roberto, and Tony Pappano.

Yes, and it created huge discussions for me at home. The various incidents happening during the first two years of our marriage had already begun to leave their mark, also because of the tension of singing so much together.

Weren't you happy to sing together?

Yes, we were—that was why I was keen to sing with him in recordings, performances, and movies, whenever I believed it was appropriate for the score and whenever we thought we could achieve something great together. Apart from the double emotions about which I have already told you, whenever I was onstage with someone close to me, I was extremely happy. Each show made us fall in love with our voices all over again, and the music was bringing us together. But if it had been up to Roberto, we ought to have sung only together, all the time, and this seemed to me slightly exaggerated. Our repertoires and voices were not always a perfect match.

You have always been very selective about the roles you sing.

I like to do what I think and feel is in my vocal and interpretive power to do. I am seeking to understand and profit from the infinite nuances of the word that underlies any opera score. The word together with the music for voices and instruments can be sung in an infinite number of interpretations, and exploring them never bores me. On the contrary, for any time of rehearsal, study, or performance, I burn completely, body and soul—I do not limit myself to just uttering some sounds. Everything is born and nourished by my heart and my brain.

I support the principle of "less is more." I do not like statistics or competitions in art. I am not interested in the thousandth performance or hundredth role, because I have never thought about quantity in my career, but only about quality. I do not want to sing a new role just to say that I sang it, just to check another role off my list, because I think it is foolish to do so. I have wanted to leave something behind, to be remembered in one role or another, to leave a strong testimony of my portrayal of a specific role, whether we are talking about Mimì, Violetta, Marguerite, Magda, Tosca, or Adriana Lecouvreur. It takes courage and I would also say wisdom to arrive at my judgment.

Certainly that decision has been particularly appreciated by connoisseurs of opera.

They understand that I have always been completely truthful, first to myself, as an artist, and then to everybody that understands and cherishes the magic of music, of art. Some very dear connoisseurs to me are Claude Martin, the former French ambassador to Germany, and his wife, Judith—passionate admirers, precious people who continue to be very close to me.

At the end of 1998 Verdi per due *came out, one of your first records as part of the contract with EMI Classics and the second disc of duets with Roberto Alagna.*

After a three-year contract with Decca, I finally signed with EMI Classics exclusively, as this was also the record company of Roberto and thus it was easier for us to sing and record together. We did *Verdi per due* under the baton of Claudio Abbado, with the Berliner Philharmoniker, which was, at that time, as I said in an interview, a Rolls-Royce of orchestras. It was a formidable disc particularly because of the selection of duets—not only did we sing the well-known *Otello, Aida,* and *Rigoletto,* but also the *I Lombardi* and *I masnadieri* scores that had not been performed so often. Three days prior to the recording sessions, Maestro Abbado asked me to add the final duet from *Don Carlo,* a highly emotional score that Roberto had been singing onstage for a while in Verdi's original French version. I accepted, I learned it quickly, I recorded it. That duet now is the first on the disc.

This record—very well received by audiences and winning multiple awards—was preceded by another EMI release that gave you the occasion to meet Luciano Pavarotti for the first time.

I first met Luciano when he awarded me the prize for our disc of *La rondine* produced by EMI in 1997—our first disc with Antonio Pappano. He was asked by the people at the Gramophone Awards to give away one of the most important awards of the evening. He came to give us the award, to me, Roberto, and Tony Pappano, as it was our first disc together. At the time of the show, I even remember that I was very upset because he only kissed the boys, not me. Who knows what was going on in his mind, maybe it was just a slip. . . . But I was very surprised by his gesture and I promised myself that I would change this situation.

After all, you also sang together, in his hometown, Modena. . . .

CLAUDE MARTIN

French diplomat Claude Martin has been present at many milestone events in Angela Gheorghiu's career and has a profound admiration for her.

◆ ◆ ◆

I had missed the legendary performance of *Traviata* at Covent Garden, which made her known to the world. Even Paris gushed with this rumor: a new star was born. I was waiting to see her path.

She finally appeared, a brilliant Violetta, full of pain, passion, and fire. Such a presence, such candor, such a soul, such a brightness that even the most improbable of staging could not dull her. I would become, that very night, one of her most passionate and dedicated admirers.

Angela is the absolute diva. She appears and dominates. Supreme, fragile, and tumultuous at the same time. Her voice gets ahold of the deepest part of one's being, it takes you, it grasps you and brings you to tears. Her face and hands speak of her pain. She is a born tragedienne. As soon as she steps onto the stage, you see only her. Her beauty stops your heart. Her long mesmerizing and resigning cry renders the cruelty of her destiny even more insufferable.

She is alternatively, and with the same force, Marguerite Gautier, Mimì, Adriana Lecouvreur, Manon. French heroines, transformed by Italian genius and sung by a Romanian fairy with the voice of gold. Is this not a testimony to the profound and magic bond which unites Romania with France and Italy? The moving mysteries of Europe.

She speaks French perfectly, with points of light which shine deliciously as she speaks. One evening in Berlin, after a brilliant performance of Verdi's *Requiem*, I had the honor and the irrefutable privilege of handing to her, on behalf of the French Republic, the distinguished decoration which testifies the admiration that my country bestows upon her. In the foyer, there were numerous musicians from the Philharmonic, who have come to associate themselves with this homage brought to her. Roberto Alagna, Claudio Abbado, Emmanuel Pahud, and Prince Frederic Georg of Prussia. I placed a star upon a fairy's dress.

The fairy resumed her journey across the world. Such is a diva's destiny. The world asks for her. Those who admire her, and do not have the possibility to follow her everywhere she goes, are far from unhappy. She offers them treasures along her way. She has, as real fairies have, the art of transforming even the plainest of objects into miracles. An example of such miracles are the Romanian arias she offered us one November evening, at the Royal Opera of Versailles. Or that "Minuit, Chrétiens" she gave us one Christmas in the Cathedral in Dresden, sung in a way in which it had surely never been sung before, a completely sublime moment that left everyone who heard her voice that night with a profound feeling of having come close to heaven.

Unfortunately, we had no opportunity to sing together in an opera, because we crossed paths professionally in a time when Luciano had fewer performances and concerts, and the roles he would take on were heavy, end-of-career-type roles, while my roles were rather light, beginning-of-career type.

Eventually we met and I did a show together with his father for Rai 1*—the show was called *Porta a porta* and was hosted by Bruno Vespa. And then, yes, I also sang in the tribute concert organized for him in Modena to celebrate the fortieth anniversary of his debut. They have remained ever since as two of my dearest memories.

Recently, I had the opportunity to sing at the Pavarotti memorial concert at the Arena di Verona, exactly ten years after his death. One of the highlights of the concert was performing "Non ti scordar di me" together with Plácido Domingo and José Carreras; this is a song that Luciano loved a lot, and it acquired a very special meaning in the context of the evening.

How was the Modena tribute concert? And what was Pavarotti like?

We all know how funny and gallant he was, always having the answer to anything. When I was in one of his last concerts at the Hollywood Bowl, after the performance I went with Roberto to congratulate him. We both were singing *Pagliacci* in Los Angeles, so we met Luciano, we kissed, we complimented each other, and during all of this Luciano

*The Italian national television network.

said, "*Ragazzi,* I want to do a concert with all tenors at the Met." As he was a good friend of Joe Volpe, everything Luciano wanted, Joe made it happen. "I will invite all generations of tenors and I will also invite you," he told Roberto, and then looked at me and said, ". . . You too."

"Well how come you would invite me—I'm not a tenor," I quipped.

"Ma si, tu sei peggio di tutti tenors, ma devi essere la" (Oh, but of course, you are worse than all the tenors, you have to be there). His remark amused me because, in my opinion, Luciano is a gift that God gave us to make us happy, to wonder at and treasure.

During his tribute concert held in Modena, I started singing the aria from *La Wally*, "Ebben, ne'andrò lontana." . . . Right in the middle of the score, there is a point where you feel that the orchestra is about to start, but actually there is a short break. The unpredictable happened just then and we had a slight sync problem. The concert was aired live on Rai but I told Eugene Kohn, who was conducting, "Let's take it from the top! Da capo!" All said and done, I resumed the aria from the beginning, as it seemed only fair. I made a mistake, I fixed it. Franco Zeffirelli, who was in the audience in the front row, stood up and shouted, "Bravaaa! Solo tu potevi fare questo!" (Bravaaa! Only you could do this!).

Has this kind of situation occurred again?

It has indeed. Once, it was during the church scene from *Faust*, in Monte Carlo, when I was singing opposite Orlin Anastassov as Mephisto. I was lying on the ground and suddenly I noticed that the orchestra, the chorus, the organ, and both myself and Orlin were in complete discordance. I stood up and said, "Da capo," but the conductor continued like nothing had happened. So I disappeared in my dressing room in the middle of the scene, and I came back for the last act, which fortunately went very well. Of course, the audience disapproved with the conductor in the end.

Luciano Pavarotti's name is also connected to your first meeting with Sting, who proved to be quite an unusual stage partner for the duet from Don Giovanni, "Là ci darem la mano."

At Petra, in 2008, in October, one year after the death of Luciano, we were both invited to participate in a grand memorial show, in an absolutely exceptional decor. We were accompanied by the Prague Philharmonia, conducted by Eugene Kohn, and joining me onstage there was a whole host of artists who had known Luciano, both opera singers and pop singers—from Plácido Domingo and José Carreras to Andrea Bocelli, Sting, Laura Pausini, and Zucchero.

How did you come to sing an opera duet with Sting? He confessed that he never believed he would ever sing opera onstage and he is not inclined to repeat the experience.

I heard what he said in the interview. I did not know what we were to sing. I was just asked to sing together with him and I was certainly crazy about the idea. I started listening to all he had written, thinking about choosing something from his work for our duet. Then we spoke on the phone and, to my dismay, he told me he wanted to sing opera with me. So my dream of performing one of his songs in duet with him remained just a dream. He prepared, he rehearsed intensely, and so came to life an extraordinary moment, which we both created for the memory of an extraordinary personality.

The day after the show, we met in Petra for breakfast. I was with my cousin Florentina, and Sting was with his wife, Trudy. I remember that he was accompanied by a kind of lute and played it the whole time we had coffee and talked. Later, I found out that he never eats without playing. It was a very nice and friendly morning, just as beautiful as the moment we shared onstage.

Afterward, I met Sting in Washington, in London, in Bucharest, in Italy. . . . Every time he sings just as cleanly and precisely as he does on his recordings, and I am fascinated by his continuous search for rhythms and instruments from all over the world. He is a very complex musician and a lover of classical music. I greatly admire him.

You mentioned Florentina before—Florentina Bucos.

In 2001, with a schedule that would only grow in intensity, I felt the need to have some constant support around me. I was in London with Roberto, both of us working with his assistant, the late Marcel Aquarone, and later with Alexander Gerdanovits, but to me it was becoming increasingly difficult to manage my schedule, the logistics of my shows and appearances—glamorous as it may seem, this is actually a complex job. It was then that my cousin Florentina reappeared in my life. She was the one with whom we went to sing in childhood on the banks of the Siret. Florentina had recently come to work in London. She had found a job that was not exactly what she had dreamed of, so I asked her to join me and become my personal assistant.

Of all the more than two dozen cousins back home, Florentina had always been the closest to me, so that she easily became the one that has helped me morally and professionally since 2001. On her shoulders she has carried both the good and the bad, and she has become—according to the words of Peter Katona—"the famous Florentina," the one who handles everything, starting with my numerous pieces of luggage. Surely it was not easy for her, because she was married, and just like me she had adopted a child—Diana, daughter of her sister Zoe. But since then, Florentina has been with me in any situation. We've been a great support to each other and I'm glad we stayed close.

Together with her and with Alexander Gerdanovits we make quite a team, bound by profound admiration and a deep friendship and, of course, by some amazing life stories, some rather difficult to tell in a book. Florentina has been responsible for my schedule, knowing everything I did and have to do, and coming with me everywhere. Two pieces of luggage for short stays, four for one week, six for long stays. She has organized everything with great precision and efficiency.

She has also accompanied you during your times of study.

Each time I have had something to study for a new role or for an important recording, we have created together a kind of ritual.

Because my study routine is completely different from that of Roberto, I could never work together with him, so I would go with Florentina to Coppet on Lake Geneva, in an idyllic place, where we had a superb apartment somewhere up in an attic and I could enjoy all the peace and the wonderful atmosphere that I needed. There I would have hours and hours of daily study with the score in my hand and I would combine this with a kind of *avant la lettre* detox, for body and soul.

In June 2002 you participated in a royal celebration, singing for the Queen of England at her Golden Jubilee.

Throughout my career I have sung in performances organized for presidents of nations and royalty. In over a quarter of a century I have had a chance to meet them all. Most often the leaders of the world would come to my shows and I would meet them in the opera theaters, but I also had concerts that have been dedicated specifically to some of them and large events that we participated in together.

Two special moments stand out, however—one was the Golden Ju-

FLORENTINA BUCOS

Cousin Florentina Bucos's memories of Angela Gheorghiu go back to their child-hoods, and during the course of Angela's career Florentina became her personal assistant.

◆　◆　◆

As little young ladies living on dreams and hopes, dancing on the Siret bridge, and looking at the huge moon that lit up the whole of Siret Valley, Gina would tell me stories about how she would grow up and shine as brightly as the stars we saw above . . . and I would watch the stars while listening to her singing and I would be fascinated. Along the years I have constantly felt as though we were above the stars, watching her shine as she had promised. One of the many examples of such an experience was in Rome in 2009 when I waited for her to arrive in front of the Colosseum in a horse and carriage: dressed divinely, she appeared triumphantly as ever. I remember that day my eyes burnt with happiness. . . . In fact this happens every time I hear the roar of applause for her and I feel such an immense happiness that I know can never be attained by anything else on this earth. And I remember that exact occasion in 2009, that same night after the wonderful concert at the Colosseum, she told all us ladies who were there with her, "Ladies, we're going to Venice on a vacation—Venice is too close and I cannot resist the temptation so we're leaving at once!" And so it happened that we just left on a spontaneous, superb vacation enjoying the streets of Venice.

What I would like to say about Angela is that when you are with her, you never experience just one moment of happiness; it is an unending sequence of such moments!

bilee of Her Majesty Queen Elizabeth, and I can say that in this case I felt most privileged, because this was the only occasion on which the Queen has ever hosted concerts inside Buckingham Palace. There were two concerts celebrating the jubilee: the first was of classical music, and one day later there was a pop concert—both took place within the palace, in its gardens.

Inside the palace we had our dressing rooms where we would put on our costumes and where we were preparing. I spent an entire day there: I never went out for a moment. I just did all sorts of rehearsal for the BBC, who were televising the event. At the concert, I also sang a Romanian song, "Muzica," by George Grigoriu!

Afterward, we all took part in a meeting with the Queen and went out with her onto the legendary balcony of the palace. I'll never forget that unique feeling. I knew quite well how we all felt when we saw the Queen appear on her balcony—now, however, I had the wonderful opportunity of experiencing this from the other perspective, from the balcony itself.

I seemed to look upon the world from heaven. The whole courtyard was open, all the space in front of the palace was full of people, just as happens during a special event . . . tens of thousands of people. . . . Joining the Queen were her husband Prince Philip and son Prince Charles, and with me were Roberto, Dame Kiri Te Kanawa, Slava Rostropovich, and Sir Thomas Allen. Huge screens had been installed in the city for people to watch both concerts, and everything was broadcast live on television. The jubilee was one of the very important historical moments in which I have been privileged to participate and which has moved me for life. Ten years later, in 2012, I would also perform at the Diamond Jubilee, in a gala at the Royal Opera House, organized in honor and in the presence of the Queen.

But this wasn't your only royal encounter.

Another important royal concert was the one I had in the Netherlands, for Queen Beatrix's Silver Jubilee, in 2005. There, unlike at the British jubilee where numerous artists had participated, I carried all the responsibility of the show on my shoulders. I only had with me a violinist, an actor with whom I sang and remained good friends until his untimely passing, and conductor Paolo Olmi. Jeroen Willems was the actor's name and together with him I interpreted a song by Jacques Brel. It was a very special song for Her Majesty and for her husband, who had died recently. The duo "La chanson des vieux amants" was the beloved song of the royal couple, and its recollection created an extremely emotional moment for everyone involved. Both of us managed to sing that duet in French and in Flemish, for and next to Queen Beatrix—and the text of Brel that made all the difference greatly inspired us and impressed everyone, creating an incredible sensitive atmosphere, which I will always keep in my heart.

I have also met Queen Sofía of Spain on several occasions. I admire her greatly and she always used to ask me, "Do you know I have a first-degree cousin in Romania?"

"Of course," I graciously replied, knowing King Mihai very well. She always told me that our King was her favorite and most beloved cousin of all.

What about the royal family of Romania?

I have a long and beautiful close relationship with the family, and as I told you before, many of us still hoped for the monarchy to be restored after the fall of Communism in Romania. I also used to stay at their home in Bucharest, at the Elisabeta Palace, when I was coming back to Romania—pretty much at the beginning of my career. We have met on various occasions, in Switzerland too, as they have a home there. Princess Margareta, the King's oldest daughter, and consort Prince Radu are focusing now on education, culture, and charity in Romania, and this is praiseworthy. As for King Michael, he was a true symbol of the Romanian people and a landmark for humanity, honesty, and dignity! I will forever adore him!

After Benoît Jacquot's film Tosca *was released, you made another film with Roberto Alagna, this time a French opera, Gounod's* Roméo et Juliette.

That was a production that had already been planned. *Roméo et Juliette* was initiated by an English producer, Alan Sievewright, who was always a loyal admirer of mine. A true gentleman, he knew me from my debut at the Royal Opera House and had asked me to do a film with a Canadian director, Barbara Willis Sweete.

I made this film with the thought of leaving something else behind me, an important record. I was interested in doing significant and valuable projects. Plus, I had always considered Roberto to be a perfect Roméo. I thought it was a nice project which suited us both, and as I always felt good opportunities must be taken, I could not turn it down.

Unfortunately, the directorial vision incurred quite a lot of movement that led to many cuts being made to the original score, so that the proper filming dynamic could be achieved.

So the physical movement was complicated?

It was certainly quite heavy and demanding, from a physical point of view. During one scene, where Roberto was supposed to run behind me, he fell on a hill and had a very bad sprain. He had a lot of physical

KING MICHAEL I OF ROMANIA

The late King Michael I of Romania had a great admiration for Angela Gheorghiu for many years, and Angela even used to stay at the Elisabeta Palace in Bucharest when she was visiting Romania at the beginning of her career.

◆ ◆ ◆

Nihil Sine Deo Decoration Speech

Wishing to reward the merits of Ms. Angela Gheorghiu,

Because she is a symbol of the perennial values of world opera, of progress through education and culture, and of Romania internationally;

For her rich career, for her outstanding talent, and for the greatness of her stage performances;

For the richness of the roles she has sung, and because through her public career she furthers the professionalism and dignity of men and women of culture;

For publicly supporting my family, for strengthening the links between Romania and the world's royal families through her international representations;

We confer the Nihil Sine Deo Royal Decoration.

Michael I

scenes, because his character in the play has duels, runs, fights—and while you can substitute all the movement elements onstage in an opera performance by convention, you cannot substitute them on the big screen.

One other scene required Roberto to take me out of the grave, carrying me in his arms, and he did indeed make all that effort although at the time he was suffering greatly from the sprain. He was nervous thinking that he would not be featured well enough in the shots . . . that the movie might not come out right, that it would not flatter him, and with all these thoughts every day, each light and each detail was examined and I was trying to make sure everything was as well as possible for him.

The footage was very beautiful, as all the shooting took place in a castle near Prague. The music was also recorded in Prague, in a fabulous venue, the Smetana Hall, to where, at the end of 2016, I returned to record a disc of verismo arias and duets. The promotion for the film was not so strong, the fast editing and the multiple cuts were not necessarily to the liking of opera lovers, and the DVD did not have the impact of *Tosca*.

Do you think this also had something to do with this opera's relative lack of popularity?

The golden trio—*Tosca*, *La traviata*, *Carmen*—have the largest appeal to mass audiences. All three works are more compact visually, and as such in terms of camerawork are more acceptable in the form of opera film. *Roméo et Juliette* is, however, very long; it is written by a French composer, not an Italian one; and unlike *Carmen*, also by a French composer but one which features popular songs, it does not have so many famous arias. The fact that Bizet borrowed and reworked pieces of Spanish popular music is one of the most powerful reasons for the continuous success of *Carmen*. *Roméo et Juliette* on the other hand brings forth a stylized French music, which is maybe less accessible, and is based on a Shakespeare play.

Still, in the end, I was very happy and proud that I could do this film of Gounod's opera that I have sung so often. With two opera movies in my career, both made according to all the standards, I consider myself very fortunate. In the history of music, it is rare for a singer not only to have a rich discography and be present on the biggest stages in new productions accompanied by the best orchestras and the best partners, but also to make opera movies.

Both on camera as well as onstage, I gave and I give as much as possible. I must admit the camera is also quite friendly with me, and in my life I have embraced any movie idea because I have always been a movie buff, devouring all the great ones.

CHAPTER 10

Becoming Tosca

◆ ◆ ◆

*Y*ou had lived through the violent days of the Romanian Revolution in *1989—and now, fourteen years later, you were in the United States when war was declared. This of course was a completely different kind of situation, but were you affected by it?*

I was doing *Faust* at the Met in 2003, in the spring, when the Iraq war began. I had neither a sense of history nor war experience; I simply thought that if a country was bombing another country it is, effectively, in a state of war, and therefore dreadful fear came upon me. As I was, by now, an only child, my mother was also extremely worried about me and kept asking me to leave America and come to Europe, where she thought I would be safer. She got very scared and she convinced me to leave America during my performances.

It was not the first time that we were living under the threat of terror and war—it had happened before, in September 2001, when I was with my bags packed and flight tickets in hand, just about to fly from Paris to New York to sing *La bohème* at the Metropolitan. Then I saw in horror the World Trade Center bombings on TV, and thanked heaven that we were not there. Two years later, therefore, when I was singing Marguerite together with Roberto and seeing how things were developing on the foreign policy stage, I told the Metropolitan that I wanted to leave, because I did not feel safe.

Did the management of the Met accept your arguments?

I was allowed to leave provided I did one last show. Roberto took advantage of the fact that my request to leave earlier had been accepted and said all of a sudden that even he could not remain behind. We both left the Metropolitan after a few performances. That production of *Faust* was already very old, from about forty years earlier—rarely such productions last as long—but I was happy to do it because it was the same production Mirella Freni did, the eclectic Freni, such a splendid soprano, together with my favorite tenor of the golden generation, Franco Corelli, so I had many sentimental reasons.

But it wasn't the only production of Faust *you were scheduled to sing at the Met. . . .*

Upon leaving, I had not noticed if they were particularly upset with me or had anything to reproach me for. Furthermore, we discussed doing a new production of *Faust* together, a proposal that I accepted immediately. As the management of the opera house was by now used to asking for my opinion when it came to new productions, I recommended Andrei Șerban for the new performances. For Faust, I would have liked to sing with Ramón Vargas, a tenor with a voice of ravishing beauty and warm musicality—a fine gentleman with great musical knowledge. But it was not to be: I was scheduled to sing with Roberto in the end.

Your history with the Met is huge, and, after Covent Garden, I think it is the house in which you have sung the most, almost all your repertoire?

Yes, Joe Volpe liked me and engaged me a lot. When his farewell concert was organized I was also invited and I wanted with all my heart to go, but I was busy at Covent Garden. I wanted to come only if I could make a real show, wearing a blonde wig à la Micaëla and to sing for Volpe either "Addio del passato" or "Addio senza rancor." They kind of wanted that too, although initially they thought I was joking, but in the end I could not come and do it. It would have been really fun because even then, nearly ten years after the wig incident in *Carmen* had occurred, it was and is still talked about.

You did sing Marguerite in Faust *also in 2004, at Covent Garden, with Sir David McVicar directing. It was the first time in eighteen years that the Royal Opera House had staged* Faust, *with Sir Antonio Pappano conducting (he was now Covent Garden's music director), and with you onstage were Roberto Alagna, Bryn Terfel, and Simon Keenlyside.*

It was a show that came out on DVD too and brought me the reunion with Bryn Terfel, but also with Simon Keenlyside, one of the most beloved of my colleagues. With a fine sense of humor, Simon is a splendid fellow; I always felt good in his company, and in addition he owns a superb voice, and is one of the best singers, if not the best acting singer, whom I have ever met. I sang with him in *Faust*, but also in *La traviata* and in *Pagliacci*.

Sometimes the dramatic importance of Marguerite in Faust *can be underestimated—in fact for many years in Germany the opera was known as* Margarethe.

When you consider the entire opera, you understand why that happened. Marguerite is really in the center, between Faust and Méphistophélès, just as David McVicar placed her in the last scene: I had Faust on my left hand and Mephisto on my right hand, so both of them want me—in a way. So I am the arm really—the weapon to be used to get something.

Among the roles you have sung with great acclaim both at Covent Garden and at the Met was Amelia in Verdi's Simon Boccanegra.

Yes, it is a role I cherish very much. At Covent Garden I sang opposite Neil Shicoff's Gabriele Adorno. Then at the Met, Adorno was sung by Marcello Giordani, and my "father," Boccanegra, was dear Thomas Hampson—wonderful colleagues, great friends, and a beautiful, stunning production. A few years later, I sang Amelia at the Teatro Real in Madrid, at the time when Plácido decided to take on baritone roles. During that time, because of a fire at the Ritz Hotel where I was staying, I had to immediately leave my suite, as the whole hotel was evacuated. So I ended up spending hours outside, during the night . . . a quite unpleasant situation for me, which I paid for with a bad cold.

In 2006 a major new production of Tosca *at the Royal Opera House was mounted especially for you, following the success of the* Tosca *film.*

Yes—Tony Pappano was there conducting and Peter Katona also came to visit during the shooting, to see how things were turning out, and then I came with a proposal to do a new production of *Tosca*, as the ROH was to replace the one made for Maria Callas, which had been designed by Franco Zeffirelli four decades before. I asked Tony to speak with Peter, having the film experience and that of our collaboration for the recordings. It was a decision that I made after some deliberation, because that was a famous production, but it had been used for too long and we had reached a point when there was a need for something new. And that "something new" had to be a great success, because it came to replace the Zeffirelli-Callas duo. I was, however, quite confident right from the beginning, trusting that everything would come out well just because I knew that my vision of the character was different from that of Maria Callas, who had stated she did not like the role very much.

That's the beauty of it, that each artist is free and able to build his or her opinion of a certain character—and, then, free to build the character itself—based upon his or her own emotions, upon those elements he or she resonates with.

What was the team for this important new production?

The director appointed for the new production was Jonathan Kent, Scarpia was my dear friend Bryn Terfel, Cavaradossi was Marcelo Álvarez with his voice of great beauty but also with a great personality, and I took the responsibility of a whole whirlwind of PR which had broken out because it was my debut in this role onstage after the movie, and after Callas, and everyone had very high expectations. The BBC made a documentary about the preparations surrounding the premiere and about the first performances, and called it *Being a Diva*.

The new production was such a great success that it was recorded on DVD, also on my initiative, in 2011. In the cast, besides Bryn, there was also Jonas Kaufmann as Cavaradossi. I have been going back to this production regularly, for the past twelve years, with the same success at the Royal Opera House; it is one of the roles that I sing with the greatest pleasure.

Your Tosca subtly combines the power and delicacy of her character—her young femininity and yet her womanliness.

In Puccini's music you can feel that Tosca is not a virgin. We don't know exactly what has happened in her personal life before. Maybe she has had a man before Cavaradossi—we don't know—but certainly she is not an innocent young girl. It is not possible for the jealousy scene in the first act to be the behavior of a girl. She can charm like a girl, certainly yes: in that first scene she is sometimes timid—but then she is not timid at all! So this is a mature woman, for sure, even though she is young. And she has the personality of a Latin woman in the way that she knows how to use words—she expresses herself with the heat of a Roman woman. Maybe she was born there perhaps, but whatever the case she is a Roman woman of that period—and that was a revolutionary period at the time of Napoleon.

Now, whenever I perform any opera, for me it is like a true story, so with Floria Tosca, like with all the characters I sing, I take myself into the mentality of who this lady was in the society of her time. She is a young woman but she has already been hugely successful and famous as a diva for some time. And just think of this: this famous lady has openly been having an affair with her boyfriend at a time when two unmarried people being together in an open relationship was not accepted in society. She is not married to Cavaradossi—but she does not care what people say about her. She is of a free mind. Now for sure, she is the lady that all the men want. But it is also complex. Because of who she is, it is easier for Scarpia to solicit her, but only because he is very clever. Of course he wants her body, but he is also a policeman and he knows how to use his position so that in his mind he can have her and also forcibly extract the truth from her to bring down Cavaradossi and Angelotti (the escaped revolutionary prisoner whom Cavaradossi is helping).

I have had my own experience of this kind of person—Scarpia is like the kind of policemen we had in Romania in the Communist era: the Securitate. He has the patience to wait until the moment that he can triumph, and he finds that moment when he can trap Tosca—through the combination of the situation and his position, and because he is cunning. He knows just when that moment is available. Because, it's impossible to think that in Rome two centuries ago anyone who was a baron could just send a message to an artist saying, "The baron wishes you to come to his home now." Do you think she would say yes just in a second? And especially that would be unthinkable in a time of revolution, because in that atmosphere people are more afraid of each other. The power of Scarpia in all this is the way he is prepared to wait —maybe a long time—until he knows the moment comes when he can catch her. He is not only very intelligent—he is very manipulative.

If you really look very carefully at Puccini's score, you see and you hear how he tells you everything about these characters—Tosca, Scarpia, and Cavaradossi—in his music. And also you realize how he has created the atmosphere of terror by the way he organized the opera. He cut a lot of Sardou's play,* and it is a short opera with everything happening very quickly. It's actually about the last twenty-four hours in the lives of three people—or four if you include Angelotti—and it's the speed with which so much happens in such a short space of time that creates the tension and the realism. The action is exactly like it is in the real world not of ordinary politicians but of police politicians—the

*Tosca was based on Victorien Sardou's drama La Tosca.

plotting, the waiting, then the decisions, and with all these different time scales very tightly put together. It's extremely lifelike.

Some people have argued that because "Vissi d'arte" was only added on to the opera for the first Tosca, Hariclea Darclée, in 1900, it would be advantageous to cut it, but it is always deeply moving and extremely convincing when you sing it—almost as though Tosca is pleading with Scarpia to spare her more suffering.

Yes, but you really see just a part of Tosca's personality there. It is in the first-act duet where we really discover her personality. In this duet she is so fresh, so girlish, and I love this difference between the first and second acts. I know that Maria Callas very much disliked this scene in the first act—and I don't know why—but for me, in fact right from Tosca's first entrance going all the way through to this duet, we can truly see her character. Even when she is jealous, she isn't furious and screaming like a lioness; she's more like a teasing seductress. From the moment that she is with Scarpia, she changes. It's as though she knows that he is going to destroy everything—which he does. He destroys himself, he destroys her, he destroys Cavaradossi—he destroys everybody, because he has no scruples. For him his whole life is a mission and all the people around him are just its elements.

You portrayed Tosca so many times and in so many different productions —Covent Garden, Vienna, San Francisco, the Metropolitan, Berlin, Japan, and so on. Do you have any absolute favorite, any particular memory?

It is unfair to compare Covent Garden's production, which was practically shaped around me and my personality, with the *Toscas* from other opera houses.

I remember that while singing alongside Željko Lučić as Scarpia, at the Vienna State Opera and later at the Met, I was always keeping the *salvacondotto*, the note of safe conduct that Scarpia writes for both Tosca and Mario at the end of act 2. And, to my surprise, Željko always wrote me a personal note on this piece of parchment—"Sei bravissima," "Sei la piu grande, la piu bella,"* et cetera. Such a beautiful and honest gesture, from a wonderful, complete artist and colleague!

How is it when you throw yourself from Castel Sant'Angelo, at the end of the opera?

---

*"You are the best, the most beautiful."

I must admit I was always afraid at first, because I am afraid of heights and darkness. But as soon as I jump, I feel that I would like to do it again and again. . . . It is a very intense moment, at the end of the opera, and you have to make it very realistic. In truth, there is always a big mattress I jump on and I also ask for people backstage to stay around it with their hands up, looking carefully after me. And always, the first congratulations after the performance come from these people, the machinists helping me come down from the mattress.

What about Margarethe Wallman's production of Tosca *in Vienna?*

It is the oldest production I sang in, dating from 1958, and it is probably the oldest opera production that is still running on an opera stage, worldwide. And this production is yet another proof that classical is the sum of all modernities, because the audience is always astonished by the settings and by the costumes, originally worn by Renata Tebaldi and Giuseppe di Stefano.

Margarethe Wallman was the first female director in opera, very meticulous onstage, a true artist. I first read her autobiography when I was little, and in 2016 I reintroduced a small stage instruction that I found in the book, which has been omitted in the past years: I asked the women from the costume department to make me a green-tone shawl, which I wore in act 2. At the moment that Tosca murders Scarpia, who was Bryn Terfel, I let my shawl fall and encircle his body. Wallman's comment on this stage indication was that the shawl was like a snake, surrounding the body of the dying Scarpia, and was the actual proof of murder. I thought it was a strong explanation, so we used it too.

In May 2006, shortly before the opening of the Tosca *production, you went to the Cannes Film Festival, where you opened the festival with a very emotional moment.*

Vincent Cassel was introducing Wong Kar-Wai, the director who was the president of the festival's jury that year and whose film *2046* included a scene with an opera soundtrack—for that film, I had sung "Casta diva," the famous aria from *Norma* by Bellini. In parallel with the projection of the movie scene in the hall, I entered the stage singing the aria. It was a very beautiful and moving moment, right at the beginning of the festival.

In the fall of 2006, two days after you celebrated your birthday, you sang again for a very large audience, in the "Proms in the Park" concert that the

BBC organized outdoors, in Hyde Park. There you had a surprise guest from Romania.

Yes, it was Ștefan Bănică Jr., a singer from Romania specializing in classic pop and rock, the son of a great actor and, at the time, the husband of a very popular television host in my country, whose name is Andreea Marin. Over the years I had done many collaborations with artists from Romania and I always insisted on singing Romanian arias or songs in my concerts, wherever I went. On this occasion, in Hyde Park, I sang a duet with Ștefan, a pop song that we had launched in my home country, called "Your Name" (Numele tău).

How did you get to meet one of your true idols, the great Romanian soprano Virginia Zeani, around this time?

That year, Ștefan's wife, together with some other people close to me, gave me a great surprise for my birthday. Two days before the concert in Hyde Park, I was in London in the Kensington apartment where we were living then and where I had agreed to shoot for Andreea Marin and the Romanian television a special edition of *Surprise, Surprise*. This TV show was produced and presented by Andreea; it had a massive audience and was based on the idea that each guest was to undergo some special experience.

I was curious to see what people could prepare for me. So, right on my birthday, Andreea came up with her TV crew to our apartment in London, we talked, we had fun, she brought me the rum-flavored chocolate of my childhood, made a few little surprises from several friends in the country, and, at one point, she introduced a special guest, just emerging from my bathroom, where she had been hiding for several minutes in silence and tension . . . none other than Virginia Zeani . . . the legendary Virginia Zeani. . . .

I was stunned, *bouche bée*, I felt like I was about to fall down, while I knew, of course, that everything, all our reactions, were recorded live. I was trying hard to control myself, but I could not. My teenage idol, Virginia Zeani, took me in her arms, just as emotional as I was, we both shed tears, we barely managed to collect ourselves so that we could continue filming.

I had previously met with Mami Virginia (as I call her), and, of course, I had talked to her several times on the phone, but I would never have expected to see her there, in front of all the cameras. It was

VIRGINIA ZEANI

Soprano Virginia Zeani was a special inspiration for Angela Gheorghiu in her formative years, and much later she and Angela became very close friends.

◆ ◆ ◆

I can tell you in all my honesty that Angela is the best singer in the present
time that I ever heard. In my period, there were Callas, Tebaldi, and Sutherland who were the best, but now it is Angela's time to shine on the world's
opera stages. She has the beauty, an incredible sound, and a large repertoire
in many languages. Like me, she began with *La traviata* and the coloratura
roles and has moved on to the deep dramatic parts. She had all the qualities
required for Violetta and now she performs *Adriana Lecouvreur*. [. . .] What
more can I say, but tell you all how proud I am of her accomplishments.

Angela is unique and has a modernity that is impressive. She has re-
venged me in many ways and made me so proud, with the pride of a mother
who has been watching her daughter succeed.

I am sure that posterity will remember her as a great voice, a very beautiful person, and the greatest representative of the Romanian artists.

a genuine moment of amazement and delight, a meeting that we will
never forget.

*And this experience must surely have made you feel particularly close to
your Romanian roots.*

Yes, my Romanian roots have always remained powerfully strong in
me. At the end of that same year I had a "full Romanian" concert on
New Year's Eve at the Opéra de Paris in the Palais Garnier. Joining me
onstage were my former colleague from the conservatory, the magnificent Iulia Isaev, and the superb baritone George Petean, an artist with
a divine voice, with whom I sang several times afterward, but maybe
not as often as I would have liked. Leading us in the music was Ion
Marin, another extraordinarily talented Romanian conductor, the son
of Marin Constantin, the founder of the Madrigal Choir, the most famous choir in Romania. With Ion Marin I sang all over the world—we
went together to New York, San Francisco, London, Paris, Tokyo, Abu

Dhabi, and dozens of other places. He is an accomplished musician, he speaks perfectly all the major European languages and has an extensive culture. A former assistant to Claudio Abbado in the Vienna Opera for ten years, he has conducted orchestras all over the world and has an important discography. It was a great Mozart celebration during the Mozart year, an incredible concert and feast for the New Year!

On that particular night, from all my colleagues only Iulia Isaev was with me, but all my former colleagues in the conservatory, who are today great Romanian artists, are loyal formidable friends of mine—Gladiola Nițulescu, Mihnea Lamatic, Mioara Manea, Gabriel Arvu-nescu. . . . I have brought them with me whenever I have been able to, in all the corners of the world, as there is an eternal brotherhood that binds us together. I am also grateful to them, because, just as they had shared moments of joy with me, they were also supporting me when I was going through indescribable sorrow and real drama. Their feelings toward me not only make me stronger, but also happier.

You have introduced a wealth of colorfully evocative Romanian songs—cântece—to audiences all over the world, who have discovered the unique timbres and flavors of this music entirely through your recitals, concerts, and recordings. Many of these songs were written by Romanian composers in the first half of the twentieth century who were influenced by the ancient folk traditions of Romania. Would you like to explain the characteristics of this highly original and idiomatic musical language?

In Romania at the time when these composers wrote these songs, many of the people who wanted to study music, painting, and litera-ture went to Paris, and they brought back some French influences into our culture. But our composers of the time in a way combined those influences with popular songs and modes of Romania—and there is a traditional perfume in Romanian music that is really very different in harmony and rhythm from Western sounds. But don't forget there is not just one kind of Romanian folk music: both in folk songs and also in church music, there are many variations in different regions of Roma-nia. For instance, Moldavian or Valachian music is very different from Transylvanian music. In Transylvania there are much more influences from Hungary. Most of the composers whose music I am singing wrote more in the Moldavian and Valachian style. On some occasions this can sound like ancient Jewish music, and that is because some of the

ION MARIN

Conductor Ion Marin has accompanied Angela Gheorghiu in many of her concert appearances.

◆ ◆ ◆

To try to write a single page about a friend of over twenty-five years is quite difficult. And when that friend is none other than Angela Gheorghiu, it becomes as rocambolesque as attempting to conduct *Tosca* in five minutes.

What do I start with? Her successes, her complex personality? That she was my wife's student in History of Music? That she is a passionate joke teller? Her generosity, her stubbornness? How can I try to express in writing both the world-class singer and a friend so dear to my heart?

Even our first collaboration looked like a family reunion. Her mother and cousins, my parents, wife, and newborn son, her first singing teacher, some of our colleagues from the Bucharest Music Academy, etc. In London's Mayfair, it led to unforgettable evenings of Romanian cuisine, hours of anecdotes and laughter. And work. Lots of hard work, under the sign of a genuine perfectionism that is one of Angela's—Gina to her friends—trademarks. It all resulted in *Mysterium*, a splendid sacred music album for Decca, where our efforts were joined by the London Philharmonic and the Madrigal Choir from Bucharest. It remains to me as one of the dearest memories, when the artists and the human beings in us were equally fulfilled.

Almost everybody on the planet Opera tries to act as if they know Angela. Her unique voice, her dresses, her caprices and other endless stories, make people feel entitled to judge. And they often do it, without realizing her true dimension. For beyond the indescribable emotion she gives when onstage, beyond her total devotion to the roles she is impersonating, beyond her respect to composers and fellow musicians, beyond her immense career, "there's more, much more than this":

She does it Her Way.

old Jewish musicians were born in Romania and they inherited some of the culture of Moldavia, where there were large numbers of Jewish people in that period. They took their memories of everything with them. And also there are Turkish influences, because we were occupied by the Turks for five hundred years, and in that period a lot of important Romanians studied in Istanbul. You see, geographically Romania is in the middle of so many different cultures: Arabic, Slavic, Hungarian, Jewish, Gypsy—don't forget the big influence the Gypsies have had on Romanian music. And also don't forget that these countries around us, they have an important influence on the way Romanians are as people —in their thinking, their feeling, even their food—altogether in the general style of their life.

A favorite Romanian song of mine, "Când perdeaua dragii mele" (When my love's curtain is gently drawn back), by Alfred Alessandrescu, is a setting of a poem by the French writer Alfred de Musset, but it's written very much in a Romanian musical dialect, with irregular rhythms and a flattened leading note.

What about Tiberiu Brediceanu, who was very deeply immersed in Romania's literary and musical heritage?

He wrote songs, operas, and operettas, and like Enescu he was much influenced by Romanian popular music. Even the harmonies, tempi, and rhythms are very much in that style. Also the words are sometimes "popular," as in popular songs, and they have a special scent. The text and music are perfectly matched.

All these Romanian songs are a special attraction for your audiences around the world. . . .

Yes, indeed. I always include a Romanian song in my concerts. The audience is fascinated to hear me sing them. They may sound exotic to some or nostalgic to others, such as Romanians who are living abroad or have made a living outside Romania. One of my fervent admirers, James Rigler, an American entrepreneur and philanthropist of Romanian origin, loves to hear me sing in my mother tongue. He is a dear friend who has followed my career very closely, and I am very much indebted to him for his honest love of my voice and of music. He is a true *mélomane* connoisseur and a wonderful man.

A kind of favorite encore you often sing at the end of your recitals is Tosti's "A vuchella" (A sweet mouth)—a Neapolitan song. Verdi considered Tosti

JAMES RIGLER

Philanthropist James Rigler (Jamie Rigler), president of the Lloyd E. Rigler–Lawrence E. Deutsch Foundation, is an ardent admirer of Angela Gheorghiu and has become a great friend in recent years.

◆ ◆ ◆

Her voice. Unmistakable, moving, dark in color, capable of many hues, touched with the quality of "morbidezza," beautiful and unforgettable. . . . No less a genius than Maestro Sir Georg Solti heard all of these qualities and personally conducted and oversaw the magnificent Covent Garden production of *La traviata*, specifically for her unique vocal and theatrical gifts. . . .

As a person, I have come to love her honesty, her deep integrity, a funny and sophisticated sense of humor, and a sensitivity that has withstood many tests of disloyalty, betrayals, and sacrifices. . . .

My joy has been to have witnessed, in the theater, her girlish Juliette, her touching and understated Mimì, her funny and adorable Adina, her world-weary Magda, her imperious and loving Tosca, and her Violetta, encompassing *all* of these qualities, coupled with a technique able to communicate and do proper musical and vocal justice to all of the above. . . .

These are some of my impressions of this dear girl, woman, and artist, who I am proud to say is also a friend. . . .

one of the finest melodists and composers of the nineteenth century. Do you agree?

You know, today we call his kind of music "crossover." But when it is really well done it is so wonderful. It is more than just "crossover." This kind of music is something opera singers love to perform because it is an easier way to put our feelings across with more fun, with more gentleness, more sweetness. But there is also pathos in this music at the same time! Tosti is the most known of the Neapolitan song composers, but there are many others too who at that time wrote these lovely and charming Italian canzonettas. They have an instant appeal, and the public loves them.

CHAPTER 11

Choices and Launches

• • •

Basically, after each performance you have a kind of New Year's cel-ebration, a sleepless night. . . .

Yes—I can never sleep after I finish a performance. In twenty-eight years, because of this habit, I have gathered many sleepless nights. What I am in my everyday life I carry onstage and vice versa. After each show, in front of my dressing room, or at the artists' door, or in the street, there is a crowd of people waiting for me for tens of minutes, sometimes in the dead of night, sometimes in the cold.

Their admiration accompanies me wherever they go, and I am both aware and in awe of it. In the same way I know when I'm going back-stage to the artists I admire, I know that they come to see me with the same emotions and the same goosebumps, and they expect me to be there for them after every performance. Their love fills me with energy, it does me a lot of good, and so I have enormous respect for them, pre-paring myself for meeting them after every performance the same way I am preparing for any major appearance.

As for the real New Year's Eves, I have spent many of them singing with wonderful stage partners—as artists don't really have weekends or holidays. One such occasion, besides the concert at Le Palais Garnier in Paris, was the New Year's concert in New York in 2005, where I sang under the baton of Maestro Lorin Maazel, or more recently in Baden-Baden, in 2014. The concerts, the people, and the magical, celebratory atmosphere surrounding them always leave me with joy and unforget-table memories.

In 2007 you took part—along with another fellow Romanian—in a bold project with the creation of a new role: Fanny in Marius et Fanny, *the only opera written by Vladimir Cosma. How did it happen?*

Roberto told me at one point, "I have a new project, but please do not tell anyone anything about it. It's a new opera written by someone you know." With these words, certainly he managed to make me immediately curious. From the discussion, I learned that it was the first operatic work of Vladimir Cosma, a famous composer of film music, of Romanian origin, who had been living in France for a long time and whose films and soundtracks obviously I knew, having watched them in the '70s. In short, the city of Marseille had commissioned Cosma to write an opera based on Marcel Pagnol's Marseille trilogy. The opera was *Marius et Fanny*.

I called Vladimir Cosma, and we called each other by our first names immediately, becoming friendly really quickly, because he is a very open and direct person and we are very much alike from this point of view. I had never talked to him before, and yet it seemed we had known each other for a lifetime.

It's a very beautiful and very demanding opera that I was happy to sing, especially being written by a Romanian composer.

At that time, to finish the opera and get everything to come out just perfectly, I went to Cosma's house. We worked together, I helped him with very specific details, I gave him tips on technique, phrasing, orchestra parts, singing elements, vowels and consonants on high notes, because he had never previously composed for opera voices. The moment he was writing something new, he was sending me the score sheets to discuss.

Slowly we reached the rehearsal time. The director had come from Monte Carlo, and he made a production that fit both the music and the libretto well. Christian Gasc was the dresser, who had made my costumes for Barbara Willis Sweete's film of *Roméo et Juliette* and for Benoît Jacquot's film of *Tosca*. He understood me and sincerely admired me: I would sit with him to discuss details, he was gentle and wise, and we worked together as a great team.

Whenever there were collaborations, I always enjoyed having a little advance discussion on ideas for costumes, an element that is so especially personal. . . . I know my body, I know exactly what I can carry best and the colors that fit me. I always ask which colors are featured in the decor, what the choir is wearing, how the scenography looks, all these just to make sure that the costumes complement the direction and highlight the meaning of the score.

You were performing a famous French character in France.

In Marseille, everyone was probably expecting me to make a faux pas during the opening night, as I am not French. This was an opera based on *The Marseille Trilogy*, a famous French novel in three parts that was made into a series of movies, and having a Romanian in the title role was quite a thing. But my main support was coming from the composer, the creator, and that comforted me a bit.

On the opening night, September 4, 2007, I felt very good because the audience reacted very nicely, as can actually be seen and heard in the recording of the performance. I had positive reviews, which is a bit unusual in France, and I confess that I was very proud, because it had been a huge undertaking, an opera that had been born before my eyes.

It sounds almost like with the role of Fanny, Cosma is recalling, probably subconsciously, some of the Puccini characters you have sung, albeit in a contemporary way.

In fact I spoke with him about that. Maybe he heard me in Puccini before?! But at the same time there was a real freshness in his music. He has written an opera with true vocal qualities and true emotions in a fresh way—so it is still possible to do this.

How did it feel singing with Roberto at this stage of your relationship?

I never wanted to talk about it, I wanted to go on with my career, which I cared more about than anything else, and I told him this very clearly. At one point we had to part our ways: I told him that the only way for us not to fight anymore would be to sing separately; I could not see any other choice. On the other hand, whatever was happening during the performances was able to mend everything between us, just at that time.

This was altogether a time of ongoing distress for you.

A few days after the series of performances of *Marius et Fanny*, I went to Chicago, where I was in a production of *La bohème*, directed by Renata Scotto. Roberto was heading toward New York, where he had two heavy roles one after the other, in *Aida* and *Roméo et Juliette*. The performances of Radames at the Met were especially important to him because they were coming after the incident at La Scala, in December 2006, when he was booed and decided to leave the stage there and then.

Surely it's appallingly demoralizing to be booed by an audience.

I certainly did not agree with the public reaction. From a human standpoint, to interrupt and offend an artist in front of other people, on a stage where the artist was giving his best, it seemed to me unjust and cruel. Surely, you are entitled to have a different opinion, you are free not to like it, you do not applaud, you leave the opera, but when you boo you insult, and an insult is a personal attack. It's not okay to attack an artist because one evening he or she was not in the emotional state required by the role or because his or her body did not respond well enough to create a perfect show. Whenever an artist cannot provide happiness to the public through his or her song and study, usually a good artist is the first to feel it, to hear it, and to suffer from it. The sharp criticism of these people in the audience does nothing but hurt him even more, rather than help him recover and be able to continue. So something like this is not acceptable. It's barbaric. I would totally vote in favor of banning such atrocious behavior the way now the corrida in Spain is prohibited. It is a violent act toward one person in front of others.

Meanwhile, there was La bohème *in Chicago.*

I did all the rehearsals both with the orchestra and the director, Renata Scotto. The only conversation that I had with her about direction was that between friends, talking about clothes and my boots rather than anything else. We both behaved like colleagues. She just told me, "Oh, how tall you are!" I was coming after giving countless performances of *La bohème*, Mimì was a role that I had been singing for seventeen years, and there was no room for any unpleasant surprises: on the contrary, I would say.

In New York, Roberto was so nervous that he asked me to come over to be with him at his performances of *Aida*. I decided to help him out and go to New York because he needed me. Obviously, I went to Renata and to the director of the Lyric Opera and I asked them to let me go for a few days. The performances were all sold in my name, I promised to come back, there was no question of me not singing all the performances I had signed for. I even waited two extra days to finish everything, both the sitzprobe and the dress fitting. I would have gone onstage with all my preparations completed, as there were only some orchestra rehearsals left to do, but I had planned to come back in time for the final dress rehearsal anyway. I talked to my colleagues, I explained to them the situation that I was in and the situation Roberto was in. I always relied on collegiality and the fact that every one of us, as an artist, can understand what it means, at some point, to have the need for moral support. They all said yes, go, okay, fine.

A day or two before the actual performance, even though I had already returned to Chicago and expected to go to the final rehearsal, I received a phone call and an e-mail which informed me in writing that I was released from my contract. "Because you left the rehearsal, you will no longer sing these *Bohème* performances. . . ."

As for Renata, with whom I had thought I had a relationship of respect and mutual admiration, I most certainly did not expect to receive such a sign of lack of collegiality, delivered via an e-mail, especially as she had been among those who had told me to my face that I could go.

Many such incidents, with untold details and reasons that were more related to unfortunate circumstances than anything else, had helped create the legend of your cancellations. . . .

In fact, if I was not singing, most of the time it was only because I had troubles at home. And if you're crying, you're sad, your voice is affected, how can you contribute to a show, how can you shine onstage? On top of the moments of personal drama, I also had to take responsibility for depriving myself of the presence on the stage, depriving myself of the positive energy that I could have received from the public. Because you must know that no artist is happy sitting at home, canceling a show, believe me. Each and every one of us wants to be perfect every day and be better, if possible, as he or she grows or despite his or her age. . . . Obviously, it's absurd, humanly it is impossible.

What I know is that when I feel I would not be okay onstage, I prefer not to sing, rather than sing poorly. If I'm wrong, I am the first to realize it, so why should I go out and do something that would not benefit the public?

Between the two options—to sing in difficulty or not to go on the stage at all—I chose the least worst one. And the most responsible one. It's very simple, that's all. I could not go onstage, I needed to rest, physically and emotionally. A singer, always carrying his instrument with him or her, is overexposed. He owes it to himself, occasionally, to have a moment of recovery or *silenzio* so that he can continue. In addition, for any performance, I do not come directly from home—wherever I would be, I come from the road. No great artist comes onstage from home. He is coming from an apartment where the kitchen is new, his bed is different, his ecosystem is different . . . every time. He materializes from nowhere, from a makeshift dwelling or a super hotel. And that's what happens when you stay in one place for one or two concerts. When you stay for a run of performances—one or even two months—you cannot stay at the hotel, because you would go crazy. Over a period of one to two months you need some sort of normality, so you live in a place that at least has the appearance of a normal home. Anyway you cannot talk about any normality when you change your suitcase from month to month.

Can a performing artist ever have normality in their life?

True artists are not normal because they do not lead a normal existence, regardless of how hard they would try or regardless of their statements that they are anti-diva or anti-divo. Without false modesty or hypocrisy, when you have to travel the world to fulfill your artistic destiny, you cannot say you're a normal person; it simply is not true. . . . To me this does not work.

By nature, I am an honest artist, truth-loving, unselfish toward my profession and my family. My purpose is to give myself to those who appreciate my art—if one evening I succeed in bringing happiness to at least one person, then I am happy and I've reached my goal.

Despite these troubles, soon afterward you attained one of your most acclaimed achievements when you recorded the role of Cio-Cio-San in Puccini's Madama Butterfly, *with Sir Antonio Pappano conducting. It was the first time you had sung the complete opera, and you received widespread accolades.*

As a Latin, for me it was very interesting to be a completely different kind of woman in a totally different world and in another period, but to become really involved in that I needed to feel it and think about it each day and not just come to the rehearsal and sing the role. So when I made the recording of *Butterfly* in Rome, for two weeks I went nowhere and was only in the studio or my hotel looking at the score, because I wanted only to feel in my mind the realm, the atmosphere, and the period of the opera. To build this role I did not want to be with my mind and body anywhere else.

And so you were experiencing completely, all the time, one of the most traumatic roles in the entire operatic repertoire.

For me, *Madama Butterfly* is one of the most emotional operas ever written. When I made the recording, right at Butterfly's first entrance in act 1 I was crying. Even here! Just to listen to Puccini's music at this moment is heartbreaking. You have to be a real heroine to sing this role, because how can you sing when you can cry with each note? You may cry with each note—with each word! Each sound that Puccini creates conjures up a whole world—of love, of life, of your family, of your religion, even of a flower. It is the most tragic opera I have ever sung in my life.

And surely one of the most demanding challenges for any soprano to sing, to capture Butterfly's delicacy and strength together?

For sure she is strong—in her character, her religion, and her mentality. Although in the first act she is only fifteen, in a way she is adult from the start. In the love duet the writing for her is very dramatic and difficult to sing, with many very high notes that have to carry over a large and rich-sounding orchestra. But also in this duet Puccini gives her many very low notes, and on almost each page you have extreme differences between the highest and lowest notes and also the loudest and quietest notes. So she is really strong and dramatic like an adult in the music even here in the first act, but she is also, as you say, so delicate, so that is hugely demanding—to be dramatic and delicate. In any case, when she becomes pregnant, even though she is still so young, she becomes completely mature immediately, as any woman does when she is pregnant, whatever her age. All this makes the role very challenging indeed, vocally and emotionally.

And also stylistically?

Yes—Puccini wrote an Italian opera with very exotic sounds. All the time you can hear the atmosphere of Japan in the orchestra, and all the time you can feel another kind of culture, which is Cio-Cio-San's world, and you have to capture that in your voice as well, in the dialogue with the orchestra—because Puccini writes the orchestra as a dialogue with the voice, not an accompaniment. This is another reason why this opera is so different and so demanding—it is an Italian opera, but it is so Japanese for the soprano.

Do you think Cio-Cio-San has had any emotional experience with men before she meets Pinkerton?

It's a tricky subject! Just because she has been a geisha, it does not necessarily mean that she has had any sexual contact before. We just don't know for sure about that. What is for sure is that for her, in the first act she has never had a relationship with a man in the way she has with Pinkerton. When she has her night of love with him and she knows that this kind of rapport can lead to a child being born, she is giving herself totally to him in this way because she is overcome with feelings she has never had before. She knows that Pinkerton paid Goro to have a geisha, but in spite of that, for her this is a real marriage and she believes that Pinkerton feels the same way. That is why she is so insistent in the first act when she says, "I am not Madama Butterfly, I am Mrs. B. F. Pinkerton."

Of course she has no knowledge or understanding of his background, which was so especially different and foreign at that time.

That's true, but although in this opera we have the conflicts that existed between the attitudes of the East and the West in the period when the action takes place, at the same time what Cio-Cio-San experiences happens to women all over the world in any period. Two persons can be in love, but not at the same level at one time, and it can happen to a man as well as a woman, to be in love and receive love for only a month, or maybe even just a day. The real tragedy, though, is dramatic for the woman in her own way when there is a child. In this instance she is experiencing more passion than the man—it is her biology, her anatomy. Women are forced to accept that, and today society in Japan accepts it too when a child has no father in a family, but in Butterfly's time an abandoned mother with her child was completely against her country's thinking. So it is inconceivable to her that Pinkerton would not return. Also, just remember, she has been with the child for more than two years and she has had him in front of her all the time—all that time the result of her love with Pinkerton has been with her. So, in the second act, when Sharpless is reading Pinkerton's letter to him out loud to her and he stops and asks her, "Now tell me, Madama Butterfly, what would you do if he were not to return?" this is already like her death here, just in one split second.

So when she answers Sharpless with, "Two things I could do—I could go back to entertaining people with my singing—or, better, to die," she means that 100 percent.

Absolutely—and for me in a way she starts to die now. She doesn't know yet what is going to happen, but it's like she has a premonition of her death and begins to experience it—just for now.

Puccini tells us that with what he puts in the score here: "Butterfly is struck numb as though from a mortal blow to the body—she sings in a voice sounding like a child's submission, almost stammering." You observe his instructions completely faithfully to the detail there: it's really frightening to listen to.

Well that's because in that one moment she accepts that she will die if Pinkerton does not come back. It's like an explosion. The shame she would have in front of her people would be unbearable.

So when she sings "Che tua madre" and she says to the child, "To think that I would have to go back to singing and dancing for the people just to feed you," she has already thought of killing herself if Pinkerton does not return?

Yes—she says, "Death is better than that." In that period, the culture and education in Japan was so different from the West, that today it is difficult for us to appreciate how she feels. Just think for a minute: in the last act, when she finds out the truth, she says to Sharpless, "If he, Pinkerton, wants the child, he needs to come here to collect him," but what she means is that he has to come and see what he has lost. To us you must have a little craziness to take your life, but something very, very powerful has happened in her mind that she should decide this in the way she does. It is to do with honor, of course, yes, but also it is because she realizes she cannot live anymore without Pinkerton. And —there is no future for the child with her. All that is very real for her, it's not crazy, and Puccini's genius is that he makes us understand this through his music—that is why it is so heartbreaking. And it's why I don't feel I can sing this role onstage, because from the second act onward the pity is unbearable—until the final scene of the opera everybody on the stage and in the audience knows the tragedy that is coming, but the only person who doesn't want to understand, who doesn't want to see this, is Madama Butterfly.

You know, Cio-Cio-San reminds me of Violetta in one respect. In their day, there were few women who felt aware of having their own opinions on life. Cio-Cio-San and Violetta had their own kind of strength to say to people, "Yes, I have the power to love whoever I want, I have the power to have an opinion." We must never forget how long it took for the rights of women to be recognized, and Violetta and Cio-Cio-San

Around the time that I had the great pleasure of arranging Angela's appearance at the "Prom at the Palace" concert celebrating the Queen's Golden Jubilee, she approached me with an idea for a project that had a very deep significance for her. She wanted to make a documentary film on Romanian choral music and she wanted the film to visit the frescoed Romanian churches in Moldova, which, unlike Italian churches, have the frescoes on the outsides of the buildings. "My dream," she said, "would be to uncover this wonderful world of music and its shrines for a worldwide audience." She said she could set aside a week in her schedule to do this, and so I enthusiastically agreed to accompany her on a reconnaissance to see if we could make it work. It was an inspiring adventure and indeed we did make the film, which Jonathan Fulford directed with myself as executive producer, and it was called *Angela Gheorghiu's Romanian Journey*. It was one of the most successful films in the early days of BBC 4, and part of its power lay in the profoundly personal importance it had for Angela. She was in fact visiting these legendary churches for the first time and she was retracing her deepest musical roots in the country where Orthodox Romanian church music had made some of the most profoundly strong impressions of her early life. It was a privilege and excitement for my colleagues and I at the BBC to be in those places in Romania with her and meet people she had made music with in earlier days as we discovered and found out new experiences in her presence. And it was all her idea.

were very courageous to show to people, "I am saying, 'This is my house, these are my feelings, this is my way to do what I believe in,'" as in those days women were supposed to be just working in the home all the time. That is what so much appealed to Verdi and Puccini in these heroines.

After this recording, which was released in 2009, there were some more special gala events.

One day I received an invitation to take part in a concert in St. James's Palace with the orchestra that was supported by Prince Charles. The concert was preceded by a dinner in honor of the richest and most influential businessmen and aristocrats in Europe and America. At eight, the beginning time of this concert, nothing happened, and forty-five minutes later still nothing—and no one came to tell me anything. It was a concert in which I was participating freely, obviously: I had been asked to do this concert because it was a special evening for Prince Charles, whom I had admired deeply. And I waited.

Then I decided that, from the moment they would say they were ready for me, I will stay in my dressing room for fifteen to twenty minutes. After twenty minutes I got out onstage like a flower. The Prince came to greet me and apologized. "Are you okay? All is well?"

"Sure, I'll do the concert."

During the dinner after the show, I had a very open conversation with him. He understood what kind of person I am and apologized once again. I had the opportunity to explain once again what I did and why I did it. He told me he liked playing the cello, and everyone around apparently had encouraged him to play it, although he had not been very keen in the beginning.

Prince Charles has great admiration for you. . . .

Yes, he does. I had in fact first met him shortly after *La traviata*, in the house of Maestro Solti. At that dinner in the palace, I learned that the same group of guests had a second gathering at a dinner at Windsor, around the longest table in the world. As a sort of reward, I also received an invitation, and the Prince's gestures of kindness did not stop there. Later on, His Royal Highness sent me a thank-you letter and some gracious words of apology, accompanied by a small gift.

At that dinner we also talked about Romania very much because after my CD with sacred music* and after the documentary the BBC television producer Peter Maniura made with me about Romanian churches, many people in the UK have shown interest in taking the same journey I took in that movie. Mother Gabriela from Voroneț Monastery was to receive Prince Charles in Bucovina,† sometime later. In time, the Prince grew even closer to Romania—maybe because, as I explained to him, everything in my country still has a taste, has some meaning, some faith.

Mysterium.
†Historical region divided between Romania and Ukraine.

CHAPTER 12

Restoring My Faith in Love

· · ·

You recorded for EMI Classics the CD Homage to Maria Callas. *What were the reasons behind this project?*

The project was exclusively the initiative of the label, and in retrospect, I think there were two important elements that the people at EMI took into consideration: the huge PR potential and the fact that, several generations apart, we were in fact . . . colleagues. We shared the same label, so legally and commercially speaking it was a disc that could be easily made. My list of vocal preferences looks quite different, as it includes Rosa Ponselle, Claudia Muzio, Renata Tebaldi, Montserrat Caballé, Mirella Freni, Maria Cebotari, and, of course, Virginia Zeani, with whom I was more connected emotionally, but this was the proposal that came from EMI and I accepted it.

Even if she may not have had the best voice in the history of opera and even though I am not a fan, I still consider Maria Callas a phenomenon because of her way of approaching any role. She already had the necessary artistic structure so that she could do whatever she wanted because she was a fine interpreter, not just a fine singer.

For me personally, the disc was not really a promotional coup; it was something related solely to EMI. Because Callas and I shared the same label, I was happy to do this thing. I was also attracted by the fact that they wanted to create a "duet" of Maria and myself singing together as a bridge between two eras of opera, as they had managed to find a recording of the "Habanera" from *Carmen* made in the 1960s, where Maria's voice was captured separately from the orchestra. Her voice recording was overdubbed by the orchestra I sang with, we all adjusted to her rhythm, and I tried to express something similar in my interpretation so as to create some kind of complicity between the two of us.

This was the first time in the history of opera that such a virtual duet was created. . . .

This is how the clip came to be, both artistic and collegial. I did not want to put the spotlight on myself; I wanted to make a real duet. It was a courageous experience, but I am a rather brave person and I'm not afraid if the expected outcome is something nice. . . .

The duet with Maria, synchronizing with the rhythm and her style, was the challenge I accepted and, moreover, I was glad that I was free to work with the people I chose for the cover, the graphics, and the video. The entire team was Romanian. We still have extraordinarily talented people in our country, and I think it worthwhile to promote them and show them to the world whenever I can.

Why have you never been given the opportunity to make your stage debut at the Bucharest National Opera?

The Bucharest Opera is, indeed, a sore spot for me, strange as it may seem, and it has been so ever since 1990, when the then-director of the opera told me, refusing to host our graduation show of *La bohème*, that the role of Mimì did not entirely match my voice.

My performances of *Tosca*, *Adriana Lecouvreur*, and *Faust* from Covent Garden were broadcast in the Bucharest Opera Hall, but I have never come to appear there onstage in a true live production. I tried many times to find a way to sing in a real opera performance in Bucharest, on that stage, but my efforts were fruitless.

Among the weirdest ideas of the management of the opera in Bucharest was to invite me, not so long ago, to debut in a show of questionable taste. It was an operetta performance: *The Merry Widow*. . . . The idea of appearing for the first time on stage in Bucharest as Hanna Glawari was . . . quite funny, to say the least. . . . Obviously, I had to say no. Thus, in twenty-eight years, I have sung there just for the anniversary gala of my dearest friend and colleague Mihnea Lamatic, in 2015, when we performed together the church scene in *Faust* and a duet from Gershwin's *Porgy and Bess*. A debut in the true sense of the word I have never made at the Bucharest Opera.

Surely when you're successful on the great stages of the world and have performed together with the most important colleagues in your profession, a debut in Bucharest is no longer an objective in itself, but to me it's still a sore spot, a touch of bitterness, that I could not be together with my colleagues, that my very countrymen have to follow me around the world to hear me sing when things could have been so different. . . .

Those great stages of the world have created many new productions around you.

Yes, among these are the productions of *La rondine* and *Adriana Lecouvreur* with which we have achieved success at Covent Garden, as we have with their new *Tosca*. They are all sumptuous productions, the costumes and set designs are gorgeous, and I still sing happily in these productions.

Moreover, the ROH seasons of transmissions in movie theaters around the world began in 2011–12 with three productions where I had the leading role: *Faust* in September, *Adriana Lecouvreur* in October, and *Tosca* in November 2011.

With the Royal Opera's mounting of Adriana Lecouvreur *for you, the opera entered the company's repertory for the first time, and because of the triumph of your performance and David McVicar's production this work was given a completely new lease on life. So how and when did you first decide to sing the role, and what is it about the opera that made you advocate it to Covent Garden?*

Initially, the Royal Opera House intended to produce first *Adriana Lecouvreur* and then, later on, *La rondine*. However, I looked at both parts and I realized that for me it would be healthier and more logical to do them the other way around—first *La rondine* followed by *Adriana*. Whenever I decide to take on a role or another, I am not very much concerned with what the opera's fortune has been in the past, but I rather want to make sure it is the right step for me from a vocal and spiritual perspective. I want to make sure it is well within my powers and I can inhabit it with ease. Both productions turned out spectacularly and I traveled the world with them.

This was a very happy mutual collaboration with the stage director Sir David McVicar.

Between the time that we had the initial discussions and the moment the production of *Adriana Lecouvreur* started to be put together, I did *Faust* at Covent Garden and this is how I got to meet David McVicar. At first, I found him really funny and maybe a bit distracted, but once we got to know each other, I realized he really liked opera and he had come to Covent Garden with all his homework done. He had a clear vision of the way he wanted to tell the story, from set design to costume design, artistic direction, even ballet. I liked so much working with him in *Faust* that we were delighted to work together again for *Adriana*.

The atmosphere Cilea creates in his music is so important in this opera. There is suddenly that rapt, dreamy, almost impressionistic magic just before the first aria in act 1, when Adriana says she feels she can hardly breathe —surely something very challenging to achieve, especially so early on in the performance, and which you did so ravishingly with your hushed floated pianissimo.

The pianissimo is my kind of "house specialty," so to speak. This is how I express the tenderness, grace, and sensitivity of my characters and it has helped me my entire life. It is not an easy technique, as it has to be soft, yet audible, as we are talking about a verismo role in *Adriana Lecouvreur*, with a theatrical authenticity. The arias no longer have repetitions, we no longer have the aria/cabaletta format, the style is different, and everything is very theatrical.

By coincidence, in this opera the protagonist herself is a very famous French actress, one of the first famous women who was brave enough to be themselves.

Do you think maybe that Adriana's dilemma is that, because of her idealism in her art, she sometimes cannot really separate fantasy from reality in her real life, which is why she is unable to see through the weakness and inconsistency of Maurizio, and also cannot see, until too late, that she is manipulated and trapped by the princess?

Here I must admit that, maybe like Adriana, I have a problem too in my life. My rich imagination and strong idealism are reflected in my art, in the way I sing and act, but also in my day-to-day behavior and lifestyle. Sometimes they tend to make me lose touch with reality. I have always paid dearly for this. To some, it might look like a weakness, or even a bit of egotism, but it is actually a coping mechanism that shelters us from the world around us.

As for the men of Adriana's time, they used to find their glory in the length of the list of their conquests. Having a famous mistress on the list was a bonus. From this perspective, Maurizio is a typical confused male. As a Pole in Paris, he suddenly finds himself rubbing shoulders with both the highest aristocracy and the elite of the artistic world. Highborn, he tries to cope with and even reap the benefits of his new environment, but he is out of luck, as he falls in love.

On the other hand, do you think that Adriana does know and accept that life is full of illusions—at least, does she accept this in the fourth act, like an artist?

Of course she accepts; there is no other option for her. Creation does not come only when you cook or clean the house—illusions must be fed as well, mustn't they. . . .

At an early rehearsal you read to everyone Adriana's words in the last act, after Maurizio offers her marriage in his royal name: "No, I can never be a royal queen, my throne is the stage—an altar of illusion." What made you choose this moment particularly?

Because to me, this seems to be the truth. Yes, even to me it is just so: "My throne is the stage—an altar of illusion." I accept and understand this. I know I have colleagues who are much more adept at planning and managing their art, but I am not like them. If I have a rehearsal with my colleagues in a theater, I can only be true to myself and true to my art; I do not play games. In order to play a role, I inhabit it, the role becomes my truth. This may sometimes prove to be emotionally exhausting, but I cannot have it any other way.

You absolutely meticulously sang Cilea's markings there of "con soave tristezza"—"with a sweet sadness."

Sweet sadness is also something that comes naturally to me. When singing *Adriana*, I am inspired by the words and sounds that come so well together in Cilea's work. It is the tear in my voice, in my timbre. . . .

You have said that you have always been very concerned that an artist should sing a specific role at the right time for the voice in the course of a life and career. Is this why you waited until 2010 before performing Adriana in the theater?

I have many ideas and stick to many principles, and that, in time, may have alienated many colleagues from me. However, I cannot and will not be anything else but true to my voice and my character. This is who I am. I have never tried to prove anything to anyone, just wanted to do what I believed was best for me and for the public. I wanted to make sure the public will like my work, down to the last detail.

You and the stage director Sir David McVicar were in close accord and agreement about the opera?

We were in perfect agreement. He is one of the most important directors of our time and we consider each other friends. He has a profound understanding of the opera, which we both love and respect.

You brought a very convincing realism and depth to this role, never making it melodramatic, which it has in the past sometimes been the victim of.

The only way to avoid melodrama or placidity is to be yourself. This is why I never wanted to have a teacher who tried to interfere with my path, or influence me. I consider myself lucky that I was able to stop discussing vocal technique at the early age of eighteen. I never ask questions or seek advice; I have always been quite sure of myself and fought tooth and nail to be allowed to do everything on my own. Spontaneity was the most important guide for me. I often said to myself, even if I fail, at least I'd be original in my actions and decisions.

Being free from any vocal stress, I succeeded in focusing on the creation of the character and on being myself all the time. I never think of notes or sounds when I first tackle a role. The words and the style of the character are there to guide me; they tell me how I need to be.

You made your debut at Carnegie Hall in New York with the role of Adriana Lecouvreur.

Yes, indeed I did. It was a concert performance of the opera and I was joined by Jonas Kaufmann as Maurizio. We had a superb concert and I remember the reaction of the audience, but also my colleagues' admiration and support. The atmosphere was beautiful throughout. I returned later to Carnegie Hall for a concert honoring Sir Georg Solti, under the baton of Valery Gergiev. The New York audience is very special for me—I always felt loved and adored there, ever since my debut in 1993 singing Mimì at the Met.

In October 2011, you performed at the reopening ceremony of the Bolshoi Theater in Moscow, at the personal invitation of President Medvedev, who paid you a great compliment—he called you the "crown jewel."

He made a courteous and unexpected gesture. This was one of the few times I sang onstage in Russian—it was an aria from *Queen of Spades* by Tchaikovsky, Liza's aria. I don't speak Russian and to me it is as difficult as Japanese, so I sang with a score so that everything would sound perfect. The compliment of President Medvedev showed me then that it was just so. There I met the great ballerina Maya Plisetskaya —such sophistication and elegance. . . . We liked each other on sight.

This was one of so many milestone events that you were invited to participate in.

Yes, and I particularly remember the one at the Kennedy Center in

GRACE BUMBRY

Mezzo-soprano Grace Bumbry and Angela Gheorghiu first performed together at the Royal Opera House in London in 1993, during the run of performances of Puccini's *Turandot*, where Angela was portraying Liù next to Grace's Princess Turandot.

◆ ◆ ◆

The first time I saw Angela Gheorghiu I so clearly remember how impressed I was not only by her outstanding talent but also by her honest and passionate desire for knowledge. It was the interval of a rehearsal of *La bohème*, in which she was making her debut singing Mimì, and she was discussing the role with her compatriot Ileana Cotrubaş. I said, "This lady is going to be someone very special indeed"—and then over the years as I saw her performing her various roles I said, "Well yes—this is just what I predicted." She truly is exceptionally special because she sings with such fire and with such intense intention. And her intention is to take the greatest care with every detail the composer wrote. This honesty in singing is the number one priority, and in Angela it is the greatest of all her qualities, which she realizes through her superlative technique. This is why I asked her to sing for me when I received my award at the Kennedy Center Honors in 2009. They gave me a list of people to consider and I immediately said, "The only artist I want is Angela Gheorghiu if she is available—I have to have her." When she agreed I was so happy.

Angela is elegant, she has fire, she has a wonderful voice—what more could you possibly want from a singer!

Washington, in 2009, when we all celebrated Grace Bumbry. There, I sang "Vissi d'arte" for her. President Barack Obama and his wife Michelle were hosting.

That same year was the 125th anniversary of the opening of the Metropolitan Opera.

I was very happy to sing the Jewel Song from *Faust*, dressed in a costume that reproduced the original costume worn at the Met premiere of *Faust*. I also sang the duet from *Simon Boccanegra* alongside dear Plácido.

Then, in 2011, I sang in Doha, at the opening of the Katara Amphitheater. This was a complete program written by Vangelis especially for me and for the occasion. Vangelis is a titan of music, and the sonorities of his compositions bring Space and God in complete harmony. He is a wonderful man, extremely friendly and a pioneer of a musical genre that will always inspire the contemporary composers. I am very proud of his friendship. There, I also had a duet with Roberto; it was called "Piccola bohème," and the presenter was the great actor Jeremy Irons, an old and dear acquaintance of mine.

Jeremy Irons is among the leading international actors whom you admire and who, in turn, admires you.

I met him in New York, at a luncheon organized for Franco Zeffirelli, and since then we have remained friends. In 2010, he invited me to a play he was doing on Broadway, booking for me some good tickets, of course, in one of the front rows. At one point in the play there is a scene with Irons opening a newspaper. I saw that he did this in a very ostentatious way, as if to draw my attention toward it. It was a genuine issue of the *New York Times*, featuring me with Plácido on the front page. The photo had been taken during the anniversary concert of the Metropolitan Opera, in the duet from *Simon Boccanegra*. In that photograph, Plácido was kissing me on the forehead. Jeremy had kept the newspaper for one year, until this performance, to make sure that I saw it when I came to his show.

I was surprised and touched and wanted to thank him for such a gesture. His talent, just like that of Anthony Hopkins, is so great that my words are not enough. We've seen each other over the years, as he has kept coming to my performances and I to his. Moreover, in an important moment, he helped me with a message of encouragement toward a group of young actors in Romania. He has always been there for me and acted like a true friend whenever I have asked for his support.

You have many admirers from the world of theater and other arts métiers.

When I met Meryl Streep, after the concert in Washington, she simply fell to her knees telling me that if she were to be born again, she would like to be a singer. Many famous actors, regardless of nationality, are great lovers of opera, and some have become my admirers—Jeanne Moreau is one such example. So is the daughter of Gérard Depardieu, Julie Depardieu, who told me how she gave birth listening to my arias and could remember exactly what notes I was singing in those moments

VANGELIS

When composer Vangelis was commissioned to write music for the opening of the Katara Amphitheatre in Doha in 2011, he invited Angela Gheorghiu to be his chosen performer and sing music he composed specifically for her. Angela Gheorghiu's friendship with Vangelis dates back many years.

◆ ◆ ◆

The first time that I heard this stunning voice was some years ago during a show on the musical channel Mezzo. I remember very well seeing a ravishing lady with a limitless striking voice. I waited until the end of the show to find out who she was, but I missed her name. Since that moment I was determined to find out who she was and where she was coming from. By asking around and trying to explain what kind of voice I heard and how she looked, the majority of my musician friends told me that my description leads to one person: *Angela Gheorghiu*!

In every century, there is a plethora of female voices from sopranos to contraltos, but only very few really exceptional voices emerge. Exceptional voice means the one that makes you shiver, that can make you cry and can give you enormous euphoria. Such voice, in other words, can touch every human feeling and above all makes the music "happy."

If you think that this miracle can happen due to an enormous amount of work, spending an enormous amount of time in various conservatories, with many different voice teachers, you are mistaken. These people are born with this gift. I am sure that Angela was born already carrying this eternal blessing.

I was extremely fortunate as a composer to work with some of the greatest sopranos. And when you have the chance to work with such rare gifted people like Montserrat Caballé, Jessye Norman, or Kathleen Battle, one question comes up; who is next? Definitely she was and she still is the next and I wish for her one thing: to be healthy and endlessly magical for the years to come.

Therefore she can, undoubtedly, join the family of the elite of all times in the history of classical voices.

Being with Angela, working with her and listening to her voice, filling the air with her exceptional color and harmonics, you don't want this moment to end. Therefore, "Angela get ready for our next one . . . . pupici pupici, Vangelis."

when she brought her babies into the world. I find it funny if I think about it, but it is equally overwhelming and gratifying. . . .

You had one special collaboration with the inspirational conductor Georges Prêtre.

Yes, indeed, and this was at the famous Vienna Opera Ball, in 2012. Sir Roger Moore was also attending this special event. It was the only time Georges and I shared the stage together, but I had met him previously on various occasions. One of them was while I was singing *Faust* in Monte Carlo—we stayed in the same hotel and used to meet at the pool there, where we would have wonderful talks and laughs. We had a feeling of mutual admiration and he was a brilliant artist, a glorious conductor, and a charming, very intelligent man.

You had a particularly historic performance of La bohème *at the Royal Opera House in 2012, when you celebrated your twenty-year career on the British stage, alongside Roberto Alagna.*

Yes, I had two performances in June. At that time, we were already rarely singing together, just on great occasions. But as the Royal Opera House had been such an important house for us for two decades, we all wanted to join the beautiful moment.

Then, in early 2013, you divorced.

I had the idea to divorce in Romania, where the process was shorter, and the pains of the divorce were milder. I had no discussions, everything went amicably, I just signed some papers. All the negative or dark moments that we had were during the marriage, not during the divorce. We started with *La bohème*, and we ended with *La bohème*—"Addio senza rancor" . . . as Mimì would sing in her third-act aria.

The only great sorrow that I bear in my soul is that Ornella has never sought me after the divorce. I understood her choice and her decision, I would never be able to judge her, it was only natural for her to stay with her father, but it's still hard to steer clear from a person who had been your daughter for nearly two decades.

And Ioana?

Ioana, Yoyo, or ivm—the love of my life*—is a very special soul; she seeks with all her strength to succeed in her own right, to find her own way. We love each other very much, and from the beginning there was

*IVM stands for *iubirea vieții mele* in Romanian—"the love of my life."

a kind of complicity between us, as between two adults. Of the two of us, I'd say I have felt all the time more spoiled and childish than she, as I have had a greater need to be encouraged and reassured.

She has understood me and, over time, has responded to all my wishes or requirements—related to her piano lessons, her singing . . . but now she goes on her way. Her beautiful evolution gives me the feeling that I leave something behind on a personal level too, not only on the artistic level. With no children of my own, all my love and all my life have gone toward Ioana and, until the moment of our separation, toward Ornella. . . .

The fact that Ioana went through those terrible experiences at such a tender age forced her to mature early and enabled her to turn into the director of our family. Until today, she guides us and inspires us and fills us with optimism—which she possesses in such large quantities that I also call her Veselică (Joy). She gives us, me and my mother equally, our sense of balance and our love, and she brings us endless satisfactions.

Recently, Ioana married Bogdan Holubaş, a young man whom I saw growing alongside her, and their love and respect between each other have become an example for me and a fantastic source of balance. I know I have a true compass in them and I thank them for it!

Of all the great tenors, José Carreras is the latest one you have performed with.

The first time I sang with him was in 2016 in a private recital in Salzburg. But I had met him previously dozens of times, including after his performances of big roles. I saw him with Mirella Freni in *Fedora*, I saw him in *La traviata*, and I've always admired him. José is an artist with a unique voice, a perfect musicality. He is a very charming and very jovial man. I have a fondness toward him even more because he looks like my father's twin brother—or my father looks just like him—although Dad is a little older than him. Once I even told him that, to which he replied, "Then this explains why you are so beautiful." He is a man who went through a very difficult period, but he is the biggest winner that I've ever met in person.

With José Carreras, even at this stage of his career, I realized that nothing is *al caso*, that the man is inhabited by grace; he is right there where any great artist should be. It's rare to see that. Still, he manages

JOSÉ CARRERAS

Tenor José Carreras and Angela Gheorghiu first sang together in 2016 after many years admiring each other's performances in theaters and concert halls around the world.

◆ ◆ ◆

When I hear and see Angela, I have the impression that we are in front of one of the last great divas. The way she expresses herself, the way she moves onstage, her beautiful instrument: all this together makes, if I may use this word, a package that is unique. And it is very touching. Everything Angela does is touching and it is always true. We have to be thankful to an artist for such truth, and I am very thankful to Angela for being this way— for the sincerity and honesty when she is singing.

to stir up magic with the same force with which he had managed to do it in the past—from the words, from a glance, from a small gesture, from the way in which he articulates a phrase. I must admit, he taught me a lesson. . . .

Exceptional artists have this power—I had encountered it a long time ago in Slava Rostropovich. These are people who, although they are older, have kept that spark, that frisson, and are still able to convey an authentic emotion and create a tangible energy and electricity around them. There are only a few artists in this category. The moment I meet them, I can feel it immediately—they have a thrill that is almost uncontrollable, that almost transcends them. . . . Some say they are crazy, but that madness is the only path that leads to immortality, to eternity. . . .

All through the years of your international life, the Royal Opera House, Covent Garden, has had a strong influence on your destiny. There you also met the person who restored your faith in love and in peace of mind and soul.

In the summer of 2013, several months after my divorce, I was there with my production of *La rondine*. After one of the performances, when I was still affected by the separation from Roberto and I had just told the world the truth about my marriage via the UK press, I met two

MIHAI CIORTEA

Romanian dentist Mihai Ciortea has been Angela Gheorghiu's life partner since autumn 2013. They are happy in love and wish to spend the rest of their lives together in harmony.

◆ ◆ ◆

Angela, the miracle, and the Miracle of Love . . .

To get two miracles in one person, whom you are devoted to, unconditionally, body and soul, is a priceless, overwhelming gift of life.

The first miracle I fell in love with, for her artistry, her beauty, and for the love of opera, is Angela, the artist, without any doubt the world's greatest opera singer. She is the only person able to take you in another dimension, with her celestial voice, her masterful technique, her genius, her stage presence, and her personality. Whenever I listen to her singing or watch her live onstage, I feel as if she is floating above us all, as if she is somehow elevated, levitating. . . . She is the only one to take me to such a state. . . . She is able to create inspiring, uplifting, very touching moments onstage, a kind of magic for which it is almost impossible to find the right words.

The second miracle followed the first one, as soon as we opened our hearts completely to each other and a bond of incomparable love formed between us. I remember the thrill of excitement of our first encounter, or our first kiss in a late summer night. It was not easy at first, but we both realized that the feelings we have for each other are really miraculous, that of absolute love, a very rare—almost endangered, I would say—kind of love, in the context of today's tumultuous world. I think I came to her right in time to give her the balance she needed in this shallow world. This is how we feel, the two of us, our family, and our true friends around us. There is no greater joy and happiness.

We already share many memories we cherish—I could write a book just about them. . . . I remember with great joy the New Year's Eve we spent with our family in Baden-Baden after Angela's concert, with one of the most beautiful fireworks we've ever seen from the terrace of the Hotel Brenners. What a romantic evening! Angela's presence in my life elevates my soul. I am happy that I can be the one who loves her and treasures her in every respect, with the purest, most honest, undying love. And I thank her for her love for me, I know that nobody could love me more.

young admirers of mine, the twin-brother dentists Mihai and Claudiu Ciortea. Sure, they had both come to see me on other occasions around the world, with their parents, Adina and Tudor Ciortea, also great lovers of opera, but that evening Mihai took one step forward. And he seemed to me just the man for whom my soul was longing. I quickly understood what a good character he had and how passionate he was about the opera and . . . me. I kept telling him he could teach a master class in gentlemanly behavior toward a woman. He is the perfect gentleman. Mihai is my guardian angel, and he brings me harmony and the beauty of life as I had always dreamed of. I love him with all my heart and I thank him for the strength and warmth that he offers me every day. Finally, I can say I am completely at peace—happy, in love, and loved as I was never before in my life.

Life must go on, just like the show must. . . .

Angela Gheorghiu

To be continued . . .

1965	Angela Gheorghiu is born as Angela Burlacu in Adjud, Romania, on September 7
1980	Enters the George Enescu High School of Art, Bucharest
1981	MARCH: Sings in a concert at the Romanian Athenaeum in Bucharest—"Solveig's Song," from Grieg's *Peer Gynt*
1984	Enters the Ciprian Porumbescu Conservatory in Bucharest
1984	OCTOBER: Appears on Romanian national television, on Iosif Sava's *Serata Muzicala*, singing an aria by Purcell
1985	Appears on Romanian national television, on Luminița Constantinescu's *Vă place opera?*, singing "Addio del passato" from Verdi's *La traviata*
1985–1990	
	Appears in a large number of concerts and radio and television programs in Bucharest
1990	JUNE 20: Debut at the Romanian National Opera in Cluj-Napoca, singing Mimì in Puccini's *La bohème* (graduation from the music conservatory)
	JULY: Prize winner at the international Belvedere Competition in Vienna
	OCTOBER 27: Appears at the Wexford Festival in the Belvedere prize-winners' concert
1991	MARCH: Debut at Basel Opera, singing Adina in Donizetti's *L'elisir d'amore*
1992	MARCH 3: Sings Zerlina at the Royal Opera House, Covent Garden, in one performance of Mozart's *Don Giovanni*
	MAY 16: Main debut at the Royal Opera House, singing Mimì in Puccini's *La bohème*
	OCTOBER 27: Debut at the Vienna State Opera, singing Adina in Donizetti's *L'elisir d'amore*
1993	MARCH 27: Sings Nanetta in Verdi's *Falstaff* at the Vienna State Opera
	AUGUST 20: Debut at the Salzburg Festival, performing "Spiegarti non poss'io" from Mozart's *Idomeneo*
	DECEMBER 4: Debut at the Metropolitan Opera, New York, singing Mimì in Puccini's *La bohème*
1994	Performs in a series of concerts with Plácido Domingo in Romania,

Germany, the Czech Republic, Switzerland, Austria, Finland, the United States, Peru, and Portugal

NOVEMBER 25: Sings Violetta for the first time, in a new production of Verdi's *La traviata* at the Royal Opera House

DECEMBER 8: The BBC televises this new production of *La traviata*, and for the first time in its history alters its broadcast schedule on short notice to air it live

1995   Records her first studio album with Decca Classics, *Arias*, singing Italian and French opera arias and a Romanian song

1996   Records her first opera in the studio with EMI Classics: Puccini's *La rondine*

APRIL 27: Sings at the James Levine twenty-fifth anniversary gala at the Metropolitan Opera

DECEMBER 1: Sings at the Gold and Silver Gala at the Royal Opera House

1999   Performs at the "Michael Jackson and Friends" concert in Munich to raise funds for children in Kosovo

DECEMBER: Performs at the reopening of the Royal Opera House

2000   Performs *Tosca* in a film of Puccini's opera directed by Benoît Jacquot, presented at the Venice Film Festival in 2001

SEPTEMBER 9: Sings at the "Last Night of the Proms" in Hyde Park, London

2001   Receives the titles of Officier de l'Ordre des Arts et Lettres, Chevalier de l'Ordre des Arts et Lettres in France, and Médaille de Vermeil de la Ville de Paris

APRIL 29: Performs at the concert honoring the fortieth anniversary of Luciano Pavarotti's debut onstage, at the Modena Opera House

MAY 3: Performs at the Royal Festival Hall fiftieth birthday gala, in the presence of HRH Prince Charles

MAY 23: Performs at the reopening of the Teatro Malibran in Venice

JUNE 1: Receives the Female Artist of the Year award at the Classical BRIT Awards, Royal Albert Hall, London

2002   Sings Magda in a new production of Puccini's *La rondine* at the Royal Opera House

JUNE 1: Performs at the "Prom at the Palace" concert for Queen Elizabeth's Golden Jubilee, held at Buckingham Palace in the presence of the Queen and the royal family

JUNE: Performs Juliette in a film of Gounod's *Roméo et Juliette*, directed by Barbara Willis Sweete

SEPTEMBER 9: Sings in concert for Pope John Paul II at Castel Gandolfo

       Timeline of Career Highlights

2003   SEPTEMBER 13: Performs at the "Last Night of the Proms," Royal Albert Hall

       DECEMBER 11: Performs at the Tenth Nobel Peace Prize Concert held in Oslo, in the presence of the royal family of Norway

       DECEMBER 31: Performs at the New Year's Eve Gala at the Deutsche Oper Berlin

2004   Performs Marguerite in Gounod's *Faust*, in a production created especially for her at the Royal Opera House

2005   APRIL 29: Sings at the concert for Queen Beatrix's Silver Jubilee in front of the palace, in Dam Square, Amsterdam

       SEPTEMBER 19: Performs act 2 of *Tosca* at the Metropolitan Opera, in a gala presentation that opens the Met 2005–6 season

       OCTOBER 8: Sings at the opening of the Palau de les Arts Reina Sofia in Valencia, in the presence of Queen Sofia of Spain

       DECEMBER 31: Performs at the New York Philharmonic New Year's Eve Gala at Avery Fisher Hall (now David Geffen Hall)

2006   FEBRUARY: Sings *La traviata* at the Metropolitan Opera

       APRIL 3: First recital at La Scala in Milan (released on CD by EMI Classics)

       MAY 17: Opens the Fifty-Ninth Cannes Film Festival

       JUNE 13: Performs *Tosca* in a new production created for her at the Royal Opera House

       DECEMBER 31: Performs at the New Year's Eve Gala at the Opéra Garnier in Paris

2007   JULY: Sings Violetta in Verdi's *La traviata* at La Scala

       SEPTEMBER 4: Performs the role of Fanny in the world premiere of Vladimir Cosma's *Marius et Fanny* in Marseille

2008   JULY: Sings Cio-Cio-San in EMI Classics' new recording of Puccini's *Madama Butterfly*

       OCTOBER 12: Performs at the "Tribute to Pavarotti" concert in Petra, Jordan, in the presence of Queen Rania of Jordan

2009   MARCH 15: Sings at the Metropolitan Opera's 125th anniversary gala

       MAY 25: Charity concert for the Abruzzo earthquake victims, at the Colosseum in Rome, alongside Andrea Bocelli

       DECEMBER 6: Performs at the Thirty-Second Annual Kennedy Center Honors in Washington, DC, paying tribute to Grace Bumbry, in an event hosted by President Barack Obama and First Lady Michelle Obama

2010   MAY 13: Receives the Female Artist of the Year award at the Classical BRIT Awards, Royal Albert Hall, London

       Sings the title role in Cilea's *Adriana Lecouvreur* at the Royal Opera

House, in a new production of the opera created for her—the first production of the opera at the Royal Opera House since 1906

Awarded the Order of the Star of Romania by the president of Romania, the country's highest civil order

Awarded the Doctor Honoris Causa title from the George Enescu Arts University in Iași, Romania

2011   OCTOBER 28: Performs at the reopening of the Bolshoi Theater in Moscow

DECEMBER 11: Performs music especially composed for her by Vangelis, at the opening of the Katara Amphitheater in Doha, Qatar, under the patronage of His Highness Emir Sheikh Hamad bin Kalifa al Tan

2012   King Michael I of Romania confers the Nihil Sine Deo royal decoration upon Angela Gheorghiu, for promoting Romanian cultural values abroad

FEBRUARY 16: Opens the Vienna Opera Ball, under the baton of Georges Prêtre

OCTOBER 31: Performs at the Our Extraordinary World Gala at the Royal Opera House, for the Diamond Jubilee of HM Queen Elizabeth II and in her presence

2014   Awarded the Doctor Honoris Causa title from the Gheorghe Dima Music Academy in Cluj-Napoca, Romania

DECEMBER 31: Performs at the New Year's Eve Gala in Baden-Baden, Germany

2015   FEBRUARY 14: Performs at the opening of the Budapest Opera Ball

MARCH 5: Performs Charlotte in Massenet's *Werther* for the first time onstage, at the Vienna State Opera

OCTOBER 2: Receives the European Cultural Award for Music, on the occasion of the twenty-fifth anniversary of the German reunification, Dresden, Germany

2017   Celebrates her twenty-fifth anniversary with the Royal Opera House and her 150th performance on Covent Garden's stage, reprising to great acclaim her production of *Adriana Lecouvreur*

MAY 29: Awarded the Doctor Honoris Causa title from the University of Bucharest

SEPTEMBER 6: Performs at the memorial concert marking the tenth anniversary of the death of Luciano Pavarotti, at Arena di Verona, singing with Plácido Domingo, José Carreras, Il Volo, and Massimo Ranieri

2018   FEBRUARY 23: Receives the Victoire d'Honneur award at the twenty-fifth Les Victoires de la Musique Classique, Évian-les-Bains, France

DISCOGRAPHY

CD albums/box sets

The Puccini Experience. Downes, Royal Opera House. Sony Classical (1995).

La traviata, Verdi. Solti, Royal Opera House. Decca Classics (1995).

Arias. Mauceri, Teatro Regio di Torino. Decca (1996).

Carmen (as Micaëla), Bizet. Sinopoli, Bayerische Staatsoper. Teldec (1996).

Duets & Arias: Roberto Alagna & Angela Gheorghiu. Armstrong, Orchestra of the Royal Opera House. EMI Classics (1996).

L'elisir d'amore, Donizetti. Pidò, Opéra de Lyon. Decca (1997).

La rondine, Puccini. Pappano, London Symphony Orchestra. EMI Classics (1997). (EMI Classics recordings are now released under the label of Warner Classics.)

The Gold & Silver Gala. Fisch, Royal Opera House. EMI Classics (1997).

Roméo et Juliette, Gounod. Plasson, Orchestre du Capitole de Toulose. EMI Classics (1998).

My World: Songs from around the Globe. Martineau, piano. Decca (1998).

Verdi per due. Abbado, Berlin Philharmonic Orchestra. EMI Classics (1998).

Il trittico, Puccini. Pappano, London Symphony Orchestra. EMI Classics (1999).

La bohème, Puccini. Chailly, La Scala. Decca (1999).

Werther, Massenet. Pappano, London Symphony Orchestra. EMI Classics (1999).

Manon, Massenet. Pappano, Brussels Théâtre de la Monnaie. EMI Classics (2000).

Verdi Heroines. Chailly, Verdi Grand Symphonic Orchestra. Decca (2000).

Requiem, Verdi. Abbado, Orféon Donostiarra, Berlin Philharmonic Orchestra, Swedish Radio Chorus. EMI Classics (2001).

Mysterium: Sacred Arias. Marin, London Philharmonic Orchestra, Romanian Madrigal Chamber Choir. Decca (2001).

Tosca, Puccini. Pappano, Royal Opera House. EMI Classics (2001).

Casta diva. Pidò, London Symphony Orchestra, Royal Opera House Chorus. EMI Classics (2001).

Angela Gheorghiu: Live from Covent Garden. Marin, Royal Opera House. EMI Classics (2002).

Il trovatore, Verdi. Pappano, London Symphony Orchestra. EMI Classics (2002).

Prom at the Palace: The Queen's Concerts, Buckingham Palace. BBC, Opus Arte (2002).

Carmen, Bizet. Plasson, Toulouse Capitole Orchestra, Les Elements Chamber Choir, La Lauzeta. EMI Classics (2003).

Last Night of the Proms 2003: Live at the Royal Albert Hall. Slatkin, BBC Symphony Orchestra. Warner Classics (2004).

Puccini: Arias. Coppola, Orchestra Sinfonica di Milano Giuseppe Verdi. EMI Classics (2005).

25 Jaar Koningin Beatrix. Olmi, Radio Filharmonisch Orkest, Holland. EMI Classics (2005).

Marius et Fanny, Cosma. Cosma, London Symphony Orchestra. Larghetto Music (2008).

Madama Butterfly, Puccini. Pappano, Accademia Nazionale di Santa Cecilia. EMI Classics (2009).

L'amico Fritz, Mascagni. Veronesi, Berlin Deutsche Oper. Deutsche Grammophon (2009).

Homage to Maria Callas. Armiliato, Royal Philharmonic Orchestra. EMI Classics (2011).

Fedora, Giordano. Veronesi, Orchestre Symphonique de la Monnaie. Deutsche Grammophon (2011).

Solti: The Legacy; 1937–1997. Decca (2012).

O, ce veste minunată (Romanian carols album). Soare, Orchestra Națională Radio. MediaPro Music (2013).

Guardian Angel (international carols album). Soare, Orchestra Națională Radio. MediaPro Music (2014).

Angela Gheorghiu: 3 Classic Albums. Box set. Decca (2014).

Autograph. Box set. Warner Classics (2015).

The Complete Warner Recitals. Box set. Warner Classics (2017).

Eternamente: The Verismo Album. Villaume, Prague Philharmonia. Warner Classics (2017).

DVDs

La traviata, Verdi. Solti, Royal Opera House. Decca (1995).

Plácido Domingo with Angela Gheorghiu: Live in Prague. Kohn, Czech Symphony Orchestra. Beckmann (1997).

Gold and Silver Gala with Plácido Domingo. Fisch, Royal Opera House. BBC (1999).

Classics on a Summer's Evening: Live from Dresden. Sinopoli, Staatskapelle Dresden. EMI Classics (2001).

Verdi: Messa da Requiem. Abbado, Berliner Philharmoniker. EMI Classics
  (2001).

Tosca, Puccini. A film by Benoît Jacquot. Arthaus Musik (2001).

Angela Gheorghiu: Live from Covent Garden. Marin, Royal Opera House.
  EMI Classics (2002).

Prom at the Palace: The Queen's Concerts, Buckingham Palace. BBC, Opus Arte
  (2002).

L'elisir d'amore, Donizetti. Pidò, Opéra de Lyon. Decca (2002).

Roméo et Juliette, Gounod. A film by Barbara Willis Sweete. Arthaus Musik
  (2003).

The Art of Angela Gheorghiu: "La traviata," "L'elisir d'amore." Box set of two
  previously released DVDs. Decca (2004).

25 Jaar Koningin Beatrix. Olmi, Radio Filharmonisch Orkest, Holland.
  EMI Classics (2005).

Great Voices of Today. Digital Classics (2005).

La bohème, Puccini. Luisotti, Metropolitan Opera. EMI Classics (2008).

La traviata, Verdi. Maazel, La Scala. Arthaus Musik (2008).

Great Opera Arias: A Gala Concert from the Royal Opera House. Reissued
  edition of *Gold and Silver Gala with Plácido Domingo* (1999). Opus Arte
  (2008).

The Tribute to Pavarotti: One Amazing Weekend in Petra. Kohn, Prague
  Philharmonia. Decca (2009).

Italian Night: Waldbühne Berlin. Abbado, Berliner Philharmoniker.
  Arthaus Musik (2009).

La rondine, Puccini. Armiliato, Metropolitan Opera. EMI Classics (2010).

Faust, Gounod. Pappano, Royal Opera House. EMI Classics (2010).

Tosca, Puccini. Pappano, Royal Opera House. EMI Classics (2012).

Adriana Lecouvreur, Cilea. Elder, Royal Opera House. Decca (2012).

Solti Centenary Concert. Gergiev, World Orchestra for Peace. Live from
  Symphony Center, Chicago. Arthaus Musik (2013).

Many of the recordings from the above discs have also been released on
various CD and DVD compilations.

INDEX

Abbado, Claudio, 92, 93, 163, 164, 183, 217, 219

Adriana Lecouvreur (Cilea), 146, 162, 164, 182, 199, 200; role of Adriana, 201, 202, 203

Agache, Alexandru, 57, 87, 119, 161

Aida (Verdi), 163, 189, 190

Alagna, Ornella, 132, 148, 149, 151, 207, 208

Alagna, Roberto, 93, 98, 99, 100, 101, 104, 105, 112, 113, 114, 126, 127, 129, 131, 132, 134, 135, 136, 137, 138, 140, 141, 142, 144, 147, 148, 149, 155, 156, 157, 160–68, 170, 171, 172, 174, 175, 187, 189, 190, 205, 207, 209, 217

Allen, Sir Thomas, 106, 170

Álvarez, Marcelo, 138, 177

amico Fritz, L' (Mascagni), 146, 157, 218

Anastassov, Orlin, 166

Angela Gheorghiu's Romanian Journey (BBC documentary), 122, 196

Anghelescu, Cristina, 76

Anna Bolena (Donizetti), 62

Aquarone, Marcel, 167

Arena di Verona, 166

Armencea, Mihail, 14, 15, 19, 20, 22

Arvunescu, Gabriel, 183

Astanei, Iulia, 54

Athenaeum, 40, 41, 43, 213

Avram, Cristea, 67

Badea, Alexandru, 51, 54, 69, 92, 136

Bălănuță, Leopoldina, 56, 73

Bănică, Ștefan Jr, 181

Barbu, Mia, 24, 25, 26, 27, 28, 30, 32, 37, 38, 39, 40, 41, 43, 44, 45, 46, 47, 50, 57, 58, 65, 84, 95, 98, 133

Bartoli, Cecilia, 159, 160

Basel Opera, 96, 98, 213

Bassey, Dame Shirley, 97

Battle, Kathleen, 206

Bayreuth Festival, 109

BBC Television, 121, 122, 123, 144, 170, 177, 181, 196, 197, 214, 218, 219

Beatrix of the Netherlands, Queen, Silver Jubilee of, 170, 215

Being a Diva, 177

Belvedere Competition, 92, 93, 213

Berliner Philharmoniker, 93, 163, 219

Bernstein, Leonard, 16

Birlic, Grigore Vasiliu, 73

Bleonț, Claudiu, 73

Bocelli, Andrea, 167, 215

Bogozavliev, Cedomir, 106

Bogoszavliev, Eva, 106

Bohème, La (Puccini), 91, 92, 94, 95, 96, 98, 99, 100, 101, 102, 103, 106, 108, 109, 110, 111, 113, 114, 115, 118, 130, 134, 137, 138, 139, 140, 143, 146, 159, 160, 162, 164, 174, 185, 189, 190, 199, 203, 204, 207, 213, 217, 219; role of Mimi in, 102, 103

Bolshoi Theatre, 203, 216

Brâncuși, Constantin, 72

Buciuceanu, Tamara, 73

Buckingham Palace, 169, 214, 218, 219

Bucos, Florentina (cousin), 16, 167, 168, 169

Budapest Opera Ball, 216

Bulandra Theater, 61

Bumbry, Grace, 204, 215

Burlacu, Constantin (paternal grandfather), 4

Burlacu, Elena "Nina" (sister), 5, 6, 7, 8, 10, 13, 14, 16, 22, 28, 36, 47, 52, 63, 64, 86, 88, 144, 145, 147, 148, 149, 150

Burlacu, Ioana (mother), 1–10, 13, 15, 16, 17, 18, 21, 22, 23, 24, 25, 26, 29, 31, 34, 35, 36, 37, 51, 57, 64, 76, 78, 88, 94, 119, 148, 174, 184, 208

Burlacu, Ion (father), 1–9, 11, 12, 13, 16, 17, 22, 24, 29, 35, 44, 45, 91, 148, 208

Burlacu, Victoria (paternal grandmother), 2, 4, 7

Buzea, Ion, 42

Caballé, Montserrat, 41, 98, 198, 206

Callas, Maria, 134, 139, 155, 176, 177, 179, 182, 198, 218

Cannes Film Festival, 97, 180, 215

Cântarea României (Song to Romania festival), 20

Caragiu, Toma, 73

Caramitru, Ion, 56, 73, 87

Carmen (Bizet), 105, 113, 147, 152, 153, 154, 173, 175, 198, 217, 218

Carnegie Hall, 203

Carreras, José, 155, 165, 167, 208, 209, 216

Caruso, Enrico, 139

Cassel, Vincent, 180

Ceaușescu, Nicolae, 16, 29, 49, 55, 67, 71, 72, 79, 81, 85, 86, 87, 102

Cebotari, Maria, 41, 198

Cercel, Florina

Chailly, Riccardo, 134, 142, 217

"chanson des vieux amants, La" (Brel), 170

Charles, Prince of Wales, 141, 170, 196, 197, 214

Chernov, Vladimir, 107, 108, 109, 110

Chiron, Martine, 106

Chung Myung-Whun, 159

"Ciobănaș cu trei sute de oi" (Little shepherd with three hundred sheep) (Lydic), 26

Ciortea, Adina, 211

Ciortea, Claudiu, 211

Ciortea, Mihai, vii, 210, 211

Ciortea, Tudor, 211

Ciprian Porumbescu Conservatory (now the National University of Music Bucharest), 8, 20, 22, 25, 27, 36, 40, 42, 43, 44, 45, 46, 49, 50–65, 69, 70, 73, 76, 78, 85, 89, 90, 91, 92, 101, 122, 144, 145, 182, 183, 213

Comăneci, Nadia, 73, 74

Condurache, Dan, 73

Constantin, George, 73

Constantin, Marin, 182

Constantinescu, Ligia, 37

Constantinescu, Luminița, 57, 61, 79, 213

contes d'Hoffmann, Les (Offenbach), 103

Corelli, Franco, 154, 175

Cortez, Mioara, 57

Cotescu, Octavian, 73

Cotrubaș, Ileana, 83, 119, 147, 204

"Country like a Rose, A" (Țara mea) (Urmuzescu), 80

Craiova Opera, 84

Croitoru, Gabriel, 79
Cyrano de Bergerac (Alfano), 157

Dan, Andrei, 85, 86, 149
Dan-Holubaş, Ioana, 88, 147, 148, 149, 150, 151, 207, 208
D'Arcangelo, Ildebrando, 134
Darclée, Hariclea, 67, 68, 179
Decca Classics, 121, 122, 134, 141, 142, 147, 163, 184, 214, 217, 218, 219
del Monaco, Mario, 155
Depardieu, Gérard, 205
Depardieu, Julie, 205
Desderi, Claudio, 106
Dessay, Natalie, 112
Detain, Anne, 106
Deutsche Oper Berlin, 215
Diana, Princess of Wales, 130
Dinescu, Mircea, 87
Dinică, Gheorghe, 73
di Stefano, Giuseppe, 180
Dodd, Tracey Claire, 106
"Doina stăncuței" (Brediceanu), 46
Doll's House, A (Ibsen), 61
Domingo, Plácido, 41, 92, 98, 103, 105, 111, 113, 114, 115, 139, 152, 155, 165, 167, 176, 204, 205, 213, 216, 218, 219
Don Carlo (Verdi), 133, 163
Don Giovanni (Mozart), 96, 97, 98, 105, 106, 166, 213
Donose, Ruxandra, 54, 57
Dragomir, Dana, 31

Electrecord, 42, 80
elisir d'amore, L' (Donizetti), 96, 98, 105, 144, 145, 146, 147, 213, 217, 219
Elizabeth II, Queen, 169; Diamond Jubilee of, 170, 216; Golden Jubilee of, 168, 196, 214

EMI Classics, 141, 142, 160, 163, 198, 214, 215, 217, 218, 219
Enăchescu, Eleonora, 89
Eugene Onegin (Tchaikovsky), 46
European Cultural Award for Music, 216
Eyre, Sir Richard, 116, 117, 118, 119, 123

Fălculete, Ion, 40, 43, 44, 45
Falstaff (Verdi), 108
Faust (Gounod), 46, 90, 146, 159, 160, 166, 174, 175, 176, 199, 200, 201, 204, 207, 215, 219
Fedora (Giordano), 208, 218
Fenice, La. *See* Teatro La Fenice
Filip, Felicia, 57
Findlay, Paul, 101, 145
Fleming, Renée, 111
Florescu, Arta, 49, 50–60, 62, 63, 69, 70, 71, 79, 80, 81, 85, 88, 89, 90
Floria Capsali Choreography High School, 25
Frederic Georg of Prussia, Prince, 164
Freischütz, Der (Weber), 68
Freni, Mirella, 134, 154, 155, 174, 198, 208
Frunzetti, Ion, 77
Fulford, Jonathan, 196
Fullerton, Fay, 103, 104

Gabriela, Mother, from Voroneț Monastery, 197
Gaetani, Raimonda, 159
Gagiu, Mihaela, 72
Galin, Carmen, 56
Gasc, Christian, 188
Gelb, Peter, 141, 142, 143
George Enescu Arts University, Iași, 216

George Enescu College of Arts, 25
George Enescu Festival, 71
George Enescu High School of Art, 24–42, 213
George Enescu Philharmonic Orchestra, 40
Georg Solti Accademia, 144, 145
Gerdanovits, Alexander, vii, 135, 136, 137, 167, 168
Gergiev, Valery, 111, 203, 219
Gheorghiu, Andrei, 78, 79, 81, 82, 99, 100, 113, 126, 127, 128, 129, 131, 136
Gheorghiu, Irina, 85, 86, 127
Gheorghiu, Manuela, 76, 77, 78, 83, 113
Gheorghiu, Nonna, 79
Gheorghiu, Ştefan, 77, 78, 79, 82, 83, 113, 130
Gheorghiu, Valentin, 79
Ghiaurov, Nicolai, 155
Giordani, Marcello, 176
Giuliani, Rudolph, 138, 139
Gold and Silver Gala, 214, 218, 219
Gorbachev, Mikhail, 81
Grigolo, Vittorio, 158, 159, 160
Grigore, Dan, 56, 79
Gustafson, Nancy, 107

Halka (Moniuszko), 71
Hampson, Thomas, 176
Herlea, Nicolae, 25, 41, 42, 57, 68
Hofburg Palace (Vienna), 67
Holender, Ioan, 92, 93, 98, 105, 135
Hollywood Bowl, 165
Holubaş, Bogdan, 208
Hopkins, Sir Anthony, 130, 141, 205
Horne, Marilyn, 111, 112
Hvorostovsky, Dmitri, 98, 103, 160

IATC (Institutul de Artă Teatrală şi Cinematografică, the Institute of Theater and Film), 60, 73
Ionescu, Ileana Stana, 73
Iordăchescu, Cristina, 54
Irons, Jeremy, 205
Isaacs, Sir Jeremy, 119
Isaev, Iulia, 51, 54, 89, 90, 92, 182, 183
Iureş, Marcel, 73
Ivan, Simina, 135, 136, 137
Ivanov, Vlad, 73

Jacquot, Benoît, 161, 171, 188, 214, 219
John Paul II, Pope, 214

Karajan, Herbert von, 144
Kasarova, Vesselina, 107
Katara Amphitheater, 204, 206, 216
Katona, Peter, 93, 94, 95, 96, 100, 104, 168, 176
Kaufmann, Jonas, 97, 159, 160, 177, 203
Keenlyside, Simon, 134, 175
Kennedy Center, 203, 204, 215
Kent, Jonathan, 177
Kleiber, Carlos, 144
Kohn, Eugene, 166, 218, 219

Lamatic, Mihnea, 51, 52, 54, 69, 90, 183, 199
Last Night of the Proms, 214, 215, 218
Leff, Susie, 106
Levine, James, 108, 109, 139, 140, 152, 214
Lipkowska, Lidia, 60
Lombardi alla prima crociata, I (Verdi), 163
London O2 Arena, 114

London Philharmonic Orchestra, 144, 184, 217

Lopardo, Frank, 99, 116, 120, 123, 135

Louise (Charpentier), 62, 63, 95, 110

Lučić, Željko, 179

Luxon, Benjamin, 107

Lyric Opera of Chicago, 190, 191

Maazel, Lorin, 120, 161, 187, 219

Madama Butterfly (Puccini), 192; role of Cio-Cio-San in, 193–96

Madrigal Choir, 79, 122, 182, 184

Măgureanu, Cristina, 54

Mălăele, Horaţiu, 73

Mandache, Rodica, 73

Manea, Mioara, 54, 63, 90, 183

Maniura, Peter, 122, 123, 196, 197

Manole, Marius, 73

Mara, Dorin, 92

Marcovici, Silvia, 96

Mărcuţa, Vergina, 9

Margareta of Romania, Princess, 79, 171

Margrethe II of Denmark, Queen, 130

Marin, Andreea, 181

Marin, Ion, 122, 182, 184, 217, 219

Marinca, Anamaria, 73

Marinescu, Florenţa, 54

Marinescu, Medeea, 73

Marius et Fanny (Cosma), 187, 188, 189, 215

Marseille Trilogy (Pagnol), 188, 189

Martin, Claude, 163, 164

Martin, Judith, 163

masnadieri, I (Verdi), 163

Mastroianni, Jack, 159

Matei, Draga Olteanu, 73

Mattila, Karita, 106

McVicar, Sir David, 175, 176, 200, 202

Medvedev, Dmitri, 203

Mehta, Zubin, 144, 161

Meier, Waltraud, 152

Menuhin, Lord Yehudi, 78, 83

Merry Widow, The (Die Lustige Witwe) (Lehar), 199

Metropolitan Opera (New York), 42, 56, 74, 105, 107–12, 127, 133, 136, 138, 141, 143, 147, 152, 154, 155, 156, 157, 159, 166, 174, 175, 176, 179, 189, 203, 204, 205, 213, 214, 215, 219

Michael I of Romania, King, 79, 171, 172, 216

"Michael Jackson and Friends," 214

Micu, Doina, 52, 59, 91

Mihaiu, Adriana (cousin), 16

Mihaiu, Mariana (cousin), 16

Mihuţ, Mariana, 73

Miller, Jonathan, 161

Modena. *See* Teatro Communale di Modena

Moise, Eugenia, 30, 31, 32, 35

Moldovan, Ovidiu Iuliu, 56

Moldoveanu, Eugenia, 33, 56, 57, 68, 69, 82, 90

Moldoveanu, Iacob, 82

Moniuszko Festival, 71, 77

Moore, Sir Roger, 207

Moraru, Marin, 73

Moreau, Jeanne, 205

"Music for a While" (Purcell), 55

Musset, Alfred de, 186

Muti, Riccardo, 133, 134, 135

"Muzica" (Grigoriu), 90, 170, 213

Muzio, Claudia, 198

Naarghita, 19

Naghiu, Octavian, 57

National Theatre (London), 117

Neblett, Carol, 111

New York Philharmonic Orchestra's New Year's Eve Gala, 215
Nichiteanu, Liliana, 57
Nihil Sine Deo, 172, 216
Nilsson, Birgit, 111
Nina, o sia La pazza per l'amore (Paisiello), 159
Nițulescu, Gladiola, 52, 54, 64, 69, 183
Nobel Peace Prize Concert, 215
"Non ti scordar di me" (De Curtis), 165
Norma (Bellini): "Casta diva," 180, 217
Norman, Jessye, 206
nozze di Figaro, Le (Mozart), 39, 46
Nucci, Leo, 99, 116, 117, 120, 123
"Numele tău" (Your Name) (Bănica), 181

Obama, Barack, 204, 215
Obama, Michelle, 204, 215
"O, ce veste minunată!" (traditional Romanian song), 12, 218
Odăgescu-Țuțuianu, Irina, 43
"oglindă, La" (Coșbuc) 15
Ohanesian, David, 83
Oistrakh, David, 78, 83
Oistrakh, Igor, 78, 83
Olmi, Paolo, 170, 218, 219
Onoghi, Atsushi, 51
Opéra de Lyon, 145, 146, 147, 217, 219
Opéra de Monte-Carlo, 146, 157
Opéra National de Paris, 161, 182, 215
Opera Națională București (Romanian National Opera, Bucharest), 60, 68, 90, 91, 102, 199
Opera Națională Română Cluj-Napoca (Romanian National Opera, Cluj-Napoca), 91, 92, 101, 102, 213
Otello (Verdi), 163
Otter, Anne Sofie von, 144
Our Extraordinary World Gala, Royal Opera House, 216
Ozawa, Seiji, 107

Pagliacci (Leoncavallo), 103
Pahud, Emmanuel, 164
PalaFenice, 138
Palais Garnier (Opéra national de Paris), 182
Palau de les Arts Reina Sofia, Valencia, 215
Pană, Cornel, 31
Pape, René, 160
Pappano, Sir Antonio, 97, 105, 160, 161, 162, 163, 175, 176, 192, 217, 218, 219
Patriarchy Choir, 63, 64, 66, 122
Patrichi, Gina, 73
Pausini, Laura, 167
Pavarotti, Luciano, 133, 139, 163, 165, 166, 214, 215, 216, 219
Peer Gynt, "Solveig's Song" (Grieg), 40, 213
Pellea, Amza, 73
Pelléas et Mélisande (Debussy), 142
Petean, George, 182
Peters, Beate, 106
Peters, Claudia, 106
Petrov, Luisa, 87, 88, 93, 95, 96, 145
Philip, Prince, Duke of Edinburgh, 170
"Piano, The" (Iancu) 80
"Piccola bohème" (Vangelis), 205
Pidò, Evelino, 146, 159, 217, 219
Piersic, Florin, 73
Pleșu, Andrei, 79
Plisetskaya, Maya, 203

Pniel, Victoria, 106
Ponselle, Rosa, 198
Porgy and Bess (Gershwin), 63, 199
Prague Philharmonia, 166, 218, 219
Prêtre, Georges, 207, 216
Prey, Hermann, 111
Prom in the Park, 180, 181

Queen of Spades (*Pikovaya dama*)
    (Tchaikovsky), 203

Radio Free Europe, 70
Radu, Axenia, 13
Răducanu, Johnny, 56
Radu of Romania, Prince, 79, 171
RAI, 165, 166
Raimondi, Ruggero, 161
Rebengiuc, Victor, 56, 73
Requiem Mass (Verdi), 93, 164, 217,
    219
Rigler, James, 185, 186
Rigoletto (Verdi), 135, 163
Romania, royal family of, 171
Romanian cântece, 183, 185, 186
Romanian Revolution, 85–88
Romanian state television, 57
Roméo et Juliette (Gounod), 126, 127,
    154, 155, 171, 173, 188, 189, 214,
    217, 219
Rostropovich, Mstislav, 144, 170, 209
Royal Albert Hall, 144, 214, 215, 218
Royal Festival Hall, 214
Royal Opera House, Covent Garden,
    93–106, 171
Royal Opera of Versailles, 165

Salle Garnier (Opéra de Monte-
    Carlo), 157
Salzburg Festspiele, 132, 134, 135, 213
Samuilă, Liviu Tudor, 63, 79
Sandu, Ilie (maternal grandfather), 3

Sandu, Safta (mother's sister), 16
Sandu, Sanda (maternal
    grandmother), 3, 74
San Francisco Opera, 102, 179, 182
Santi, Nello, 138
"Sara pe deal" (In the Evening on the
    Hill) (Eminescu), 38, 118
Sava, Iosif, 37, 55, 56, 57, 58, 61, 63,
    79, 105, 110, 213
Savu, Sorana, vii
Scala, La. *See* Teatro alla Scala
Scènes de la vie de bohème (Murger),
    101
Schaaf, Johannes, 97
Schönbrunn Palace, Vienna, 67
Scotto, Renata, 189, 190
Securitate, 49, 55, 57, 65, 66, 67, 79,
    178
Şerban, Andrei, 79, 175
"Se tu m'ami" (Pergolesi), 40
Shicoff, Neil, 176
Sievewright, Alan, 171
Simon Boccanegra (Verdi), 176, 204,
    205
Sims, Barbara, 106
Sissi, Empress, 67, 121
Slătinaru-Nistor, Maria, 40, 57, 68,
    85, 89, 90, 144
Smetana Hall, Prague, 173
Sofia of Spain, Queen, 171
Solti, Lady Valerie, 116, 130
Solti, Sir Georg, 99, 101, 114–23, 130,
    141, 142, 144, 145, 160, 185, 197,
    203, 217, 218, 219
Sony Classical, 141, 143, 217
Spiess, Ludovic, 68
Stabat Mater (Rossini), 63
Star of Romania, 216
Stephansdom (Archdiocesan
    Cathedral), 67
Sting, 166, 167

St. James's Palace, 196
Stoia, Ion, 62
Stoleriu, Georgeta, 50, 51, 89
Strauss, Max, 112
Strauss, Sissy, 110, 111, 112
Streep, Meryl, 205
Sutherland, Dame Joan, 182

Tănase, Maria, 25
Tapacian, Roxana Gaiane, 51
Te Kanawa, Dame Kiri, 170
Teatro alla Scala, 31, 120, 133, 134, 135, 160, 189, 215, 217, 219
Teatro Communale di Modena, 163, 165, 166, 214
Teatro dell' Opera di Roma, 158, 160
Teatro La Fenice, 138
Teatro Malibran, Venice, 214
Teatro Real, Madrid, 176
Tebaldi, Renata, 134, 143, 180, 182, 198
Televiziunea Română, 55
Tell, Lucienne, 140, 155
Teoctist, Patriarch, 66
Terfel, Sir Bryn, 96, 97, 106, 175, 177, 180
Théâtre de la Monnaie, Brussels, 105, 217
Tolansky, Jon, 122
Tomoroveanu, Ilinca, 73
Tonitza, Nicolae, 136
Tosca (Puccini), 42, 67, 68, 97, 102, 161, 162, 171, 173, 174, 176, 184, 185, 188, 199, 200, 214, 215, 217, 219; role of Tosca in, 177–80
Toscan du Plantier, Daniel, 161
Trăilescu, Cornel, 102
traviata, La (Verdi), 33, 38, 42, 46, 58, 62, 63, 67, 68, 83, 84, 92, 99, 101, 102, 114–23, 173, 175, 182, 185, 197, 208, 213, 214, 215, 217,

218, 219; role of Violetta in, 122, 124, 125
"Trout, The" ("Die Forelle") (Schubert), 28, 32
Tudorache, Olga, 73
Turandot (Puccini), 107, 113, 138, 148, 204
TVR2, 55, 56, 58

University of Bucharest, 216
Urechescu, Adriana, 92

Văduva, Leontina, 54, 57, 71, 87, 90, 119, 126, 131
Valurile Dunării (Waves of the Danube) (Grigoriu), 90
Vaness, Carol, 106
Vangelis, 205, 206, 216
Vargas, Ramón, 107, 108, 138, 139, 161, 175
Vengerov, Maxim, 144
Venice Film Festival, 214
Vespa, Bruno, 165
Vienna Opera Ball, 207, 216
Vienna State Opera, 92, 98, 102, 104, 105, 107, 108, 118, 137, 146, 160, 179, 180, 183, 213, 216
Voice of America, 70
Voinea, Silvia, 89
Voineag, Ionel, 57, 89
Volpe, Joseph, 138, 139, 140, 153, 154, 155, 156, 157, 159, 166, 175
Vraca, George, 73
"vuchella, A" (A sweet mouth) (Tosti), 186

Wallman, Margarethe, 180
Wally, La, "Ebben, ne'andro lontana" (Catalani), 166
Warner Classics, 141, 217
Weber, Babett, 103

Werther (Massenet), 216, 217

Wiegenlied, "Guten Abend, gut'
    Nacht" (Brahms), 15

Wiener Blut (Voices of Spring)
    (Strauss, Johann Jr.), 21

Willems, Jeroen, 170

Willis Sweete, Barbara, 171, 188, 214,
    219

Windsor Castle, 197

Wong Kar-Wai, 180

World Trade Center, 174

Zancu, Dan, 90

Zeani, Virginia, 41, 42, 60, 134, 181,
    182, 198

Zeffirelli, Franco, 152

Zucchero, 167

Zurich Opera House, 143, 159, 160